Top Five Tips for Sellers

1. **Find the best site**   It's tempting to sell everything on eBay, but another site may be a better fit for the item you're trying to sell.

2. **Open low**   To generate bidding, set your minimum bid much lower than what you expect the item to sell for (10% of your desired price is a good start).

3. **Be honest**   Don't misrepresent your item in its description.

4. **Pick your start time carefully**   List your item during the prime time hours (9 p.m.–11 p.m. EST/6 p.m.–8 p.m. PST). That way, your auction will *close* during prime time, when as many potential bidders as possible are home and online, and you'll get more last-minute bids.

5. ***Don't* set a reserve price**   If you want top dollar for your merchandise, don't do a reserve price auction. Many people won't bid if they think your reserve is too high.

Top Five Tips for Buyers

1. **Don't bid on the first thing you see**   Resist placing a bid on the first item you see. Look through the listings; you might find the same item with a lower opening bid.

2. **Check out the seller**   Most auction sites provide feedback ratings for their sellers and bidders; avoid sellers who don't have good feedback ratings.

3. **Don't bid whole dollar values**   Always bid a few pennies more than an even dollar; that way, your bid will beat out any-one else who came in at the same dollar figure.

4. **Be disciplined!**   Set a maximum price you're willing to pay for an item, and *don't exceed it!*

5. **Bid late—and snipe if you have to**   Track the final hours of bidding on items you want so you won't be outbid at the last minute. If you want to virtually guarantee a win, hold *all* your bidding until the last minute. This is called *sniping*. While auction sites discourage it (some auction sites—but *not* eBay—automatically extend the end of an auction if there is last-minute bidding, reducing the effectiveness of sniping), it works more often than not.

cut here

W9-BUC-089

eBay Quick Reference

To Do This...	Use This Command...	Example:
Search for part of a word	*	bat*
Search for either word	(word1,word2)	(batman,robin)
Search for either word	@0	@0 batman robin
Include at least two of the words	@1	@1 pez furby plate
Search for an exact phrase	" "	"batman pez dispenser"
Must include a word	+	batman +pez
Must exclude a word	-	batman -pez
Include a year or number	#	#1972

To List an Item

1. Click **Sell** on eBay's home page.
2. In the Sell Your Item page, type a short title for your ad.
3. Select the category where you want the item listed.
4. Enter a description for your item. (This is the text of your ad; you can include HTML coding.)
5. If you have a picture of your item, enter its URL.
6. Select any of the special options that you would like for your auction: Gallery, Boldface Title, Featured, Featured in Category, or Great Gift Icon.
7. Enter your location (city/state/country).
8. Select the payment methods, payment terms, and shipping terms you will accept.
9. Enter the quantity of items you have for sale. (Enter **1** unless you're holding a Dutch auction.)
10. Enter the minimum bid for your item (the least amount of money you'll accept; this will be the starting bid).
11. Select the length of your auction—3, 5, 7, or 10 days.
12. If you want to hold a reserve price auction, enter the reserve price for your item.
13. If you're auctioning something of a sensitive nature, check the **Private Auction** box.
14. Enter your user ID and password.
15. Click **Review** to proceed to the next page.
16. Verify the content of your listing. To change anything, click your browser's **Back** button to return to the Sell Your Item page. Otherwise, click **Submit My Listing**.

To Place a Bid

1. Scroll to the bottom of the listing you want to bid on, enter the maximum bid you're willing to make on the item, and then click **Review Bid**.
2. Review your bid. If you decide *not* to make the bid, click your browser's **Back** to return to the item listing. Otherwise, enter your user ID and password, and click **Place Bid**.
3. The next page informs you as to whether you are now the high bidder, or if your bid has already been outbid.

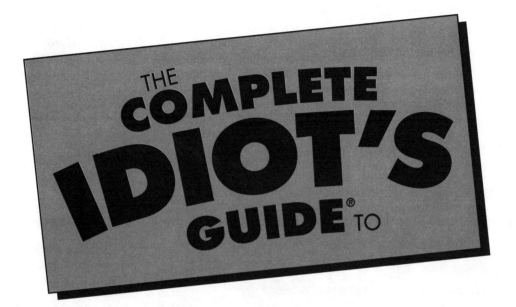

THE COMPLETE IDIOT'S GUIDE® TO

Online
Auctions

by Michael Miller

201 West 103rd Street, Indianapolis, Indiana 46290

The Complete Idiot's Guide to Online Auctions

Copyright © 1999 by Que

International Standard Book Number: 0-7897-2057-4

Library of Congress Catalog Card Number: 99-61625

Printed in the United States of America

First Printing: July 1999

01   00   99   4   3   2

Trademarks

Warning and Disclaimer

Development Editor
Kate Welsh

Managing Editor
Thomas F. Hayes

Project Editor
Karen S. Shields

Copy Editor
Julie McNamee

Indexer
Chris Barrick

Proofreaders
Jeanne Clark
Ryan Walsh

Technical Editor
Ian Welsh

Interior Design
Nathan Clement

Cover Design
Michael Freeland

Illustrator
Judd Winnick

Copy Writer
Eric Bogert

Layout Technicians
Cyndi Davis-Hubler
Tricia Flodder

Contents at a Glance

Table of Contents

Part 3: Essential eBay: Buying and Selling on the Internet's Largest Auction Site 125

ix

Part 4: Buy Low, Sell High: Secrets of Successful Online Auctioneers   227

22 Winning an Auction: Strategies for Buyers   229

About the Author

Michael Miller is a writer, speaker, consultant, and the President/Founder of The Molehill Group, a strategic consulting and authoring firm based in Carmel, IN. You can find more information about the author and The Molehill Group at www.molehillgroup.com, or email the author directly at author@molehillgroup.com.

Mr. Miller has been an important force in the book publishing business since 1987. In his most recent position of Vice President of Business Strategy for Macmillan Publishing, he helped guide the strategic direction for the world's largest reference publisher and influence the shape of today's computer book publishing market. There are few who know as much about the computer industry—how it works and why—as does Mr. Miller.

As the author of 30 best-selling nonfiction books, Mr. Miller writes about a variety of topics. His most recent books include *The Complete Idiot's Guide to Online Search Secrets, Lycos Personal Internet Guide, Sams' Teach Yourself MORE Windows 98 in 24 Hours,* and *Webster's New World Vocabulary of Success.* Upcoming releases include *The Complete Idiot's Guide to Surfing the Internet with WebTV* and a new edition of his all-time best-seller, *OOPS! What to Do When Things Go Wrong.*

From his first book (*Ventura Publisher Techniques and Applications,* published in 1988) to this, his latest title, Michael Miller has established a reputation for practical advice, technical accuracy, and an unerring empathy for the needs of his readers. Many regard Mr. Miller as the consummate reporter on new technology for an everyday audience, as well as an expert on the online auction industry.

Dedication

To my nephews Alec and Ben Hauser—I hope this book helps you find more Beanies, Pokemon, and Crazy Bones online!

Acknowledgements

Special thanks to the usual suspects at Macmillan including, but not limited to, Greg Wiegand and Kate Welsh. Also, thanks to David Israel and Larry Schwartz for their invaluable background on the online auction business.

Tell Us What You Think!

As the reader of this book, *you* are our most important critic and commentator. We value your opinion and want to know what we're doing right, what we could do better, what areas you'd like to see us publish in, and any other words of wisdom you're willing to pass our way.

As a Publisher for Que, I welcome your comments. You can fax, email, or write me directly to let me know what you did or didn't like about this book—as well as what we can do to make our books stronger.

Please note that I cannot help you with technical problems related to the topic of this book, and that due to the high volume of mail I receive, I might not be able to reply to every message.

When you write, please be sure to include this book's title and author as well as your name and phone or fax number. I will carefully review your comments and share them with the author and editors who worked on the book.

Fax: 317-581-4666

Email: gwiegand@mcp.com

Mail: Greg Wiegand
          Que
          201 West 103rd Street
          Indianapolis, IN 46290 USA

Introduction

There's a new way to buy and sell merchandise over the Internet—one that provides access to millions of individual items worldwide and virtually guarantees a fair market price for each product placed for sale.

What is this new approach to buying and selling?

It's called an *online auction*.

You're probably familiar with traditional auctions, where people bid against each other for merchandise, increasing their bids until the auction is over—and the highest bid wins.

Well, an online auction is a lot like one of those traditional real-world auctions. A seller puts an item up for auction, and potential buyers express their interest by placing bids for that item. At the end of the auction, the user who placed the highest bid wins the right to purchase the item.

The difference is, all this happens online, at a Web site. And much of the bidding takes place automatically—after bidders establish both the minimum and maximum amounts they're willing to bid for an item.

It sounds relatively simple, but the concept of auctioning items over the Internet is taking the world by storm. Today there are hundreds of different auction sites with millions of total users placing bids daily. In fact, for some types of items—collectibles, especially—online auctions have created a completely new model for conducting business.

The largest auction sites, such as eBay, have produced self-contained communities of buyers and sellers. In fact, many online auction users have been able to form free-standing businesses based on the volume of transactions they're able to execute through these online auction sites.

Do you want to know more about how online auctions work? Do you want to get in on the action yourself? Do you want to make sure that you're *consistently successful* when buying or selling items via online auction sites?

If so, this is the book for you.

Who This Book Is For

The Complete Idiot's Guide to Online Auctions is written for anyone who's interested in buying or selling merchandise at an online auction site. Whether you're a first-time bidder or an experienced seller, you'll find information in this book that will help you make more money from your online auction activities.

If you're completely new to online auctions, this book will explain to you how online auctions work and guide you to the best auction sites on the Web. You'll also learn how to join and use eBay, the most popular online auction.

If you're an auction bidder, you'll learn the secrets and strategies you need to win the auctions you want to win—at any online auction site. I'll show you what you need to do to virtually guarantee a winning bid, without spending a penny more than necessary.

If you're an auction seller, you'll learn secrets and strategies that ensure that your merchandise will be sold—and that you'll receive the highest possible bids. I'll also show you how to minimize the costs associated with listing items for bid, including shipping costs.

Whether you're a buyer or a seller, you'll get maximum value from my advice on how to protect your interests when using online auctions. You'll also find useful information about sites and software that help you find and manage auctions across multiple Web sites.

I do assume a few things about you, the reader. I figure that you already have a personal computer (and know how to use it!), that you have an Internet connection, that you have a Web browser (Internet Explorer, Netscape Navigator, or the America Online browser), and that you know your way around Internet basics—how to click hyperlinks and enter Web page addresses and that sort of thing. I *don't* assume that you know everything there is to know about online auctions—because if you did, you wouldn't be reading this book!

What You'll Find in This Book

The Complete Idiot's Guide to Online Auctions is composed of 28 chapters, each of which concentrates on specific information relating to the topic of online auctions. The chapters are organized into four general parts, as follows:

➤ Part 1, "Going Once, Going Twice: All About Online Auctions," is a general introduction to the topic of online auctions. In these chapters, you'll learn what an online auction is, how it works, and what happens after the auction—who pays whom, how, and when. This is a great place to start *before* you start futzing around with individual online auction sites.

➤ Part 2, "Auctions, Auctions, Everywhere: Finding the Right Auction for You," shows you all the different types of auction sites accessible via the Internet. You'll learn about general and collectible auctions, antique auctions, art auctions, sports auctions—in short, you'll learn about just about every type of auction that exists today!

➤ Part 3, "Essential eBay: Buying and Selling on the Internet's Largest Auction Site," is where you'll find everything you need to know about using eBay. You'll learn how to search for items, how to bid on items, how to sell items, how to use HTML in your item listings, and how to personalize your experience with My eBay. You'll even discover the "undercover eBay"—the secrets that eBay doesn't want you to know about!

➤ Part 4, "Buy Low, Sell High: Secrets of Successful Online Auctioneers," is where you can really gain an advantage over your fellow users of online auctions. In these chapters I'll show you all the secrets and strategies you can use to become a real winner on eBay and other online auction sites!

In addition, I've included "The Complete Idiot's Directory of Online Auctions," which lists the URL for every single online auction site mentioned in this book, in alphabetical order. You should also find invaluable the tear-out card in the front of the book, which serves as both a "quick reference" to eBay, and a handy "tip sheet" for online buyers and sellers—keep it next to your computer at all times to help you become a more efficient and effective online auctioneer!

How to Do the Things You See in This Book

To get the most out of this book, you should know how it is designed. I've tried to put things together in such a way as to make reading the book both rewarding and fun. So, here's what to do when you see any of the following:

➤ Web page addresses (URLs) are presented in a `special font`; you can enter the text with this font into your browser's Address box to go to that page. Anything you need to enter—into a search box, for example, or into a form—are presented in the same special font that is used to designate URLs; enter this text as-written to proceed.

➤ Anything you click (such as dialog box buttons or links to Web pages) is presented in **bold and colored text**.

➤ New terms are presented in *italicized text*; pay close attention to these terms.

Extras

To pack as much information as possible into *The Complete Idiot's Guide to Online Auctions*, you are presented with additional tips and advice as you read the book. These elements enhance your knowledge, or point out important pitfalls to avoid. Along the way, you'll find the following elements:

Going Once, Going Twice

These boxes contain warnings, notes, and other information you'll find useful for successful Web searching. Be sure to read each of these boxes—failure to do so might result in missing out on some important points.

Behind the Podium

These boxes contain high-tech info that provides more in-depth information about a topic related to the chapter. If you don't want to dig deeper into how online auctions *really* work, you can skip over these boxes. If you want to impress your friends and loved ones with your mastery of arcane technical information, though, this is the place to look.

Get Ready to Search the Net

Still here? It's time to get started, so turn the page and prepare to learn how to find the things you want—and make good money—buying and selling items through online auctions!

Part 1

Going Once, Going Twice: All About Online Auctions

Just what is this online auction thing all about, anyway? What exactly is an online auction—and how does it work? If you don't know much about online auctions but you want to learn more, this part of the book is for you! You'll learn what an online auction is, how it works, and what happens after the auction—who pays whom, how, and when. These chapters are a good general overview to the topic of online auctions, so start here before you read the rest of the book.

Chapter 1

What's All This Fuss About Online Auctions?

In This Chapter

➤ Learn why online auctions are taking the world by storm

➤ Discover how an online auction works

➤ Find out about the two major types of auctions

➤ Locate the most popular auction site on the Web

Looking for a retired Bumble the Bee Beanie Baby? How about a copy of *Detective Comics #33*, from 1939—the one with the first appearance of Batman? Or a Civil War–era sword and scabbard? Or maybe even a brand-new hard disk drive for your computer—but at a bargain price? Or, perhaps, you have one of these items that you would like to sell?

Whatever you're buying or selling, a new way to trade merchandise is taking the Internet by storm.

It's called an *online auction*.

How Popular Are Online Auctions?

Online auctions have created an entirely new market for many types of merchandise, allowing both individuals and small businesses to sell items to and buy items from other Internet users worldwide. Every single day millions of items are listed at online auctions, and millions of users—people like you and me—place bids on these items.

Just how big is the market for online auctions? By the Spring of 1999, eBay—the world's largest online auction site—had 3.8 million registered buyers and sellers, and was on track to do more than $2 billion worth of transactions for the full year. Forrester Research, a market research firm, projects that the online auction market will reach *$8.5 billion* by 2001, and Jupiter Communications (another market research firm) projects that by 2002 more than *6.5 million* people will purchase items in Internet auctions. That's not small potatoes, folks.

What Is an Online Auction, Exactly?

An online auction is an Internet-based version of a traditional auction—you know, the type where a fast-talking auctioneer stands in the front of the room, trying to coax potential buyers into bidding *just a little bit more* for the piece of merchandise up for bid. The only difference is, there's no fast-talking auctioneer online (the bidding process is executed by special auction software on the auction site), and your fellow bidders aren't in the same room with you—in fact, they might be located anywhere in the world, as long as they have Internet access.

At today's online auctions, you're likely to find a wide variety of items up for bid—everything from discontinued Beanie Babies to vintage sports memorabilia, from rare antiques to the latest computer equipment. If you're a bidder, you can choose from literally millions of individual items available for sale on any given day; if you're a seller, your potential customer base is millions of users strong.

More than fifteen hundred different categories of merchandise are listed on eBay's online auction site.

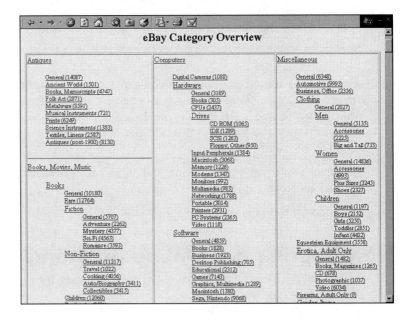

I find the entire online auction phenomenon truly astounding. Hundreds of different Web sites are operating just as many different types of online auctions; some are generalists, listing items from A to Z, while others target special types of items. Believe it or not, some Web sites are devoted just to wine auctions, and auctions of classic automobiles!

What Makes Online Auctions So Popular?

The already immense and rapidly growing popularity of online auctions is due in part to the mania with which some people collect things. Hardcore collectors—whether they collect PEZ dispensers, vintage Barbie dolls, Faberge eggs, or antique chairs—often exhibit obsessive-compulsive behavior (you know you do—admit it!), expending huge amounts of time and effort to track down the most obscure items for their collections. Even if you're not that hardcore, there are still precious things that you collect, and it's relatively easy to get caught up in the thrill of bidding on a one-of-a-kind item that you find online.

Of course, another factor in the surge of online auction popularity is the all-too-human love of a bargain. In many ways, an online auction is just a high-tech version of a garage sale—and people *love* to scrounge through others' leftovers, hunting for that one item at a rock-bottom price.

On the selling front, online auctions are popular because there is no better or cheaper way to guarantee such wide exposure to merchandise. The more people you have looking at something, the more likely it is that someone will buy it—and, thanks to the auction format, more bidders equals a higher selling price.

In addition, many merchants are using online auctions to move overstocked, refurbished, and discontinued merchandise. Goods that used to sit unsold in moldy old warehouses are now being dusted off and auctioned off at discounted prices to users looking for bargains.

In fact, online auctions are really helping to create a new buyer-and-seller economy. Whether you're talking about buyers devoted to their hobbies or sellers running small retail businesses out of their homes, online auctions are providing unique new opportunities for millions of people to buy and sell things that they simply couldn't buy or sell before.

Why Should *You* Use an Online Auction?

If you have something to sell, why would you choose to auction it instead of just selling it outright, through a classified ad or some similar means? Conversely, if you want to buy something, why would you want to bid on it in an auction, as opposed to just buying it normally?

In other words, *what's in it for you?*

Why Sellers Like Online Auctions

For a seller, the value of an auction is readily apparent.

You have something to sell, and you want to get the highest possible dollar for it. If you list it in a classified ad for a fixed amount, that amount is the most you'll receive for it—and you could get less, if a buyer tries to haggle you down on the price. But in an online auction, the price you set is the *minimum* you'll receive—and if several potential buyers are interested in your item, it's possible that they'll bid up the price over and beyond what you would have gotten if you sold the item in a more traditional fashion.

The bottom line for sellers is that online auctions provide the possibility of *upside* that you don't get when you sell something outright.

Why Buyers Like Online Auctions

For a buyer, the value of an auction isn't as obvious. After all, if you buy something outright, you know how much you're going to pay, and you know you can get it right now, just as soon as you pay for it.

With an online auction, the price you pay is less certain. Yes, the seller wants a certain amount for the item, but another buyer might come along and offer a higher amount. Even if you hold out to be the high bidder, you still have to wait until the end of the auction—which could be a week from now!—to receive the item. Truth be told, online auctions may not be as easily predictable or immediately gratifying as just buying something outright.

On the other hand, the sheer number of items available at online auction sites benefits you as a potential buyer. If you want something relatively common, you'll probably have your choice of several different items to buy. If you're looking for something a bit more rare, chances are you'll actually find it when you look at an online auction.

And as for price—well, with the huge number of items up for auction on any given day, the reality is that prices, driven by supply and demand, adjust to market levels. If an item is rare and has a lot of interested bidders, the price will go up accordingly; if it's a common item with few bidders, the price stays low (or it doesn't sell!). Say what you like, that's *fair*.

How Many Different Types of Auctions Are There?

Even though there are hundreds of different auction sites, from general auctions to those specializing in particular types of merchandise, they all fall into one of two general auction types:

➤ **Person-to-person auctions**   Person-to-person auctions work a little bit like classified ads or garage sales, in that you're dealing with an individual (*not a business*), and the merchandise is second-hand. After the auction, you pay the individual directly, and then you get the merchandise shipped to you. Person-to-person auctions are great places to find rare and collectible items for sale.

➤ **Merchant auctions**   Merchant auctions are run by commercial businesses that put their merchandise up for auction. In some cases, these auctions are of surplus or refurbished merchandise; in other cases, it's brand new stuff, right off the shelves. In any case, most merchant auctions take credit cards, offer return policies for defective merchandise, provide after-sale customer service, and so on.

Both merchant and person-to-person auctions operate on the same principle: The auction is for a limited period of time, and at the end of the auction, the highest bidder wins.

Person-to-Person Auctions—Without People!

eBay holds over two million auctions every day. Even though eBay is a person-to-person auction site, not all of those two million auctions are held by individuals; some of the items listed for auction are actually being sold by merchants!

There are a large number of small merchants who use eBay and other person-to-person auctions to sell their merchandise. These merchants usually—but not always—sell collectible or antique items, and find that online auctions are a great way to enhance their real-world retail business. There's nothing wrong with these people using online auctions in this manner; in fact, it's generally a little safer and more convenient (in terms of payment options) to buy from one of these established merchants.

You'll also find some individuals who might as well be running businesses on eBay and other large person-to-person auction sites. These folks buy and sell dozens of items a month, and could be viewed as professional online traders. You'll see these users buy an item one week, then put it back up for auction the next—trying to make a few bucks profit in the meantime. Dealing with one of these pros is generally a pleasant and efficient experience; they definitely know what they're doing!

How Do Person-to-Person Auctions Work?

Most person-to-person auction sites, such as eBay, require you to register before you can list items for sale or place bids. Some sites are free to both buyers and sellers; other sites charge the seller a small *listing fee* when items are placed up for bid, and a small *transaction fee* on all items sold. Sites that charge selling fees often require the seller to place a credit card on file, so the site can automatically charge all fees against the card; buyers are seldom or ever asked to leave a credit card number with the site.

You're Buying from an Individual or a Merchant—Not from the Auction Site!

A person-to-person auction site is kind of like a newspaper that runs classified ads—the site isn't the actual seller, and isn't even really a "middleman." All the auction site does is facilitate the transaction, and therefore can't be held responsible for anything that goes wrong with any particular auction or sale. Obviously, most major sites actively discourage fraud and criminal activities, but offer little protection to the users of the sites. To avoid fraudulent transactions, try to deal only with those buyers and sellers who have built up good ratings on the site. For larger transactions, consider using an *escrow service* to manage the transaction for both parties. See Chapter 26, "Protecting Yourself from Unscrupulous Buyers and Sellers," for more information on escrow services and other ways to take the risks out of your online auctions and transactions.

Although every person-to-person auction site has its own unique operations and rules, most sites tend to follow the same general procedures. Here's how a typical person-to-person auction works:

1. You begin (either as a buyer or seller) by registering with the auction site.
2. The seller creates an ad for an item and lists the item on the auction site. (Some sites charge a small listing fee for each item, anywhere from $.25 to $2.) In the ad, the seller specifies the length of the auction (anywhere from one day to two weeks), and the minimum bid he or she will accept for that item.
3. Potential buyers searching for a particular type of item (or just browsing through all the merchandise listed in a specific category) read the ad and decide to make a bid. The bidder specifies the *maximum* amount he or she will pay; this amount has to be above the seller's *minimum* bid.

4. Software at the online auction site automatically places a bid for the bidder that bests the current bid by a specified amount—but doesn't reveal the bidder's maximum bid. For example, the current bid on an item might be $25. A bidder is willing to pay up to $40 for the item, and enters a maximum bid of $40. The "proxy" software places a bid for the new bidder in the amount of $26—higher than the current bid, but less than the specified maximum bid. If there are no other bids, this bidder will win the auction with a $26 bid. Other potential buyers, however, can place additional bids; unless their maximum bids are more than the current bidder's $40 maximum, they are informed that they have been outbid—and the first bidder's current bid is automatically raised to match the new bids (up to the specified maximum bid price).

5. At the conclusion of an auction, the high bidder is informed of his or her winning bid. The seller is responsible for contacting the high bidder and arranging payment. When the seller receives the buyer's payment (generally by check or money order), the seller then ships the merchandise directly to the buyer.

Bidding by Proxy

For more information on how this automated proxy bidding works, see Chapter 4, "Bidding by Proxy: Robot Bidders Rule!"

Paying and Shipping

For more information on post-auction activities, see Chapter 5, "After the Sale: Who Pays Whom, How, and When."

6. Concurrent with the close of the auction, some auction sites bill the seller for a small percentage (generally one or two percent) of the final bid price. This selling fee is directly billed to the seller's credit card.

That's how it works, in general. For a more detailed example of a typical person-to-person auction, see Chapter 2, "Here's How It Works: An Easy Auction Example."

How Do Merchant Auctions Work?

Merchant auctions are different from person-to-person auctions. The main difference, of course, is that you're not buying from an individual—you're buying from a company. In fact, you're typically buying from the same company that's running the auction. A large number of merchant auctions deal primarily or exclusively in computer hardware and software. Whether you're looking for modems, memory chips, or complete computer systems, you can probably find what you're looking for at an online merchant auction.

As for the merchandise found at merchant auctions, many of the items, for one reason or another, aren't ideally suited for traditional retail sale. You'll find some good deals on merchant auction sites, but the goods might be overstock items, or prior-season models, or discontinued products, or even refurbished units. Most (but not all!) items will come with some sort of warranty or return privilege, and you'll often find multiple quantities of the same item up for auction.

After the auction, the transaction is similar to dealing with a traditional merchant. Most merchant auctions take credit cards, and ship the merchandise out in an expedient and professional manner. You seldom have to worry about being shafted at a merchant auction.

Although every merchant auction site has its own unique operations and rules, most sites tend to follow the same general procedures. Here's how a typical merchant auction works:

1. You, the buyer, register with the auction site. Some sites require you to register your credit card information, so your card can be charged automatically if you win an auction.

2. You search for a particular type of item on the site. When you find something you want, you place your bid for the item, specifying the *maximum* amount you're willing to pay; this amount has to be equal to or above the auction's *minimum* bid.

3. When the auction is over, the highest bidders in the auction are notified of their winning bids. If you're a winner (and you probably are—merchant auctions often have multiple quantities of most items), you arrange payment with the auction site, probably by credit card. Once payment is finalized, the auction site ships out your merchandise.

The entire procedure is just a little different from what you find at person-to-person auctions. You typically stand a better chance of winning an auction, since there are often multiple quantities of the same item up for sale. In most cases you also benefit from the convenience of paying by credit card, which is safer than mailing a check to a complete stranger in a person-to-person auction—and allows the merchant to ship your merchandise faster than would an individual waiting for your personal check to clear.

For a more detailed example of a actual merchant auction, see Chapter 11, "PC Auctions: Computer Hardware and Software at a Great Price."

Which Are the Most Popular Online Auction Sites?

So, now that you're convinced that online auctions are a big deal, who are the major players? Where should you go if you want to place a bid—or put an item up for bid?

Well, in the online auction world, there's one big dog, and lots and lots and *lots* of little dogs.

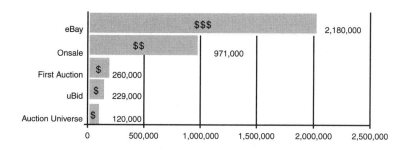

eBay	$$$ 2,180,000
Onsale	$$ 971,000
First Auction	$ 260,000
uBid	$ 229,000
Auction Universe	$ 120,000

Registered users for the five largest online auction sites at the end of 1998 (as reported by the sites themselves; note that Yahoo! Auctions and Classified 2000 Auctions are not included, because they don't reveal their own auction numbers).

eBay (www.ebay.com) is far and away the largest and most popular online auction site of any type. On any given day, eBay has more than fifteen hundred different categories of merchandise, 2 million items for sale, and over a million bids made. If you do the math, that comes out to an average of *eleven bids every second*!

Since its launch in 1997, eBay has logged more than *100 million items for sale*, with more than *800 million total bids made*. From December 31, 1997, to December 31, 1998, the number of registered eBay users grew from approximately 340,000 to more than 2.1 million; in the first half of 1999 alone its user base *almost tripled* to more than *5.6 million!*

eBay is definitely the big dog, and continues to get bigger. The site recently launched country-specific auctions in the United Kingdom and Canada, and additional services such as local auctions and live auctions are in the works. And if that wasn't enough, a recently announced $75 million marketing pact with America Online will make eBay the auction of choice for the 20+ million users of AOL, CompuServe, Digital City, and Netscape Netcenter.

In spite of eBay's dominance, almost a thousand *other* auction sites are on the Web today, with more being launched weekly. Competing directly with eBay are general person-to-person auction sites such as Auction Universe (www.auctionuniverse.com), Yahoo! Auctions (auctions.yahoo.com), Amazon.com Auctions

More on eBay Later

To learn just everything there is to know about eBay—how to join, how to sell, how to bid, and how to protect yourself while you're there—turn to the eight chapters in Part 3 of this book, "Essential eBay: Buying and Selling on the Internet's Largest Auction Site."

Hundreds of Auctions in One Single Book

To learn more about all the different types of online auction sites, check out the eight chapters in Part 2 of this book, "Auctions, Auctions, Everywhere: Finding the Right Auction for You."

(auctions.amazon.com), and Classifieds 2000 Auctions (www.classifieds2000.com); hundreds of smaller person-to-person auctions also serve a variety of specialty markets.

In the merchant auction arena, the larger sites are typically computer-oriented auctions, such as Onsale (www.onsale.com), uBid (www.ubid.com), First Auction (www.firstauction.com), and Egghead's Surplus Auction (www.surplusauction.com). All of these sites are safe and quite professional to work with.

Taking all the options into account, if you're not sure which auction site to try, you probably won't go wrong by going directly to eBay. More experienced buyers and sellers, however, will try to target the specific auction that best suits their individual needs.

The Least You Need to Know

➤ Online auctions facilitate one-to-one trading of all types of merchandise between buyers and sellers around the world.

➤ Online auctions are big business, projected to grow to an $8.5 billion market by 2001.

➤ There are two general types of auctions (merchant and person-to-person), hundreds of different auction sites, and one market leader (eBay).

➤ Online auctions are similar to traditional auctions, except that automated bidding software replaces the role of the human auctioneer.

Chapter 2

Here's How it Works: An Easy Auction Example

> **In This Chapter**
>
> ➤ Discover how sellers place ads on online auction sites
>
> ➤ Learn how the bidding process works
>
> ➤ Find out what happens after the auction is over

Never participated in an online auction before? Well, don't get nervous—the online auction sites actually make it easy to join in on the fun. You'll probably need to register first (which costs you nothing but a few minutes of your time), and then you're ready to jump in and join the bidding—or pull some old stuff out of the attic and try to sell it!

Now, I can't give you precise instructions that will fit every one of the thousand or more auction sites currently operating on the Web, but I can show you in general terms how auctions on most sites operate. (That said, I *do* provide detailed instructions for buying and selling on eBay, the world's largest auction site. You can find this information in Chapters 18, "A Tutorial for Sellers: How to Put an Item Up for Bid," and 19, "A Tutorial for Buyers: How to Make a Winning Bid.")

So read through this chapter, get familiar with the way things work, and soon you'll be doing your own buying and selling—on any auction site that you choose!

The Seller Places an Ad

The way an auction starts is that someone has something he or she wants to sell. It could be something big, or it could be something small—it really doesn't matter, as long as there's a market for it.

The seller enters the auction site, and clicks a "sell your item" or "list your item" link. This displays a form or series of forms that must be completed for each item to be listed. The seller typically has to fill in the following information for each item for sale:

➤ **User ID and password**   On some sites, you get a specific user ID when you register; on other sites, you use your email address. In any case, the seller has to tell the site who he or she is.

➤ **Title**   This is the "headline" of the ad, the brief one-line description that buyers see when they're browsing the ad listings.

➤ **Location**   Where the item is located, geographically. This helps narrow down potential buyers for items that are too big or bulky to be shipped long distances.

➤ **Category**   This is the category under which the item will be listed. Typical categories include Antiques, Collectibles, Computers, Sports Memorabilia, and Toys. Some of the larger sites have over a thousand different categories and more narrow subcategories; sellers must make sure their items are listed under those categories where interested buyers are most likely to look for them.

➤ **Description**   This is the body of the listing, the detailed description of the item for sale. Some auction sites let sellers add HTML coding to their descriptions, so the ads display in color and with different font types. Some sites also let sellers include a picture of the item for sale.

➤ **Minimum bid**   This is the minimum price the seller is willing to take for the item, and is the price at which the auction starts.

➤ **Reserve price**   Some sites let sellers elect to put a *reserve price* on their items. This is a price above the minimum bid that is the lowest price the seller is willing to take for the item; if no bids come in above the reserve price (which is hidden from bidders), then the seller is not obligated to sell the item. (For more information on reserve price auctions, see Chapter 3, "Those Other Types of Auctions: Dutch and Reserve.")

➤ **Duration**   This is how long the seller wants the auction to last. Depending on the site, auctions can last from one day to two weeks.

Different sites might have different names for some of these items, and might also include some options specific to their sites, but in general this is the information that is needed to list an item. After a seller has entered all this information, he or she clicks the appropriate button and the item is automatically listed on the auction site.

Oh, there's one last thing that happens at this stage: If an auction site charges a listing fee—and not all sites do—that fee is automatically charged to the seller's account.

The Buyer Searches for an Item

Now let's turn our attention to the potential buyer. A buyer looking for something in particular can try to find it in one of two ways:

➤ By browsing through the master list of categories of items for sale
➤ By searching all the items for sale for items matching a specific query or keyword

If the buyer is new to all this, the browsing option is probably best—it's a good way to get a feel for all the different types of merchandise available on the auction site. All you have to do is click through the categories and subcategories of items.

Browsing Is Free

On most auction sites, potential bidders don't have to pay any fees. In fact, you don't even have to register with the site just to browse. Most sites will require that you register—name, address, and phone number—in order to place a bid, but even then you don't have to leave any credit card information (like sellers have to).

More experienced buyers, however, learn to search for specific things they want. For example, let's say the buyer wants to find a gray-colored Furby. The buyer would enter the query gray Furby into the site's Search box, and then click the **Search** button. The site's search engine then returns a list of gray Furbies currently up for auction.

Item for sale   Initial bid   Current bid

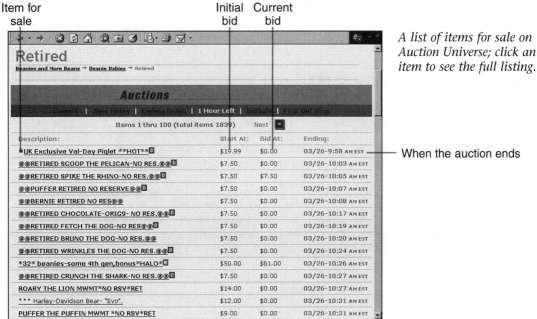

A list of items for sale on Auction Universe; click an item to see the full listing.

When the auction ends

Description:	Start At:	Bid At:	Ending:
UK Exclusive Val-Day Piglet **HOT**	$19.99	$0.00	03/26-9:58 AM EST
@@RETIRED SCOOP THE PELICAN-NO RES.@@	$7.50	$0.00	03/26-10:03 AM EST
@@RETIRED SPIKE THE RHINO-NO RES.@@	$7.50	$7.50	03/26-10:05 AM EST
@@PUFFER RETIRED NO RESERVE@@	$7.50	$0.00	03/26-10:07 AM EST
@@BERNIE RETIRED NO RES@@	$7.50	$0.00	03/26-10:08 AM EST
@@RETIRED CHOCOLATE-ORIG9- NO RES.@@	$7.50	$0.00	03/26-10:17 AM EST
@@RETIRED FETCH THE DOG-NO RES@@	$7.50	$0.00	03/26-10:19 AM EST
@@RETIRED BRUNO THE DOG-NO RES.@@	$7.50	$0.00	03/26-10:20 AM EST
@@RETIRED WRINKLES THE DOG-NO RES.@@	$7.50	$0.00	03/26-10:24 AM EST
32 beanies-some 4th gen,bonus*HALO*	$50.00	$61.00	03/26-10:26 AM EST
@@RETIRED CRUNCH THE SHARK-NO RES.@@	$7.50	$0.00	03/26-10:27 AM EST
ROARY THE LION MWMT*NO RSV*RET	$14.00	$0.00	03/26-10:27 AM EST
*** Harley-Davidson Bear- "Evo".	$12.00	$0.00	03/26-10:31 AM EST
PUFFER THE PUFFIN MWMT *NO RSV*RET	$9.00	$0.00	03/26-10:31 AM EST

19

When a buyer finds an item that looks interesting, he or she clicks the link for that item. This displays a full description of the item for sale, including a picture (if the seller posted one), the initial bid, the current bid, and how much time is left on this particular auction.

A typical item listing at Auction Universe—enter your email address, password, and maximum bid amount to place a bid.

Enter your bid amount here   Buyer information

Item information —

Bid information —

Seller information —

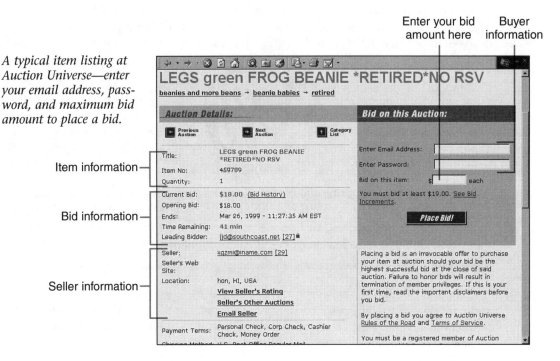

If the buyer isn't interested in that item, no harm done—clicking the browser's **Back** button takes the buyer back to the master list with no bid registered. If the buyer *is* interested, however, we move to the next step.

The Buyer Makes a Bid

To make a bid, the buyer has to enter his or her user ID (sometimes email address) and password, and the *maximum bid* he or she is willing to make.

After the buyer enters a maximum bid amount, he or she then clicks a button confirming the bid. The bid is registered, and a new current bid is displayed on the item's listing screen.

At this point, the potential buyer gets immediate feedback as to whether he/she was the high bidder. It's possible that a previous bidder registered a higher maximum bid than did this buyer, so the buyer's bid was immediately and automatically outbid. (That is, it's possible to bid the current asking price and find out you didn't bid high enough!) If this happens—and the buyer still wants the item—it's time to make another, higher bid and see what happens.

Maximum Bids

Now, you might be asking, why would you enter a *maximum* bid when the listing is displaying the current *minimum* bid?

Think about it this way: The buyer enters the maximum amount he or she is willing to pay—even though the buyer hopes the bidding doesn't go up that high! Here's an example: Let's say the seller has listed a minimum bid of $20 for an item. The potential buyer reads the listing and determines that the item is actually worth $30—so the buyer enters $30 as the maximum bid. The automated bidding software, however, enters the buyer's bid as $20, which is the minimum *required* bid. If no one else bids on this item, the buyer gets it for $20—and doesn't have to spend all the $30 he/she was willing to pay. However, if another bidder enters the fray and bids, let's say, $25, then the initial bidder's bid will be automatically increased to meet and beat the competing bid—up to the $30 maximum that was specified.

The Bidding Continues...

Now the waiting begins. Other potential buyers might read the item's listing, and place competing bids—or maybe no one else bids. In any case, the auction continues until its time expires.

Automated Bidding Explained

This automated bidding procedure—formally called *proxy bidding*—is explained in more detail in Chapter 4, "Bidding by Proxy: Robot Bidders Rule!"

What happens when someone outbids the current minimum bid? Well, several things *can* happen. First, however, the site's automated bidding software automatically adjusts the initial buyer's bid to outbid the new bidder—unless the new bidder's maximum bid exceeds the initial buyer's maximum bid, or until the current minimum bid exceeds the maximum bid specified by the initial buyer. At the point where the initial buyer is outbid, he or she is notified (via email) that he/she no longer has the high bid.

Then the initial bidder has a choice. He or she can choose to return to the auction site and place a new, higher bid on the item—or to bow out of the bidding completely, no other actions necessary.

Bidding in Increments

If you know what the current bid is, how do you figure out what the next higher bid should be? It's easy—the auction sites calculate an official *bid increment* for each bid. This bid increment varies by price point; the bid increment is lower when the current bid price is lower, and higher when the current bid price is higher. For example, a $5 bid might have a $.50 bid increment (making the next bid $5.50), while a $50 bid might have a $1.00 bid increment (making the next bid $51), and a $100 item might have a $5 bid increment (making the next bid $105).

The High Bidder Wins

Days go by. The auction runs its course, and at the appointed time the highest bid is recognized as the official winning bid.

Going, Going...and Still Going?

On some sites (such as Classifieds 2000 and Auction Universe), bidding on an item can actually continue *beyond* the stated auction close. On these sites, if there is any bidding in the 5 minutes prior to the close of the auction, the auction is extended in 5- or 10-minute increments.

Of course, it's not that simple. The final few minutes of any auction often see a flurry of activity, with several bidders trying to get in on the action at the last minute. For that reason, many bidders monitor the final minutes of any auction they're really serious about.

When the auction is finally over, both the seller and the winning bidder are notified via email of the final status of the auction. It is their responsibility to contact each other to arrange payment and shipping. (On most sites, it's common operating procedure for the seller to make the initial contact with the winning bidder, although it's okay for either to initiate communication.)

Typically, the seller notifies the buyer of the final *total* price of the item, including shipping and handling. Sometimes shipping/handling has to be negotiated, but more often than not the seller has a firm cost—and often states it up front in the item's description.

After the Auction at a Merchant Auction

If the auction was on a merchant auction site (such as Onsale or Surplus Auction), then the merchant contacts the high bidder to arrange payment and shipping. If the buyer has previously left credit card information with the site, the card is charged automatically and the merchandise sent on its way.

If an auction site charges selling fees, those fees (typically a small percentage of the final selling price) are assessed at this time. This happens automatically, and the fees are recorded to the seller's credit card account.

The Buyer Pays, the Seller Ships

After the total price is disclosed, the buyer then sends the seller a personal check, cashier's check, or money order. (If the seller is actually a business, the buyer might be able to pay with a credit card; most individuals cannot process credit-card transactions.)

After the seller receives payment (and, in the case of personal checks, waits for the check to clear), the seller then packs and ships the merchandise to the buyer. The buyer receives the merchandise a few days later, and—assuming it all arrives in one piece as described—another online auction is successfully concluded.

How Much Does Shipping Cost?

How do you know how much shipping and handling will be in advance? Experienced sellers are able to "guesstimate" shipping costs to different parts of the country for those items they sell a lot of. You can also use services such as the Postal Service's Priority Mail, which has a flat fee for sending items that fall within certain parameters anywhere in the country. See Chapter 27, "Shipping It Out—Without Spending a Fortune," for more information.

Use Escrow for Credit Cards

Individuals can accept credit card payments for items by using an *escrow service*. Escrow services are also good ways for buyers and sellers to protect themselves during a transaction, as the service acts as a "middleman," ensuring that both payment and shipment are made. See Chapter 26, "Protecting Yourself from Unscrupulous Buyers and Sellers," for more information on escrow services.

More Post-Auction Info

For more detailed advice on what to do when the auction is over, see Chapter 5, "After the Sale: Who Pays Whom, How, and When."

One last thing: Most online auction sites encourage users to provide *feedback* about the people they deal with. So if you're a buyer, you should provide feedback—positive or negative, depending on your experience—about the seller, and vice versa. You can get a good gauge on the reliability of a buyer or seller by observing his or her overall feedback ratings, gathered from multiple transactions.

The Least You Need to Know

➤ Online auctions start when the seller places an ad.

➤ The potential buyer begins by searching for a certain type of item.

➤ After displaying the item's detailed listing, the buyer can choose to place a bid on that item.

➤ The buyer enters the maximum amount he or she is willing to bid; the site's automated bidding software then manages the bidding process so that the buyer's current bid is no higher than it needs to be in order to be the high bid on the item.

➤ At the end of the auction, the high bidder wins.

➤ The seller and the high bidder contact each other and arrange payment terms and shipping.

Chapter 3

Those Other Types of Auctions: Dutch and Reserve

Most auctions on most auction sites are normal auctions—there is only one item for sale, and the high bidder wins. It's simple, and everybody understands how it works.

However, you might run into some variations on the normal auction from time to time. The most popular variations are *Dutch auctions* (used when there are multiple quantities of an item for sale) and *reserve price auctions* (used when the seller wants to ensure a higher selling price while still enticing potential buyers with a low opening bid).

When You Have More Than One to Sell, Go Dutch!

A Dutch auction is a special type of auction for sellers who have multiple quantities of an item to sell. Although most sellers on Dutch auctions are small businesses that want to unload multiple quantities of items, you'll also find some individuals with several like items to sell.

Here's how Dutch auctions work: A seller might have five copies of a particular video-tape title for sale (which, please note, is *not* the same as having five different video-tape titles that happen to be at the same price!); the seller can create one listing for a single Dutch auction with five quantities of the listed item.

In a Dutch auction, the seller specifies both the minimum bid and the number of items available in the auction. As in a normal auction, bidders bid at or above that minimum for the item—although, in a Dutch auction, bidders can specify a specific *quantity* that they're interested in purchasing.

An example of a Dutch auction at eBay—note the quantity available in the left-hand column.

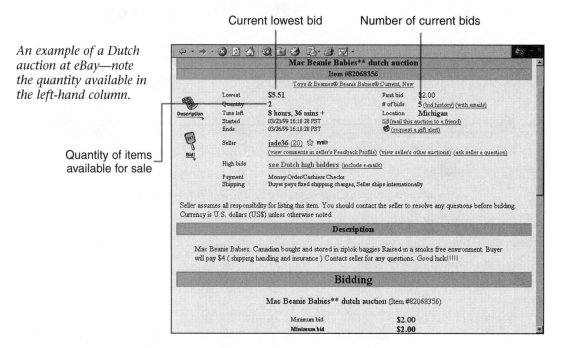

Current lowest bid

Number of current bids

Quantity of items available for sale

Dutch Auctions, By Example

Determining who "wins" a Dutch auction is a little different from determining who wins a normal auction. In a Dutch auction, the highest bidders purchase the items, but all buyers pay only the amount that matches the lowest successful bid.

Let's work through an example. Say a seller has 10 identical copies of *Star Wars* on videocassette. The seller indicates the number of items available (10), and the minimum bid (let's say $10). Potential buyers enter their bids, which must be equal to or higher than the minimum bid of $10; each buyer also indicates the quantity (from 1 to 10) that he or she is interested in purchasing.

If 11 people bid $10 each, then the first 10 bidders will win the auction, each paying $10 for their items, and the last bidder will be out of luck. But if the 11th person had placed a higher bid—$11, let's say—then that 11th bidder would be listed as the #1 bidder, and the last $10 bidder (chronologically) would be knocked from the list. All ten winning bidders, however—including the person who bid $11—would only have to pay $10 for the item. (Highest bidders, lowest bids—get it?)

In a Dutch auction, the minimum price ends up being raised only if enough bidders place bids above the minimum bid. In our example, if 9 bidders bid over the minimum, but the 10th bidder bid $10, then all bidders would still pay $10. But if the lowest bid was $11 (and the other bidders bid from $11 to $20), then all 10 bidders would pay $11 (the lowest current bid). So posting a higher bid increases a buyer's chances of winning an item at a Dutch auction, but it also increases the risk of raising the price for everybody.

All or Nothing at All

Remember, the higher bidders get first dibs on multiple quantities. So if the lowest bidder wants multiple quantities of the item on the block, he or she might find that there aren't enough to go around. If only a partial quantity is available, the bidder can officially walk away from his/her bid.

When a potential buyer bids on multiple copies of the item, those toward the end of the list might not get the quantity they desire. Still using our *Star Wars* example, if the top bidder wants three copies, the remaining seven copies are distributed among the next seven bidders—leaving the last or lowest two bidders out in the cold.

Tips for Bidding on Dutch Auctions

Dutch auctions actually benefit the buyer more than any other type of auction by letting higher bidders pay the lowest bid price. Should you bid on a Dutch auction? Why not? If someone is selling something you want, then by all means, bid!

How much should you bid? Ah, there's the issue! I actually like bidding on Dutch auctions later in the game, so that I can get a handle on how many other bidders I'm competing with. The number of bidders versus the quantity of items available determines my strategy:

➤ If the seller has a large quantity of items and a small number of bidders, bid the minimum. In this scenario, everybody wins because there's more than enough merchandise to go around.

➤ If the seller has a small quantity of items and a large number of bidders, then you probably should bid higher than the minimum. In fact, in this scenario, treat it like a normal auction and bid the highest amount you're willing to pay. The worst thing that could happen is you lose the auction; the second worst is that you're a winning bidder and you have to pay your maximum bid; the best scenario is that you're a winning bidder but get to pay a lower amount (due to a lower bid entered by another winning bidder).

When You Know It's Worth a Lot, Make a Reserve

In a *reserve price* auction, the seller has reserved the option to set a second price (the *reserve price*) that is higher than the opening bid. At the end of an auction, if the high bid does not meet or exceed the seller's reserve price, the seller does *not* have to sell the item to the high bidder. Sellers sometimes use a reserve price on high-end items if they want to make sure the market does not undervalue what they are selling.

In other words, the reserve price is the lowest price at which a seller is willing to sell an item (unrelated to the opening bid price). The seller specifies the reserve price when the item is initially listed (naturally, the reserve price should be above the minimum bid price). The reserve price is known only to the seller (and to the auction site), and is never disclosed to bidders—even though reserve price auctions are typically identified as such in the item's description.

Reserve, No Dutch

Reserve price auctions are not available for Dutch auctions. In a Dutch auction, the minimum price is the minimum price.

A reserve price auction begins just like any other auction, at the minimum bid price. When a bidder's maximum bid is equal to or greater than the reserve price, the item's current price is raised to the reserve price, and the reserve price has officially been met. If, through the course of the auction, the reserve price is *not* met, neither the seller nor the high bidder is under any further obligation to consummate the transaction.

Reserve Price Auctions, By Example

Let's look at a brief example of a reserve price auction. Suppose a seller has an item to sell that he feels is worth $50—but he wants to set a lower initial bid, to get the bidding going early. So the seller sets $25 as the initial bid, and $50 as the reserve price.

The first bidder on this item sees the $25 initial bid (the reserve price isn't displayed, of course), and bids $25. The bidder is notified that he has the current high bid, but that the reserve price has not been met. If the auction were to end right now, the item would *not* be sold—the seller is obligated to sell only if the reserve price is met.

The bidding continues, and the bid price increases until it hits $50. At that point, the last bidder is notified both that he is the high bidder, and also that the reserve price has been met. If the auction ends now—or at any point afterwards—the seller *is* obligated to sell, because the reserve price ($50) has been met.

So, in this example, any bids under $50 don't win the auction; any bids $50 and over can be winning bids.

Current bid

Indicates current bid is below the reserve price

Opening bid

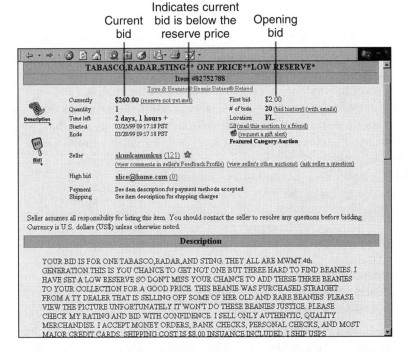

Example of a reserve auction at eBay—even though the current bid is higher than the opening bid, the reserve has not yet been met; the current high bidder needs to bid higher if he/she wants to win the auction.

Tips for Using Reserve Price Auctions

Why would a seller run a reserved price auction? There are two possible scenarios:

➤ When a seller is unsure of the real value of an item—and doesn't want to appear to be asking too much for an item—he or she essentially reserves the right to refuse to sell the item if the market value is below a certain price.

➤ When a seller wants to use a low initial bid price to get the bidding going more quickly than if the true desired minimum price (now the reserve price) was listed; the reserve price still guarantees the seller that he or she won't have to sell below a minimum acceptable price.

Some sellers might like reserve price auctions because they tend to protect the seller's minimum investment without listing unreasonable minimum bids, but they leave a lot of guesswork for the buyer as to how high he or she must bid to obtain the item. Because of the uncertainty factor, many buyers avoid auctions with reserve prices.

What Do You Do If Your Reserve Isn't Met?

If your auction ends and the high bid is below your reserve price, you don't have to do anything—you are not obligated to sell the item. However, you might want to contact the high bidder and see if he/she is willing to pay the reserve price for the item, or perhaps you can negotiate a fair price inbetween the high bid and your reserve. If you don't want to do this, you can always *re-list* the item in a new auction, in the hope that a new round of bidders will push the price up to what you expect to receive. Most auction sites make it fairly easy for sellers of non-sold items to re-list, often with the click of a button. If you do re-list, however, you might want to edit the item's description to make it more appealing, or even rethink your reserve price to make the item more affordable.

If you do want to bid in a reserve price auction, what should your strategy be? It depends on how badly you want the item. If you really, really, *really* want the item, you should place your first bid and see if you hit the reserve price. If you didn't, then place a new, higher bid, and see if *it* hits the reserve price. If you *still* didn't, repeat until your bid is high enough to guarantee a win.

For most bidders, however, this is simply a strategy to ensure writing a large check. In most cases, play a reserve price auction like you would a normal auction, and let the high bid be the high bid. If you have the high bid and the reserve price isn't met, then you can contact the seller and see if he/she is willing to sell at the current bid price, even though the reserve hasn't been met. The seller isn't obligated to do so, of course, but some might be willing to let the merchandise go to forgo starting a whole new auction (and paying another listing fee)—or they might be willing to negotiate a selling price somewhere in between your bid and the reserve. You never know until you ask!

More Types of Auctions

Dutch and reserve price auctions aren't the only unusual types of auctions you'll find on some sites. Here are some examples of other non-standard types of auctions you might run into:

➤ eBay has what it calls a *private auction*, where the bidders' email addresses are not disclosed to other bidders. (This is a useful option for auctions of "sensitive" items where potential bidders might not want their identities disclosed to the general public.)

➤ eBay also has *restricted access auctions* for items in the Erotica: Adults Only cate-gory; you need a credit card on file with eBay to view or bid on these items.

➤ Auction Universe has a *FirstBidWins* auction, which functions more or less like a traditional classified ad—the first bid that meets the seller's minimum bid wins the auction, right then and there, no further bidding allowed. For some buyers and sellers, it's a less stressful way of buying and selling items—absolutely no guesswork is involved, and no uncertainties exist.

The Least You Need to Know

➤ Dutch auctions are used when a seller has more than one identical copy of an item for sale.

➤ In a Dutch auction, the highest bidders win, but pay the lowest successful bid price.

➤ Reserve price auctions let sellers set a higher (hidden) minimum selling price than is listed for the initial bid price.

➤ If the highest bid is lower than the reserve price, the seller doesn't have to sell the item.

➤ Some sellers like reserve price auctions, but most buyers don't, due to the uncertainty factor.

Chapter 4

Bidding by Proxy: Robot Bidders Rule!

> **In This Chapter**
>
> ➤ Learn how automated bidding makes it easy to use online auctions
>
> ➤ Discover the secrets of the proxy bidding process
>
> ➤ Find out why smart bidders let their proxies help protect them from undisciplined spending

In these first few chapters, you've read about the so-called automated bidding software employed by many auction sites. This software is what makes online bidding relatively easy—you don't have to constantly monitor the auctions you're bidding on, because the software does it for you. But how does this bidding software work? Read on, and I'll explain.

Bidding with Robots: Proxy Bidding Explained

The automated bidding software used by many auction sites is called *proxy* or "robot" software. If you're a bidder, using proxy bidding can save you time and help ensure that you get the items you want. (If you're a seller, it doesn't really matter, because all you're interested in is the highest price at the end of the auction—no matter how it got there!)

Proxy software operates as an *agent* that is authorized to act in your place—but with some predefined bidding parameters. You define the maximum amount you are willing to bid, and then the robot agent takes over and does your bidding for you.

The proxy robot bids as little as possible to outbid new competition, up to the maximum bid you specified. If it needs to up your bid $1, it does. If it needs to up your bid $5, it does—until it hits your bid ceiling, then it stops and bows out of the bidding.

The robot bids in the official bid increments used by your auction site. If the next bid is $.50 higher than the current bid, then the robot ups your bid $.50. In no instance does the robot place a bid *over* the next bid increment. (It's pretty smart software!)

Of course, because all bidders are using these proxy robots, what happens when you have two robots bidding against each other? Simple—you get a robot bidding war! In this instance, each robot automatically ups its bid in response to the last bid by the other robot, which rapidly (seemingly instantaneously!) increases the bid price until one of the robots reaches its maximum bid level. Let's say one robot has been programmed with a maximum bid of $25, and another with a maximum bid of $26. Even though the initial bid might be $10, the bids rapidly increase from $10 to $11 to $12 and on to $26, at which point the first robot drops out and the second robot holds the high bid.

Proxy Bidding, by Example

Let's walk through a detailed example of proxy bidding. The process is totally automated, and goes like this:

1. You see an item with an initial bid of $100, and you instruct your robot that you're willing to pay $150 for it. The $150 becomes your maximum bid.

2. The bid increment on this $100 item is $10, so your robot bids $110. This becomes the current high bid.

3. Another bidder sees this item, and bids the next bid increment, $120.

4. Your robot sees the new bid, and ups its bid automatically to $130.

5. A third bidder sees the item, and instructs his robot to enter the auction with a maximum bid of $175. In accordance with the current bid increment, his robot enters a bid of $140.

6. Your robot responds with a bid of $150.

7. The third bidder's robot responds with a bid of $160.

8. Your robot drops out of the bidding, and the auction site notifies you (via email) that your bid has been surpassed. (If the auction were to end right then, the third bidder would win the auction with a bid of $160. Even though he specified a $175 maximum bid, the bidding never got that high.)

9. At this point, you can place a new maximum bid for the item, or you can throw in the towel and let the new bidder have the item.

Dutch, No Proxy

You can't use automated proxy bidding in Dutch auctions.

Proxy Bidding Advice

The nice thing about proxy bidding is that you can engage in a fierce bidding war—and never have to get your hands dirty! The robot does all the dirty work for you, and just notifies you of the results.

When you're placing your bid, realize that just because you set a maximum bid price doesn't mean you'll have to actually pay that price. The robot bidder works in your favor to keep your final price as low as possible; don't assume that just because you specified a price, the bidding will always rise to that level.

Also feel comfortable that your robot bidder will never exceed your maximum bid price. It just won't happen; the software is smart enough to know your limits.

The best advice for proxy bidding is the same advice I give every bidder—only bid as much as you think the item is worth. If you're willing to bid $100 for an item, say so! Don't hedge your bets—and don't exceed your predefined limits if the bidding goes higher. If you use proxy bidding appropriately, it will help you exercise discipline in your bidding activities.

By bidding your maximum right away, you guarantee that you won't get carried away and pay too much at the end of a heated competition. Remember, if you lose an auction because the bidding goes higher than your maximum, you didn't want to pay that much for the merchandise, anyway. Get comfortable with that—and be glad the proxy robot helped you stay within your limits.

Bidding Manually

On most that offer proxy bidding, use of the proxy is automatic for all bidders. So how can you bid manually when you're forced to use a proxy?

It's simple—just make your maximum bid the same value as the next minimum bid (that is, the current bid plus the bid increment). For example, if the current bid is $10 and the bid increment is $1, the next minimum bid is $11; your maximum bid, then, should be $11.

Bidding only the minimum doesn't give the proxy anything to do; there's no "up" to go from your bid amount. While this gives you more control over the auction process, this also means that you have to manually manage all your auctions, which can be somewhat time consuming.

Of course, some bidders don't like proxy bidding. It is true that if two or more people are bidding for the same item, then the bids will automatically (and quickly) rocket up until they max out. For this reason, some bidders prefer to view every single one of their bids as a manual minimum bid—they don't want the robot proxy bidding things up without their approval. Of course, if you choose to operate this way, you have to be a lot more hands-on with your bidding, essentially checking back on all your bids as frequently as necessary to ensure that you always end up on top. (This isn't a bad strategy for the closing moments of an auction, anyway, as discussed in Chapter 22, "Winning an Auction: Strategies for Buyers.")

The Least You Need to Know

➤ Proxy bidding lets you automate the entire bidding process, and eliminates the need for you to "birddog" all your auctions all the time.

➤ When you place a maximum bid, your proxy robot bids only the minimum amount necessary to ensure that you're the high bidder—and never exceeds your maximum bid amount.

➤ Use proxy bidding to help you enforce self-discipline in the bidding process—enter the maximum amount that you're really prepared to pay, and let your robot worry about the details.

Chapter 5

After the Sale: Who Pays Whom, How, and When

In This Chapter

➤ Learn what happens when an auction ends

➤ Find out what to do if the winning buyer reneges on the bid

➤ Discover the preferred methods of payment for both buyers and sellers

---

The auction is over. You've either won a bid, or sold an item.

Now what happens?

Making Contact

As soon as an auction ends, the auction site emails both the seller and the winning bidder. This email confirms that the auction is over, verifies the high bid, and identifies the winning bidder.

A typical post-auction email looks something like this:

> This message is to notify you that the following auction has ended:
>
>   ROBIN comics—lot of 45 issues (Item #37185048)
>
>   Final price: 14.00
>
>   Auction ended at: 8/28/99 14:35:06 PST
>
>   Total number of bids: 6
>
>   Seller User ID: trapperjohn2000
>
>   Seller E-mail: mmiller@somewhere.net
>
>   High-bidder User ID: bidderguy
>
>   High-bidder E-mail: bidguy@somewhere.net
>
> Seller and high bidder should now contact each other to complete the sale.
>
> IMPORTANT: Buyer and seller should contact each other within three business days, or risk losing their right to complete this transaction.
>
> The official results of this auction (including email addresses of all bidders) can be found for 30 days after the auction closes at `http://special.link.address`.

Take Responsibility

It is the responsibility of the seller and the buyer to contact one another—the auction site assumes no responsibility to get the two of you together.

After you receive this message, you should send an email to the other person in the transaction. Sellers should contact the winning bidders within *three business days* after the auction ends; winning bidders should also contact sellers, especially if they haven't heard from the seller within three business days.

When the seller contacts the winning bidder, he or she should provide the following information:

➤ Total cost of the item, including shipping and handling

➤ What kind of payment the seller prefers (for example, a seller could say that he or she will ship the item immediately with payment by cashier's check or money order, or that he or she will hold checks for two weeks to clear)

➤ Details on where the buyer should send the payment

➤ Details on shipping method

Remember, the buyer pays the seller directly—the buyer does *not* pay the auction site! In fact, the auction site has no role in the resulting transaction; the binding contract of the auction is between the winning bidder and the seller only.

...Or *Not* Making Contact

If you *can't* make contact with the high bidder or the seller, you should first double-check the other person's email address by sending an email to the auction site and requesting the user's contact information. Then send another email—including your personal contact information (phone number, address, and so on) just in case the other person has had trouble contacting you via return email.

High bidders can forfeit their position as winning bidders if they don't make prompt contact with the seller; the seller is not obligated to hold the merchandise beyond a reasonable period. So, if you're a seller and you've sent an email to the winning bidder, if at least *three business days* go by without a return message, you can officially move on to the next highest bidder.

If you're a seller and the buyer vanishes, you can't do much about it other than file a complaint with the auction site and leave negative feedback about that person. At least you won't be out any money!

Paying the Piper

Now the buyer has to pay for the item. Note that the buyer pays before the seller ships; that's just the way it is. In effect, this means that the risk of the transaction is on the buyer; the buyer is trusting the seller to actually ship the merchandise (in the agreed-upon condition) when the payment is made.

Most sellers state that they prefer cashier's checks or money orders, and try to discourage

Moving On to Number Two

You're not obligated to sell your item to anyone except your high bidder, but oftentimes it's easier to go to someone with proven interest than to start a brand-new auction from scratch. If your winning bidder tanks and you decide to contact the #2 bidder, explain your situation and offer to sell the item at his or her highest bid price. (Note that #2 bidders are not obligated to pay the delinquent winning bidder's price, only the highest price that they themselves bid.)

Dealing with Deadbeats

For more information about dealing with deadbeat buyers and sellers, see Chapter 26, "Protecting Yourself from Unscrupulous Buyers and Sellers."

payment by personal check. This is understandable; cashier's checks and money orders are just like cash, but a personal check isn't good until it clears the bank.

The reality is, however, most buyers pay by personal check. Let's face it, cashier's checks and money orders are a bit of a hassle—you have to make a special trip to the bank or the post office, stand in line, pay a fee, and only *then* can you send your payment. With a personal check, you write the check from the comfort of your own desk, pop it in an envelope, and have the payment in the mail almost immediately.

Know, however, that some sellers will hold items paid for by a personal check for 1–2 weeks, until the check clears the bank. Other sellers will look at a buyer's feedback rating, and if it's strong, they'll go ahead and ship the merchandise when they receive the check. (That's one good use for the auction site's feedback ratings, discussed later in this chapter.) But don't expect all sellers to ship immediately if you pay by personal check, especially if they haven't dealt with you before or you're a relatively new user of the auction site.

In any case, let the seller know how you'll be paying, and get them to confirm how many days after payment it takes them to ship—just so there are no surprises.

Most private individuals, of course, can't accept credit-card payment, which is why you have to use paper payment. Many small businesses sell items on auction sites, however, and many of these firms *do* accept payment by credit card. If you need something in a hurry, choosing a seller who accepts credit cards can be the key to success. (If in doubt, email the seller while the auction is still in progress and ask!)

Paying by Escrow

If you're unsure of the other person in the transaction, you can protect yourself by using an *escrow service* to function as a go-between for both the buyer and seller. The buyer pays the escrow service (and can pay by credit card if desired—which is one way for individual sellers to accept credit cards), and the service confirms that the payment was made and cleared the appropriate banks. On the okay from the escrow service, the seller ships out the merchandise. When the buyer receives the item, he/she confirms receipt with the escrow service, and the service then releases the buyer's payment to the seller. You can find out more about escrow services in Chapter 26.

Shipping It Out

After the seller receives payment for the item, it's time to pack it up and ship it out. The seller must pack the item in an efficient yet sturdy manner, so the item doesn't get damaged in shipment. Then the seller takes the item to the post office or one of the major shipping services, and arranges shipment. (It's also considered good form for the seller to email the buyer, confirming receipt of payment and notifying them when and how the item was shipped out.)

Typically, the method of shipment is decided upon by the seller, although a buyer can request a particular shipping method. Most experienced sellers have the shipping down to a science, and thus have their preferred shipping services.

Some sellers offer buyers several shipping options. A basic option might be U.S. Postal Service Priority Mail, which can ship many items out for just $3.20. A step-up option might be adding insurance, which costs an extra $.75 or so. A further option might be using Federal Express or U.S. Postal Service Express Mail, for guaranteed next-day delivery. Naturally, the faster the delivery, the higher the shipping costs.

I find that an increasing number of sellers use U.S. Postal Service Priority Mail to ship their items. Priority Mail does offer a good compromise between low cost and rapid delivery. If you need an item guaranteed for overnight delivery, however, you'll have to go up to the Postal Service's Express Mail, or to Federal Express or a similar service—both of which are costly.

The Buyer Pays

In the world of online auctions, the buyer pays for everything—including shipping. Don't expect the seller to throw in shipping for free! Remember to mentally add the approximate shipping costs to your bid price on any item, so you're prepared for the total cost when the auction is over.

An All-in-One Shipping Resource

If you want to access all the major shipping services from a single page, go to the TradeSafe ShippingLinks page (www.tradesafe.com/ShippingLinks.htm). This page includes links to all the major shipping services, from the U.S. Postal Service to heavy freight carriers.

If you're a buyer, don't be surprised to see the seller quote a shipping charge that is slightly higher than what you know the actual shipping costs to be. Remember, the seller has to cover various costs—the cost of the box and packing materials, the fees to the auction site, that sort of thing. So paying a buck or so above the actual shipping costs shouldn't be onerous.

To read more detailed information advice about packing and shipping, see Chapter 27, "Shipping It Out—Without Spending a Fortune."

Waiting for Your Doorbell to Ring...

Now the buyer waits for the item to arrive. If the wait is too long, the buyer should contact the seller and confirm that the item was actually shipped out on a particular date; if an item appears to be lost in shipment, the buyer and seller can work together to track down the shipment with the shipping service.

In most cases, however, the item arrives promptly. Now the buyer should unpack the item and inspect it for any damage. If it's something that can be tried out, the buyer should make sure that the item actually works. (Nothing is more frustrating to a seller than to receive an email from a buyer *months later* complaining that an item didn't work as claimed!)

If anything is wrong with the merchandise, the buyer should contact the seller immediately (and politely!) to work out a mutually agreeable solution. In most cases, buyers should expect sellers to refund their money upon return of defective merchandise.

If nothing is wrong, the buyer should still contact the seller to confirm delivery—and to say thanks for a successful and enjoyable auction experience!

Leave Feedback

After the merchandise has been received and accepted, one last task remains for both the buyer and the seller—leaving feedback. Most auction sites encourage their users to leave feedback about the people they deal with. You can typically leave positive, neutral, or negative feedback, complete with brief comments. If you had a successful auction, leave positive feedback about the buyer or seller. If something went horribly wrong, don't be afraid to leave negative feedback—it warns other users about possible bad apples.

In any case, you want to build up your own cache of positive feedback, and the best way to do that is to leave positive feedback about others (when warranted). Model online auctioneers take the time and effort to participate in the feedback process, for the benefit of all.

The Least You Need to Know

➤ When an auction is over, the auction site notifies both the seller and the winning bidder via email.

➤ The seller and winning bidder must contact each other within three working days.

➤ The seller tells the buyer the total cost, including shipping.

➤ The buyer sends payment to the seller, normally via personal check, cashier's check, or money order.

➤ Upon payment, the seller packs and ships the item to the buyer.

➤ After the buyer receives the merchandise, the two parties leave feedback for each other at the auction site.

Part 2

Auctions, Auctions, Everywhere: Finding the Right Auction for You

Did you know that more than 300 auction sites exist on the World Wide Web? You've proba-bly heard about eBay, but did you know about Auction Universe, Up4Sale, or uBid? Many auc-tions even specialize in certain types of merchandise, such as antiques, rare coins, or vintage automobiles? Well, if you're looking for just the right auction for what you want to buy or sell, this section of the book is for you!

Chapter 6

General Auctions: A Little Bit of Everything, All in One Place

In This Chapter

➤ Discover which auction sites have the most listings—and the most bidder traffic

➤ Find out which features and services are important when choosing an auction site

➤ Learn about nearly 100 different general auction sites

What is it you need?

A new modem for your computer? A vintage German military helmet? A prop from your favorite movie? A specific trading card or comic book or retired Beanie Baby? How about some jewelry, or an antique desk, or an answering machine for your office?

You can find all these items—and more—at the many "general" auction sites on the Web. Although some smaller auctions tend to specialize in a certain category of merchandise, these general auctions accept listings for just about anything. In fact, some general auction sites carry so many different types of items that they divide their listings into literally thousands of different categories!

Knowing this—and also knowing that there are hundreds of different auction sites on the Web—how do you pick the right site for your needs?

Let's take a look at the biggest and the best (and the rest) of the Internet's general auction sites.

Just What Is a "General" Auction?

To be a truly general auction, a site must have a large number of items listed in most if not all of the following categories:

➤ Antiques

➤ Art

➤ Autographs

➤ Autos, boats, and planes

➤ Books and manuscripts

➤ Business supplies and equipment

➤ Coins and stamps

➤ Collectibles and memorabilia (general)

➤ Comics and trading cards

➤ Computer hardware and software

➤ Consumer electronics (including audio, video, and photography)

➤ Dolls and action figures

➤ Furniture

➤ Jewelry and gemstones

➤ Model kits, cars, and airplanes

➤ Movies and television memorabilia

➤ Music and musical instruments

➤ Pottery and glass

➤ Sporting goods and memorabilia (especially sports cards)

➤ Toys (especially Beanie Babies)

Comparing the Big Five Auction Sites

When it comes to general auction sites, there are five really big players—and hundreds of smaller ones. In fact, if you really want to get right down to it, there's one really, really big player—and then there's everybody else.

The biggest player, far and away, is eBay. eBay has more items listed and more bidders than all the other auction sites combined—several times over! In fact, eBay has over 10 times the number of items for auction as the #2 site (Yahoo! Auctions), with more than to 2 million individual listings on any given day.

So if eBay is so dominant, why should anyone bother with any other auction?

You might want to pick a site besides eBay for a number of reasons:

➤ **Retire to an exclusive community**   Few hard-core enthusiasts and collectors want to shop at a mass merchant—and eBay can sometimes be the equivalent of a mass-merchant auction. If you want a more exclusive environment, go to an auction site that specializes in your hobby.

➤ **Go Local**   So far, eBay is a global auction, not a local one (although a recent alliance with AOL should change all that). That means if you have items you can only sell locally—big, heavy stuff, for example—eBay doesn't cut it. Until eBay discovers how to localize its process, you might want to check out one of the growing number of local auction sites (CityAuction, for example, or one of the Auction Universe Network affiliate sites).

➤ **Reduce the confusion**   With close to two million items for sale, how is a bidder to find anything? If you find eBay too big and confusing, opt for a smaller site, where it's easier to find what you're looking for.

➤ **Get noticed**   When eBay has more than 85,000 different Beanie Babies listed, it's hard to stand out in the crowd. If you're selling something and don't want to get lost in the shuffle, go to a smaller site, where you *can* get noticed.

➤ **Save some money**   The huge number of bidders on eBay means that sometimes items get bid up to ridiculous prices. (I've actually seen brand-new items being sold for higher than retail price on eBay due to a last-minute bidding frenzy!) If you want fewer competitors for the items you're bidding on—and thus a better bargain for your bid—skip eBay and go to a less competitive auction.

➤ **Find the exact thing that you want**   Not even eBay has *everything* listed. If you're looking for a specific baseball card or coin and it isn't on eBay, it may be on Auction Universe, Yahoo! Auctions, or a more collector-focused site. If you're searching for a specific item, it pays to shop around.

Beyond eBay, then, who are the major auction players?

The balance of what I call the Big Five auction sites is comprised of Amazon.com Auctions (auctions.amazon.com, the newest player), Auction Universe (www.auctionuniverse.com, the most established competitor), Classifieds 2000 Auctions (www.classifieds2000.com, where auctions grew out of classified ads), and Yahoo! Auctions (auctions.yahoo.com, driven by the enormous traffic from the Web's most popular portal). These sites all offer a broad variety of merchandise in all popular categories, and all operate in much the same fashion as does eBay.

That's not to say, however, that there aren't differences between these sites. Yahoo! Auctions, for example, is simply bigger than the remaining three players (although is itself much smaller than eBay); neither Classifieds 2000 nor Yahoo! Auctions charge listing fees; and Amazon.com Auctions and Auction Universe both offer buyer protection programs of various sorts (something eBay doesn't do).

Table 6.1 offers a more detailed look at the differences between the Big Five sites.

Table 6.1   Comparison of Big Five Auction Sites

Feature	eBay	Amazon.com Auctions	Auction Universe	Classifieds 2000 Auctions	Yahoo! Auctions
URL	www.ebay. com	auctions. amazon.com	www. auctionuniverse. com	www. classifieds2000. com	auctions. yahoo.com
Number of items listed	2,000,000+	20,000	30,000	25,000	135,000
Seller fees charged	Yes	Yes	Yes	No	No
Automatic auction end	No	No	Yes	Yes	Seller selectable extensions
Escrow option and/or guarantee	Yes, free protection up to $200	Yes, free protection up to $250	Yes, $19.95 /year	No	No

Which auction site should you choose? Well, if you want the most bidders or items to bid on, go to eBay. If you want to avoid paying any listing or selling fees, go to Classifieds 2000 Auctions or Yahoo! Auctions. If you want the safest auctions, hit Amazon.com Auctions, Auction Universe, or eBay. Beyond that, many buyers and sellers frequent all five of these sites with some regularity—because you never know *where* that one special item you've always wanted is going to show up!

When the End Isn't Really the End

On some auction sites—specifically, Auction Universe, Classifieds 2000, and Yahoo! Auctions (on a seller-selectable basis)—auctions don't always end at the specified end time. On these sites, auctions don't close until either five or ten minutes (depending on the site) after the last bid is placed—which means that as long as people keep bidding, the auction keeps going. These sites claim they do this to prevent users from being locked out of an auction in the closing minutes, due to a slow connection or other issues. To me, the real reason they implement this automatic auction end extension model is to eliminate "sniping" (discussed in Chapter 22, "Winning an Auction: Strategies for Buyers") as an auction-winning strategy. (Because eBay's auctions are not automatically extended, you can still snipe on the largest auction site.)

Bigger Than All the Others Put Together: eBay

What is eBay? I think its official mission statement sums up what eBay does quite well:

> *"We help people trade practically anything on earth."*

With over 2 million items for sale on any given day, it's hard to argue that eBay isn't achieving what it set out to do.

eBay was one of the first auction sites on the Internet, launched way back on Labor Day of 1995. It almost single-handedly pioneered the concept of online auctions, and in doing so, carved out a dominant market share. (It also made a lot of money for those who invested in the firm over the years!)

It's All Due to PEZ

As the official story goes, founder Pierre Omidyar launched eBay as the result of a conversation with his then-girlfriend, an avid PEZ dispenser collector. She supposedly commented to Pierre about how great it would be if she were able to collect PEZ dispensers using the Internet; Pierre saw the light and a Web empire was born.

How to Use eBay

I won't go into detail here on how eBay works, because eight chapters of this book are devoted to using eBay in explicit detail. (See Part 3, "Essential eBay: Buying and

Selling on the Internet's Largest Auction Site.") Suffice it to say that eBay essentially created the online auction model, and all the other sites followed in eBay's footsteps.

The biggest auction site in the world—eBay.

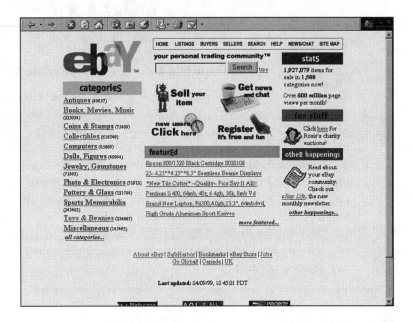

eBay on AOL

As this book is being written, eBay has just announced a $75 million "strategic marketing alliance." As part of this alliance, eBay will provide AOL users with a customized "eBay at AOL" site containing special content, features, and access to promotional auctions just for AOL's 16+ million users. In addition, eBay users will now be able to access AOL's ICQ instant messaging service, and eBay will use AOL's Digital City subsidiary to create local and regional auction sites. Look for more information on this key alliance as time passes.

The Good and the Bad About eBay

Given the fact that eBay is the most popular auction site around, what are its true merits and detriments? Here's my personal take on eBay:

➤ **Good: It's big**   eBay's size brings many benefits, chief among them a large variety of items for sale and a large number of potential buyers to bid on any item you decide to list. Being big (and a public company) also means it's going to stick around for awhile, and not go out of business over the weekend. In short, almost all of eBay's strong points—large selection, large bidder pool, rich feature set, and so on—come from its size.

➤ **Bad: It's big**   eBay's size is also its greatest weakness. Sometimes it seems like there are too many items for sale, making it hard to find any specific item and causing items to get "lost" within large categories. Also, the large number of bidders often results in prices being driven too high too fast, which isn't good if you're trying to buy something cheap. In addition, *you* can get lost among eBay's two million other registered users; don't expect a lot of personal service here.

➤ **Good: It's getting safer**   eBay's Safe Harbor program protects buyers for up to $200 (less a $25 deductible) if the sale goes bad in any way—if they fail to receive the merchandise, or if the merchandise isn't as advertised. While other sites (such as Auction Universe) have higher levels of insurance, eBay's program covers the majority of items up for auction, and is the first of what will be several steps taken to make eBay a much safer environment for its users.

Bottom line—I use eBay all the time. Yeah, its size is starting to get in the way somewhat, but it's still the best place in the world to buy and sell just about anything.

Some Interesting Facts About eBay

Want some cocktail party conversation? Then whip out these interesting items:

➤ eBay has more than 5.6 million registered users.

➤ On any given day eBay has more than 2 million individual items for sale—with 250,000 new items added every 24 hours.

➤ An average day sees 800,000 individual bids—which computes to 33,000 bids per hour, 554 bids per minute, or 3 bids every second.

➤ The average visit to eBay is 27 minutes long—an eternity for Web site visits.

➤ Since its launch on Labor Day, 1995, eBay has logged more than 200 million items for sale, with more than 800 million bids made.

New Kid on the Block: Amazon.com Auctions

One day in March, 1999, the face of online auctions was forever changed. On that day, without much warning but with a lot of fanfare, the largest Internet shopping site added auctions to its portfolio of online offerings.

Amazon.com is an amazing site. Starting with books (and billing themselves as "the world's largest bookstore") and expanding into music and video, Amazon.com has a huge base of 8 million registered users. When Amazon.com launched Amazon.com Auctions, every one of those 8 million users was automatically pre-registered to buy and sell in its online auction.

From the first day, however, Amazon.com was a little different from eBay. Where eBay deals primarily in person-to-person auctions, Amazon.com launched with more of a merchant-to-customer model. On day one, all of Amazon.com's merchandise came from one hundred "charter merchants," not from individuals. That means that just about all of the items listed on Amazon.com are retail items, not used items like you find on eBay. (Don't think Amazon.com just auctions books, CDs, and videos, however—its auction site offers merchandise in a large variety of categories, not just those categories offered by Amazon's retail operations.)

This is partly due to Amazon.com's desire to create a safer, more familiar auction environment for its current retail customers. It's also due to the fact that it's difficult to start an auction from scratch, so "seeding" the site with merchant listings gave them thousands of items for sale overnight.

As time goes on Amazon.com is adding thousands of individual listings to its core merchant listing base. And, if you're looking for a particular item at a particular price, what do you care if it comes from a merchant or from an individual? (If anything, buying from merchants is safer than buying from individuals.)

An online auction that looks like an online bookstore—Amazon.com Auctions.

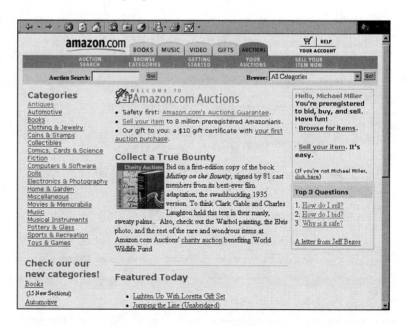

How to Use Amazon.com Auctions

In terms of buying and selling, Amazon.com Auctions works much like eBay. You have to register to buy or sell items (although if you've ever purchased from Amazon.com, you're pre-registered), and Amazon.com charges sellers both listing and completion fees.

To list an item, just click the **Sell Your Item Now** link. The Sell an Item form asks for much of the same information you would supply at other sites, and you can include a picture with your ad. Amazon.com allows reserve price auctions, Dutch auctions, and private auctions. Auctions can last from 1 to 14 days, and you can use HTML code in your listings.

To find an item, you can either browse through Amazon.com's many categories, or search for the item from the Auction Search box. You can perform a more sophisticated search (specifying categories, auction status, or seller name) by clicking the **Auction Search** link.

To bid on an item, enter your maximum bid on the listing page and click the **Bid Now!** button. Amazon.com uses a proxy bidding system called Bid Click to automate the bidding process. Note that, like eBay, when an auction ends, it ends—no automatic extensions here.

At Amazon, It's Guaranteed!

One of the nice features of this site is the Amazon.com Auctions Guarantee. This states that for all auctions carrying the Amazon.com Auctions Guarantee logo and closing under $250, a buyer is guaranteed that the item purchased from the seller was described accurately, and that it was shipped in a timely fashion after payment. If you have problems, contact Amazon.com directly and they'll reimburse you for what you paid. The best thing about the guarantee? It's free!

The Good and the Bad About Amazon.com Auctions

What's to like—and not to like—about Amazon.com Auctions? Here's my personal list:

➤ **Good: It's Amazon**   Everything you like about Amazon.com is present in Amazon.com Auctions—terrific site design and logical navigation, the backing of the Internet's largest retailer, automatic registration for Amazon.com customers, and smooth integration with the rest of the Amazon.com site (including auction recommendations listed on book, music, or movie listing pages). If you go to Amazon.com anyway (and 8 million of you have already), then how much trouble is it to click the **Auctions** tab?

➤ **Good: The Guarantee**   Amazon.com's unique guarantee assures bidders that they'll be protected (up to $250) should a transaction go bad. And, for sellers, the guarantee is free. What better way to take the fear out of buying something online?

➤ **Bad: Not enough listings from individuals** All those listings from merchants are fine, but an auction's not an auction without a lot of stuff offered by individuals. Until and unless Amazon.com builds its user auctions, this will be a major roadblock for a lot of potential bidders.

The bottom line? I'll give Amazon.com a chance (and I certainly won't bet against it, given Amazon's track record in book and music retailing), but it doesn't impress just yet. Check back in a few months and see if things have changed.

An Expanding Universe of Listings: Auction Universe

After eBay, Auction Universe is the oldest and most established of the Big Five auction sites. Owned by Classified Ventures, Inc. (a company created by several major newspaper syndicates), Auction Universe has one of the best-designed sites of any auction.

Auction Universe (also called *AU*) divvies its site into more than 6,000 different categories (compared to eBay's 1,500 categories). This doesn't necessarily mean that the site has more things for sale (because AU is much, much smaller than eBay), but rather that the things it has are grouped into more precise categories, for easier location.

AU also has a lot more editorial content than the other sites, eBay included. Although it's unclear how useful this is to users, it's always informative to head to one of AU's "hubs" and read what its editors have to say about the topic at hand.

One of the best-designed auction sites around— Auction Universe.

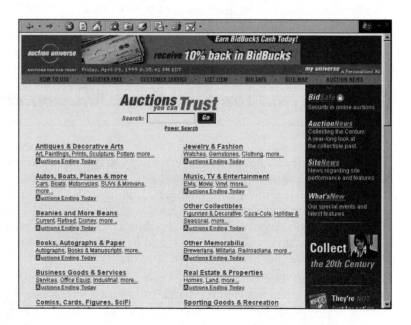

How to Use Auction Universe

Using Auction Universe is much like using eBay. You have to register to buy or sell items, and AU charges sellers both listing and completion fees.

To list an item, just click on the **List Item** link. You first choose a category for your listing, and then enter the usual info in the List an Item form. You can include a picture with your ad, and use HTML code in your listings. AU allows reserve price auctions and Dutch auctions, and auctions can last from 1 to 14 days.

To find an item, you can either browse through AU's 6,000 different categories, or search for the item from the Search box. You can perform a more sophisticated search (specifying categories, auction status, or seller name) by clicking the **Power Search** link. The Power Search function on AU offers the unique feature of searching for auctions by location (state and country).

To bid on an item, enter your maximum bid on the listing page and click the **Place Bid** button. Auction Universe uses a proxy bidding system called RoboBid to automate the bidding process. Unlike eBay, AU auctions continue for five to ten minutes after the last bid, preventing sniping.

Auction Universe offers optional protection for buyers and sellers in the form of its Bid$afe service. For $19.95 a year, you get $3,000 in insurance coverage and various other benefits. This replaces the need for an escrow service for insured transactions.

In addition to its normal auctions, AU offers a fixed-priced auction called FirstBidWins. Basically, this works kind of like a classified ad; the first bidder offering the requested bid wins the auction. It's a good way to take the guesswork out of the whole auction process.

The Good and the Bad About Auction Universe

So, what are Auction Universe's strong points—and weak points? Here's what I think:

➤ **Good: Terrific site design** I love the way AU works; it's clean and easy to navigate. Also, dividing its listings into 6,000 separate categories makes it easy to find just the right category for each piece of merchandise.

➤ **Good: Bid$afe** Cheap insurance. It's a nice safety net.

➤ **Good: Local auctions** Not only can you search for listings by location (which no other Big Five Auction offers), but you can also enter local auction sites through the Auction Universe Network. Great for things you couldn't put up for auction, otherwise.

➤ **Bad: Not enough listings, not enough bidders** In spite of all these great features, the main problem with AU is that, in many categories, there simply aren't enough items for sale, nor are there enough potential buyers for those items. Why list if there's no one to buy—and why buy if there's nothing to bid on? With only 30,000 items for sale (compared to eBay's 2 *million* listings), there's just no comparison. (Note that this isn't true in every category; there are some categories—such as comics and sports cards—where both the listings and the bids are robust.)

My bottom-line opinion of Auction Universe is simple—good design, good features, not enough stuff!

Go Local with the Auction Universe Network

Auction Universe offer something that none of the other Big Five auction sites offers at this point in time—local auction sites. Through the Auction Universe Network (www.aun.com), Auction Universe helps dozens of affiliates create local auction sites. These sites are often associated with major metropolitan newspapers (such as the *Chicago Tribune, Los Angeles Times,* and *Washington Post*) or radio/TV stations.

If you want to see the items for sale in your particular region, just enter the Auction Universe Network through one of the affiliate auction sites. Most affiliate sites include both local items and items listed on the main Auction Universe site.

As of this writing, the Auction Universe Network includes the following affiliate sites:

➤ Auction Hunter (www.auctionhunter.co.uk)

➤ Auction OK (www.auctionok.com)

➤ Auctions Orlando (www.auctionsorlando.com)

➤ Auctions VA (www.auctionsva.com)

➤ AuctionsSouthFlorida (www.auctionssouthflorida.com)

➤ Auctionuniverse.co.uk (www.auctionuniverse.co.uk)

➤ AZ Auctions (www.azauctions.com)

➤ Bargain News Auctions Online (www.bnauctions.com)

➤ BV Auctions (www.bvauctions.com)

➤ Channel 3000 Auctions (www.channel3000auctions.com)

➤ Channel 6000 Auctions (www.channel6000auctions.com)

➤ Columbian.com Auctions NW (www.auctionsnw.com)

➤ Courant CTAuctions (www.ctauctions.com)

➤ Dr. Laura Schlessenger Foundation Auctions (www.drlauraauctions.com)

➤ LancAuctions (www.lancauctions.com)

➤ Los Angeles Times Auctions (www.laauctions.com)

➤ Maine Market Auctions (www.maineauctions.com)

➤ MFCP Auctions Midwest (www.auctionsmidwest.com)

➤ Minneapolis Star Tribune Strib Auctions.com (www.stribauctions.com)

➤ Monitor Auctions (www.monitorauctions.com)

➤ Morning Call Penn Auctions (www.pennauctions.com)

➤ Nando: Scoopy's Auction Universe (www.scoopysauction.com)

➤ Netis AuctionWeb (www.netisauctions.com)

➤ NewsNet 5 Auctions (www.newsnet5auctions.com)

➤ NFL Alumni Charity Auctions (www.nflalumniauctions.com)

➤ Palladium Interactive bbauctions.com (www.bbauctions.com)

➤ Philadelphia Online Philly Auctions (www.phillyauctions.com)

➤ Postnet Auctions (www.postnetauctions.com)

➤ Sporting News Auction House (auctions.sportingnews.com)

➤ St. Lucie Marketplace (www.stluciemarketplace.com)

➤ Triangle Auction (www.triangleauction.com)

➤ VermontAuctions (www.vermontauctions.com)

➤ VTCO Auctions (www.vtcoauctions.com)

➤ White's Guide Auction House (www.whitesauction.com)

➤ WLAJ Auction (www.wlajauction.com)

➤ WWMT Auction (www.wwmtauction.com)

Your Choice of Classifieds or Auctions: Classifieds 2000 Auctions

Classifieds 2000 is the Internet's largest site for classified advertising, and also runs one of the Big Five auction sites. Owned by Excite, Classifieds 2000 (or just C2K) really feels more like a classifieds site than an auction site; in fact, the site design is such that you're often not sure whether you're looking at straight ads or auction listings.

This site is also the smallest of the Big Five auction sites, and offers the fewest bells and whistles. To be honest, after using eBay, Amazon.com Auctions, and Auction Universe, this is a hard site to like.

Classifieds 2000 has kind of an average auction site—but you can also use it for classified advertising.

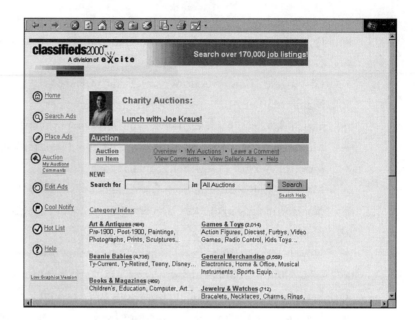

Ad or Auction—Choose One Only!

You can't choose to list an item in both a classified ad and an online auction, because Classifieds 2000 forbids duplicate ads. If you have an item listed in an ad, you must wait for the ad period to expire before you place the item for bid in an auction. Alternately, you can convert your classified ad to an auction ad by clicking the **Edit Ads** link on the main Classifieds page, clicking the **Change One of My Ads** link, and following the onscreen instructions.

How to Use Classifieds 2000 Auctions

Because of its background in classified ads, using Classifieds 2000 Auctions is a little different from using eBay. You still have to register to buy or sell items, although C2K does *not* charge either listing or completion fees. Note that there isn't a simple URL for the Auctions site itself; just go to the main Classifieds 2000 page (www.classifieds2000.com) and click the **Auctions** link.

To list an item, just click the **Place Ads** link. You first choose a category for your listing, and then click the **Place an Auction Ad** link. (At this point you could opt to place a classified ad instead.) Next you choose a subcategory, and then log on with your user ID and password. When the Place Ads page appears, enter the usual information. You can include a picture with your ad, and use HTML code in your listings. C2K allows reserve price auctions (but not Dutch auctions), and auctions can last from 3 to 14 days.

To find an item, you can either browse through C2K's limited number of categories, or (better) search for the item from the Search box. This site doesn't offer an advanced search page.

To bid on an item, enter your maximum bid and personal information on the listing page and click the **Submit Bid** button. Classifieds 2000 uses a proxy bidding system called AutoBidder to automate the bidding process. Unlike eBay, Classifieds 2000 auctions continue for ten minutes after the last bid, preventing sniping.

The Good and the Bad About Classifieds 2000 Auctions

What's to like—and not to like—about Classifieds 2000? Here's my personal list:

- ➤ **Good: Not much**   I suppose if you're used to the C2K classifieds service, moving to its auctions is an easy jump. Also, if you're not sure whether you want to run a fixed-priced classified or risk an auction, you can come here to make your final decision.

- ➤ **Bad: Doesn't really feel like an auction**   This site is way too complicated compared to other auction sites, and you often can't tell whether you're doing an auction or a regular classified. Really poor feel and navigation, in my opinion.

- ➤ **Bad: Too few listings, too few categories, too few bidders**   This is the smallest of the Big Five sites, poorly constructed in terms of categories, and therefore hasn't been attracting too many bidders or sellers. It isn't picking up much of a positive buzz, either.

The bottom line? This isn't the best auction site in the world. Frankly, I don't like it, and don't use it much. (Even though I *do* use C2K's standard classified ads—which they do very well.)

Free Listings: Yahoo! Auctions

When Yahoo!—the most-visited site on the entire Internet—decided to get into auctions, people took notice. After all, Yahoo! knows how to design an easy-to-use site, and it can certainly deliver a lot of traffic. Yahoo! also did a quick deal with Onsale—an experienced auction company—to help develop and run its auction site.

The result? Yahoo! Auctions is now arguably the #2 auction site on the Web. It lists five times as many items as the smaller Big Five sites (but still less than 10% of what is listed at eBay), and delivers a fair amount of bidders.

The #2 auction site—Yahoo! Auctions.

Should Auctions Be Free?

Some observers have blamed Yahoo! Auctions's slow growth on the fact that it's free—it doesn't charge any listing or selling fees. To some extent, free listings encourage abuse of the system; it's too easy for kids and pranksters to put up false auctions, or back out of bids. Certainly, that type of abuse is more prevalent on Yahoo! than it is on eBay, percentage-wise. So it may be the case that free isn't always better—charging a slight fee keeps out the riff-raff!

How to Use Yahoo! Auctions

Using Yahoo! Auctions isn't that terribly different from using eBay. You still have to register to buy or sell items, although Yahoo! Auctions does *not* charge either listing or completion fees; its auctions are all free.

To list an item, just click the **Submit Auctions** link. You first choose a category for your listing, then sign in to the system. When the Yahoo! Auctions Submissions page appears, enter the usual info. You can include a picture with your ad, and use HTML code in your listings. Yahoo! allows both reserve price and Dutch auctions, and you can choose whether you want to use Yahoo!'s Auto-Extension feature or have a "hard" end time for your auction. Auctions can last from 2 to 14 days.

To find an item, you can either browse through Yahoo's well-thought-out categories, or search for the item from the Search box. Click the **Options** link for some limited advanced search options.

Add Pictures from the Photo Album

Yahoo! makes it easier than most auctions to add pictures to your listings, through the use of the Yahoo! Auctions photo album. You can use this service to store photos of your auction items, as well as your logo, on the Yahoo! servers—which means you don't need to know HTML to show your images on the auction pages, as you do with eBay. You can access the photo album from the submission form, from the Auction Manager (located on your auction pages), or through your My Auctions pages. To add photos to your album, just click the **Add Images to Your Photo Album** link. This takes you to your photo album edit page, where you can upload photos directly from your computer. After you have uploaded your images to your photo library, pull down the **First Picture** list and select the image you want to display.

To bid on an item, enter your maximum bid and personal info on the listing page and click the **Place a Bid** button. Like eBay, Yahoo! uses an automated bidding system; unlike eBay, Yahoo! auctions can continue for five minutes after the last bid (if the seller chose the Auto-Extension option), preventing sniping.

The Good and the Bad About Yahoo! Auctions

So, what's good and bad about the #2 auction site?

➤ **Good: Good site design and categorization**   As you would expect from Yahoo!, this is an easy site to use.

➤ **Bad: Too few bidders**   So, does everybody just go to eBay to bid, no matter what? Too many categories have items with zero bidders, which would make me leery of putting anything here for sale.

The bottom line? Despite the typical non-eBay lack of traffic, I like this site. (Of course, I'm a sucker for an attractive site design.) However, the lack of traffic is worrisome—this is probably a better site at which to bid than to list.

All the Other General Auctions

Okay, you've seen the best—now it's time for the rest! The Big Five aren't the only auction sites around, and sometimes you can find some great bargains at the hundreds of other general auction sites on the Web. Note, however, that many of these sites are *really* small, and some are even run by individuals out of their bed-rooms and garages—which means your risk increases somewhat when you're buying things there.

That said, Table 6.2 lists a lot of the "other" general auction sites on the Web today.

Table 6.2   Top General Auction Sites

Site	URL	Comments
4u2Bid Auction	`www.ultra-web.com/auction/`	General auction, focus on collectibles
A1Auction	`www.a1auction.com`	Based in northwest Arkansas, billed as a "Flea Market Auction"
ActionBid Online Auctions	`www.actionbid.com`	General auction, started as computers only, now expanding into other categories
Advantage Auction	`advantageauction.com`	General auction, focus on collectibles
Auction Bidding	`www.auction-bidding.com`	Core auctions feature computer accessories, electronics, and auto parts; expanding into general and collectible categories
Auction First	`www.auctionfirst.com/html/categories.htm`	Collection of auctions from various small merchants
Auction InfoCom	`auction.infocom.net`	Very small, limited number of listings
Auction Nation	`www.auctionnation.com`	General auction, focus on collectibles
Auction Online De Veiling	`www.auction-online.com`	International auctions in Dutch and English
Auction Universe Network	`www.aun.com`	Local affiliates of Auction Universe, generally large metropolitan newspapers; great for local auctions
AuctionAddict	`www.auctionaddict.com`	General auction, focus on collectibles
AuctionBuy	`www.auctionbuy.com`	General auction, focus on collectibles
AuctionLand	`www.auction-land.com`	Network of sites, including PlanetBike, Rhythm & Books, and Past's Presents
AuctionPage	`www.auctionpage.com`	Offers standard auctions as well as "Countdown" auctions, where the price falls as the auction progresses
Auctionscape	`www.auctionscape.com`	General auction, focus on collectibles
AuctionWare	`www.auctionware.com`	General auction, focus on collectibles and computers

Site	URL	Comments
Bargoon	www.bargoon.com	Local auctions in Canada
Bid to Buy	www.bidtobuy.com	General auction, focus on collectibles; includes a fixed-price shopping mall
Bid.com	www.bid.com	Includes both American and Canadian versions
BidAway	www.bidaway.com	General auctions
BidBonanza	www.bidbonanza.com	General auctions
BidMore	www.bidmore.com	General auction, focus on collectibles
Bidstream.com	www.bidstream.com	Consolidating items for auction from hundreds of online merchants
BidsWanted	www.bidswanted.com	General auctions, focus on home and office, computers, and travel
Boxlot Online Auction	www.boxlot.com	General auctions, focus on collectibles and art
CanAuction	www.canauction.com	Canadian auction site with a large range of categories
CityAuction	www.cityauction.com	Offers local, national, and international auctions; also features a "Shopping Agent" to notify you when new auctions meet your criteria; worth considering if you need a local-only auction
CT Auctions Today	www.ctauctions.com	General auctions
CyberAuctions	www.cyber-auctions.com	General auctions, focus on collectibles
DC Values	www.dcvalues.com	Washington, D.C. general auctions
Dream Pages Online Auction	www.dreampages.com/auction/	Very small, few listings
eBid: UK Online Auctions	www.ebid.co.uk	U.K. general auctions
edeal	www.edeal.com	Global auctions and classifieds
Eleventh Avenue Marketplace	www.eleventhavenue.com	General auctions
Encore Auction	www.encoreauction.com	Specializing in overstock, end-of-life, and refurbished computers, consumer electronics and office equipment
Fainco Auction	www.faincoauction.com	General auctions, focus on collectibles
First Auction	www.firstauction.com	Hosted by the Internet Shopping Network (a division of TV's Home Shopping Network); a decent auction where bidders tend to overbid

continues

65

Table 6.2 Continued

Site	URL	Comments
Florida Auctions Online	www.comspec-marketing .com/auction/	General auctions, focus on computers
France Auction Web	www.auction-fr.com	French general auctions
Global Auction Club	www.gaci.net	General auctions, focus on computers, power tools, electronics, and trading cards
Global Auction Online	www.global-auction.com	General auctions, focus on collectibles
goMainline	www.gomainline.com	General auctions, focus on toys and collectibles
Graham Auctions	www.grahamauctions.com	Western Canada general auctions; very, very small selection
Great Deals Auction	www.great-deals.net	General auctions, focus on antiques and jewelry
Haggle Online	www.haggle.com	General auctions, focus on computers
Hardware Canada	www.hardwarecanada.com	100% Canadian owned and operated; all auctions are in CDN$
Hybrid Liquidation	www.liquidation.com	Business-to-business liquidation auction
Internet Auction	www.internetauction.net	General auctions
JC Shopping Club	www.jcshopping.com	General auctions in a Christian environment; a division of JC Book Club
Klik Klok On-line Dutch Auctions	www.klik-klok.com	Featuring auctions where the price falls as the auction progresses
LiveBid	www.livebid.com	General auctions, focus on vehicles and business-to-business
Local Auction Online	www.localauctiononline .com	General auctions
Lycos Auctions	www.lycos.com/auctions/	General auctions, plus meta-auction search engine
Mallpark Live Online Auctions	auctions.mallpark.com	General auctions
NeedFulThings	www.needfulthings.net /auction.shtm	Oklahoma general auctions; very small selection
Net4Sale	www.net4sale.org	General auctions
NetWORLD Online Auction Center	auctions.networld.com	General auctions; very few listings
NowUBid	www.nowubid.com	General auctions

Site	URL	Comments
Ohio Auction, The	`www.ohioauction.com`	General auctions, including wholesale, closeouts, and liquidations
Online Auction Services	`www.online-auction.com`	Mainly liquidations of computers, automobiles, and aircraft
Online Market & Auction	`www.theonlinemarket.com`	General auctions
OnTrack Auction	`www.ontrackauction.com`	General auctions; very small selection
Quixell	`www.qxl.com`	Europe general auctions, focus on computers and travel
RightAuction.com	`www.rightauction.com`	General auctions
SellAndTrade.com	`www.sellandtrade.com`	General auctions; small number of listings
SoldUSA	`www.sportauction.com`	General auctions, focus on sports collectibles
Trader's Cove Online Auction	`niximage.com/auction/`	Canada general auctions; very, very few listings
TradersPage	`www.traderspage.com`	General auctions, focus on collectibles
U.S. Government FinanceNet Auctions	`www.financenet.gov /sales.htm`	U.S. government's FinanceNet Project provides information on the sale or auction of public assets and surplus
u-Auction-it	`www.uauction.com`	General auctions
uBid	`www.ubid.com`	Offering excess, refurbished, and limited merchandise
Up4Sale	`www.up4sale.com`	General auctions, claims to have 30,000 items available
VegasToday.com	`www.vegastoday.com`	General auctions, focus on collectibles, coins, and casino chips (!)
Virtual Warehouse	`www.4sale-or-auction .com`	General auctions; very, very few listings

Most of these sites work in similar fashion to the Big Five. You can browse through their topic categories by clicking specific links, or you can search for items using their built-in search engines. After you locate an item, bidding works much the same from site to site—you enter a maximum amount you're willing to bid, and let the auction software take over the process from there.

Nose around a site before you decide to use it—browse or search through the listings, and check out the fees and policies. Find the site that has the merchandise you want and that you're comfortable with, and settle in for some auction fun!

The Least You Need to Know

➤ eBay is the largest online auction site in the world, bigger than all the other auction sites combined.

➤ The other Big Five auction sites are Amazon.com Auctions, Auction Universe, Classifieds 2000 Auctions, and Yahoo! Auctions.

➤ Consider all the factors when choosing an auction site, including number of listings, amount of bidder traffic, listing/selling fees, types of auctions offered, and insurance or escrow services offered.

Chapter 7

Collectible Auctions: Beanies, Coins, Steins, and More

In This Chapter

➤ Discover why collecting can be both fun and profitable

➤ Learn which Web sites specialize in collectibles auctions

➤ Uncover the auctions that true enthusiasts use to find specific types of collectibles

Why do people become collectors? Whether they collect vinyl LPs or Native American pottery or coins or trading cards, collectors are often a breed apart.

Some people collect out of nostalgia. Some collect to preserve history. Some collect out of fun, some from obsession, and still others as a serious investment.

People collect everything from aardvark figurines to zipper pulls. Anything can be a collectible—books, buttons, and Beanie Babies are all collected by someone, somewhere. You name it, someone collects it.

How do you know if you truly have a collectible item in your possession? First, remember that if someone wants to collect it—no matter what it is—that item is by definition a collectible. However, it may have no value to anyone but you.

If you want to collect things that have value to others, however, make sure you're collecting something that is truly rare. When objects get mass produced, they are just too common to become valuable.

Then make sure that what you have is in the best possible condition. Those old comic books you had when you were a kid *might* be worth something today—if you hadn't read them a hundred times and torn off the covers.

Finally, check the Web sites listed in this chapter. The best way to gauge an object's worth is to compare it to similar objects. If it's a valuable collectible, you'll be able to tell from the prices similar objects fetch at these collectible auctions.

At the end of the day, however, collecting should be fun. Why collect things you don't like? If you want to get started with collecting, find something you like, and have some fun with it. And remember—you can often find that rare collectible at an online auction!

What's the Difference Between a Collectible and an Antique?

The simple answer is *time.* Although most antiques are collectible, not all collectibles are antiques—*yet.* In chronological order, here are some terms you'll come across to help you better classify your items:

➤ **Antiquities**   Artifacts from the ancient world, commonly extending to the fall of the Roman Empire or the Middle Ages.

➤ **Antiques**   Typically, items at least 100 years old (although some people label selected post-1900 items as antiques, as well).

➤ **Collectibles**   Anything a collector feels is worth collecting, regardless of age.

➤ **Vintage Collectibles**   Any collectible from 1989 or earlier.

➤ **Contemporary Collectibles**   Items from the 1990s.

Collecting All Sorts of Things at General Collectibles Auctions

Almost all the general auction sites offer collectible items for auction. However, other sites specialize in collectibles, without all the other general stuff (you know, like computers and cameras and consumer goods).

These collectibles sites often provide more than just auctions. Some offer editorial or reference content of value to collectors; others offer complete collectors communities. In any case, these sites are great places to start if you're serious about collecting.

Don't Forget the Big Five!

Actually, some of the better sites for collectibles are the Big Five general auction sites—eBay, Amazon.com Auctions, Auction Universe, Classifieds 2000 Auctions, and Yahoo! Auctions. eBay in particular is a powerhouse in most collectible categories, listing more Beanie Babies than all the specialized Beanie sites combined. Auction Universe isn't bad in some categories, either—especially antiques, sports cards, and comics. Bottom line: In your quest for the perfect collectible, don't forget to look at the Big Five!

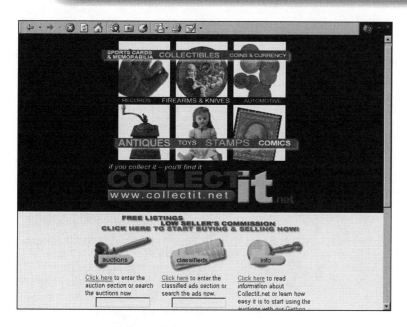

Collectit.net is one of the better general collectibles sites, featuring a large selection of coins, records, toys, and sports cards.

Table 7.1 lists some of the major general collectibles auctions on the Web.

Table 7.1 General Collectibles Auctions

Site	URL	Comments
Antique Canada/ Antiques Ontario	www.antique-canada.com	Two Web sites in one, offering both collectibles and antiques from Canada. Open 24 hours a day.

continues

Table 7.1   Continued

Site	URL	Comments
Antique Trails	www.nidlink.com/~trails/	Offering both collectibles and antiques; categories include Books/Paper Memorabilia, Porcelain, Metal, and Textile.
Auction Network	www.auction-network.com	Specializing in collectibles, sports cards, and antiques.
Auction Works	www.auctionworks.com	Collectibles categories include pottery, porcelain, glassware, Royal Doulton, holiday ornaments, and Beanie Babies.
AuctionAdventure	www.auctionadventures.net	Relatively new auction, good site design, specializing in collectibles, sports memorabilia, and antiques.
AuctionIsland	www.auctionisland.com	Collectibles-only site, with listings for general collectibles, trading cards, memorabilia, seasonal, auto racing, glass/crystal/china, and antiques.
AuctionPort	www.auctionport.com	Licensed auctioneers with over 15 years' experience in antiques and collectibles.
Auctions Unlimited	www.auctions-unlimited.com	Specializing in vintage toys and collectibles, with periodic auctions (usually monthly) and a "dynamic closing"—the entire batch of items on auction ends at the same time. Most of this site's merchandise is consigned by collectors and dealers from around the world, and they physically have the items that are being sold, taking full responsibility for descriptions and authenticity. One of the best collectibles auctions on the Web—recommended.
Bid on Collectibles	www.bidoncollectibles.com	Offering both collectibles and antiques, including books, pottery, glassware, jewelry, and toys.
Collectit.net	www.collectit.net	One of the newer collectibles auctions, also offering sports memorabilia. Recommended.

Site	URL	Comments
CollectEx	www.collectex.com	Collectibles-only site.
Collectibles.Net	www.collectibles.net/auction/	Collectibles-only site.
Collectors Universe.com	www.collectorsauction.com	One of the best collector-to-collector auctions on the Web, offering coins, currency, sports memorabilia, and more. Also includes links to Coin Universe, Beanie Universe, Sports Collectors Universe, Record Universe, and Collectors Auction. Recommended.
Golden Age	www.goldnage.com	Specializing in both collectibles and antiques. The operators of this auction are collectors themselves; good quality items can often be found here.
Hobby Markets Online	www.hobbymarkets.com	Collectibles-only auction.
Interactive Collector	www.icollector.com	Offering collectibles, antiques, and art.
Jim's Historic Collectibles	www.ica-ark.com/ jimhistoricpage.htm	Offering collectibles and antiques, specializing in historic items such as old newspapers, documents, prints, maps, books, magazines, and other paper items.
Keybuy Auction House	www.keybuy.com	Offering both collectibles and computers (what a combination!); always willing to create new categories for sellers.
My Shop	www.myshop.com	Specializing in Beanie Babies and collectible toys, with a large number of listings and bidders.
OHI EXchange	www.ohiexchange.com	Founded in 1989, this is the original broad-reference collectibles exchange; specializes in plates, steins, figurines, and dolls; also publishes a bimonthly newsletter detailing trends in the collectibles marketplace and listing more than 2,000 popular collectibles and their actual current selling prices.

continues

73

Table 7.1   Continued

Site	URL	Comments
OneWebPlace	www.onewebplace.com	Good site, lots of listings in key categories, such as Beanie Babies and Magic The Gathering.
Palm Beach Auctions	www.palmbeachauctions.com	Offering collectibles, antiques, art, furniture, and sculptures from the respected Galleries of Palm Beach, Florida.
Past's Presents	www.auction-land.com/antiques/	Collectibles and antiques; part of the AuctionLand site.
PeddleIt	www.PeddleIt.com	One of the best collectibles sites, featuring pedal cars, die-cast toys, Beanie Babies, motor vehicles, kitchen collectibles, and antiques.
Phoebus Auction Gallery On-Line Auction	www.phoebusauction.com	Offering collectibles and antiques, including dolls, fine art, glass and ceramics, militaria, and erotica.
Popula	www.popula.com	Collectibles and antiques, specializing in first editions, vintage clothing, and antique photos; a well-designed site.
Rotman Collectibles	www.wwcd.com/rotman/	Specializing in sports and non-sports cards, sports memorabilia, autographs, comic books, movie posters, pins, political memorabilia, statues and figurines, and more.
Royal Auction	www.royalauction.com	Live online auction offering collectibles, antiques, and jewelry.
Russian Auction	www.russianauction.com	European gifts and collectibles.
Sellathon Auction Services, Inc.	www.sellathon.com	Offering die-cast cars, dolls, toys, comics, and more.
SkyBid	www.skybid.com	A new entry into the collectibles auction category, with a limited number of items for sale; potential for growth.
Sotheby's	www.Sothebys.com	The granddaddy of all auctions is coming online; will offer big-ticket collectibles, art, antiques, and jewelry.
SPEEDBID	www.speedbid.com	U.K.-based collectibles auction, with secure multi-currency credit card capability.

Site	URL	Comments
Teletrade Auctions	www.teletrade.com	Offering coins, sports cards, memorabilia, movie posters, stamps, and comic books with 800-line telephone bidding.
ThinkBID	www.thinkbid.com	Offering books, coins, stamps, trading cards, memorabilia, sporting goods, music, dolls, comics, antiques, and jewelry.
Up4Auction	www.up4auction.com	More than 1,000 different categories of collectibles and antiques.
Wcollect.com	www.wcollect.com	Offering collectibles from the worlds of entertainment, sports, and fine art.
Webquest's Auctions	www.webquests.com/auction/index.shtml	Collectibles-only site.
World Wide Auctions	www.wwauction.com	Collectibles-only site, large focus on coins; international auction.
WowAuction	www.wowauction.com	Categories include Beanie Babies, autographs, toys, sports cards, antiques, and jewelry.

Some of these sites are rather small and run by individual collectors; some are large and run by commercial establishments. The best to check out are Auctions Unlimited (www.auctions-unlimited.com), Collectit.net (www.collectit.net), and Collector's Universe (www.collectorsauction.com).

Auction Sites for Specialized Collectors

Beyond these general collector's sites, however, are even more specialized auctions for specific types of collectors. These are often smaller sites that specialize in certain types of collectibles, such as just coins or just glass or just Beanie Babies.

Collecting Beanie Babies

Hundreds of Beanie Baby sites exist on the Web; almost all general auction sites have huge Beanie Baby categories. There are also a handful of sites offering Beanie Baby–specific auctions, including the following:

➤ **Beanie Baby Bidding (www.beaniebid.com)**   Colorful auction and chat site.

➤ **Beanie Forum and Chat (www.advant.net/beanie.htm)**   Auction and classifieds offering both hard-to-find and retired Beanies.

➤ **Beanie Nation (www.beanienation.com)** One of the largest Beanie auctions—and the #1 Beanie site, period—with close to 10,000 items for sale at any given time (recommended).

➤ **Beanie Universe (www.auctions.beanie-universe.com)** Auctions from major Beanie dealers worldwide.

➤ **My Shop: Beanie Babies Auction (www.myshop.com/html/categories.html)** Another large Beanie auction, with over 12,000 registered users and over 50,000 items sold to date.

➤ **Unofficial Beanie Baby Online Auction (www.defend.net/beanie/)** Auctions and classifieds for both Beanie Babies and Teenie Beanie Babies.

Check out the almost 10,000 Beanie Babies for auction at Beanie Nation.

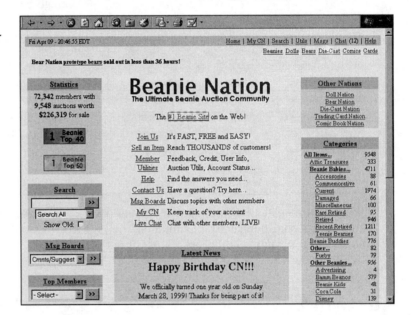

Collecting Coins

Numismatists worldwide have been collecting coins for ages. A healthy Web community has built up around this hobby, and several major coin-only auctions are on the Web today:

➤ CCE-Auction (www.cce-auction.com)

➤ Coin Universe Auctions (auctions.coin-universe.com)

➤ Numismatists Online (www.numismatists.com/hkP92aTc/)

➤ Waverly's Online Antique Auction (www.waverlys.com)

➤ www.CoinAuctions.com (www.coinauctions.com)

I recommend you check out Coin Universe Auctions. This site features auctions by both individuals and major dealers around the world, as well as a weekly certified consignment auction.

The Next Beanie Babies—Pokémon?

If you have youngsters, you've probably already heard plenty about Pokémon (pronounced poh-kay-mon). If you haven't heard of them, you will. There are Pokémon videogames, comic books, trading cards, and stuffed toys—all springing from the Pokémon cartoon. To date there are 151 different Pokémon to collect, and the trading card craze is just getting started. As I write this, I find no dedicated Pokémon auctions, but the general auction sites (eBay in particular) have huge Pokémon sections. Look for dedicated Pokémon auctions to spring up rapidly, possibly by the time you're reading these words! (To learn more about Pokémon, go to the official Web site at www.pokemon.com.)

Collecting Stamps

Philatelists have been collecting stamps almost as long as numismatists have been collecting coins. The stamp collecting community has found a home on the Web, and there are numerous stamp-only auctions to check out:

➤ auction-123.com (www.auction-123.com)

➤ Dennis R. Abel Stamp Auction (www.drabel.com/cgi-bin/auctions/auction.cgi)

➤ Philatelic.Com/Rainbow Online Auctions (auction.philatelic.com)

➤ Philately Stamps (www.philea.se)

➤ Sandafayre (www.sandafayre.com)

➤ www.StampAuctions.com (www.stampauctions.com)

Two of the best sites are Sandafayre (with over $1 million worth of stamps online each week) and the Philatelic.com/Rainbow Online Auctions (with several thousand lots available at any given time).

Not quite the U.S. Postal Service: expensive stamps at Philatelic.com/Rainbow Online Auctions.

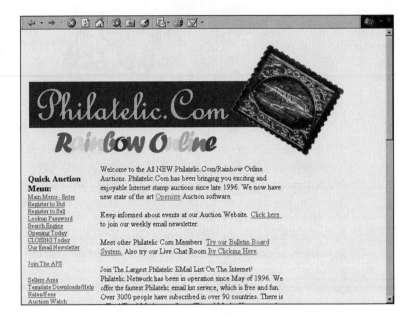

Collecting Comics

Remember all those twelve-cent comics you had as a kid? Those comics are now worth big bucks to collectors—especially if you were smart enough not to read them, and to hermetically seal them as soon as you brought them home from the drugstore! The two best comics auction sites are AuctionComic.com (`www.auctioncomic.com`) and ComicExchange (`www.ComicExchange.net`). In addition, eBay's comics section is robust, and I've been told that sellers on Auction Universe are for some reason able to command top prices for their comics listings.

Collecting War Games and Miniatures

Looking for auctions of war games and miniatures? In addition to eBay, check out Crusader29's Auction Page (`home.earthlink.net/~crusader29/`). This auction is run by a dedicated hobbyist, but it's well done and has some good merchandise.

Collecting Militaria

When it comes to historical militaria collectibles, the best auction is the one on the Militaria Collectibles Auction Haus site (`www.militaria-collectibles.com`). The big categories here are U.S. militaria and German militaria, but there are also categories for other countries and other types of items, including autographs, firearms, and G.I. Joe action figures.

Collecting Autographs

Autograph collecting is a hobby—or, for some, an obsession—with a long tradition. Although autograph categories are a staple at eBay and the other general auction sites, you can sometimes do better by visiting specialized autograph auctions. The best of these is probably AutographAuction (www.autographauction. com), with a large variety and sample photos on most items listed. Also of interest are New Age Sportscards and Autographs Auction (www.newagecards.com), specializing in sports autographs, and Stardoodles for Kids (www.stardoodle.com/index.shtml), which auctions celebrity doodles for the Champions for Children Foundation charity.

Collecting Sports Cards

Sports cards are another popular type of collectible—so popular they're covered in their own chapter in this book. See Chapter 10, "Sports Auctions: Bats, Balls, and Memorabilia for Sale," for more information.

Collecting Movie and Music Memorabilia

Most movie memorabilia sites also feature a wide variety of celebrity autographs, along with movie posters, film props, original scripts, and similar items. (I've also had good luck finding film props on eBay, of course.) Some of the best of these sites include

➤ **Hollywood Auction (www.travel.to/Hollywood/)**   A monthly online Hollywood charity auction, offering everything from VIP tickets to TV shows to prime memorabilia.

➤ **MCW Online Poster Auction (www.mcwonline.com)**   Specializing in movie posters, stills, and so on.

➤ **Time Tunnel (www.nextlevel.com/espace/)**   Specializing in musician autographs and memorabilia, including the Beatles, the Rolling Stones, and more.

➤ **Universal Studios Online Auction (www.unistudiosauction.com)**   Includes props, costumes, and other memorabilia and collectibles from Universal movies. Past auctions have included a life vest from *Titanic*, a phaser from *Star Trek*, the 1968 Olympic torch, and scripts from *Seinfeld*.

Collecting Records and CDs

For those of you old enough to remember vinyl records, a variety of sites offer auctions of vintage LPs, 45s, and 78s. (To be fair, many of these sites also auction CDs, the heretics!) The main music auction sites include

➤ **AllJazz Jazz Record Auctions** (`www.alljazz.com`)   Bimonthly auctions of old jazz records, mainly 78s and early LPs.

➤ **4Tunes.com** (`www.4tunes.com`)   Auctions by both dealers and individuals, featuring both vinyl LPs and compact discs.

➤ **Record Universe** (`auctions.record-universe.com`)   LP and CD auctions by dealers, worldwide.

➤ **Rhythm & Books** (`www.auction-land.com/cdbooks/`)   Auctions of records, CDs, music memorabilia, and rare books.

➤ **Steal-A-Record** (`www.wizvax.net/mpekar/index.html`)   Monthly auctions featuring collectible LPs and 45s with no minimum bids.

Bid for groovy tunes on vinyl or CD at 4Tunes.Com.

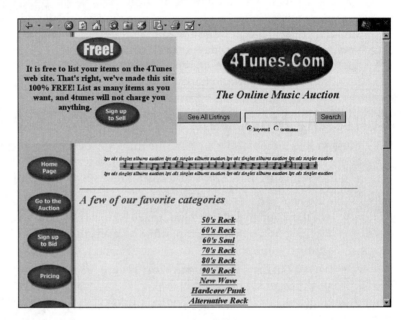

Collecting Vintage Radios

For vintage radio enthusiasts, check out King's Attic (`www.kingsattic.com`). This specialty site offers bimonthly auctions of vintage radios—and nothing but vintage radios!

Collecting Model Trains

The best model train auction on the Web is at the Lionel Toy Train Auction site (`www.buznorma.com`)—not affiliated with Lionel, but just a good hobbyist's auction site.

Collecting Bottles and Other Containers

Bottles, jugs, crocks, jars, glasses—all these have great value to collectors. Of course, eBay is a great site for these collectibles, but a surprising number of sites are dedicated solely to glassware and bottle auctions.

If you're interested in antique bottles and stoneware, then you can check out AB!C (www.auctionsbyabc.com). This is a Canadian site specializing in antique bottles and stoneware, including insulators, crocks, merchant jugs, ginger beers, lightning rod balls, sodas, medicines, milks, poisons, inks, hairs, whiskies, beers, bitters, flasks, black glass, fruit jars, and whimsies.

If beer mugs are more your fashion, Buck a Bottle Auction (www.buckabottle.com) and Stein Auction (www.steinauction.com) might be your cup of tea (or rather, your stein of beer). These sites feature all sorts of brewianna, including Anheuser-Busch and German steins, and brewery glasses.

Collecting Pottery

If you're a pottery collector, there's no better site than Pottery Auction (www.potteryauction.com). Here you can find all types of American art pottery for auction, including Roseville, Weller, Rookwood, Van Briggle, McCoy, and Hull.

Collecting Glass

Vintage glass collectors can find everything they want on auction at Just Glass Auctions (www.justglass.com). As the name says, this site contains just glass auctions—including auctions of depression, carnival, opalescent, modern, and art glass.

Collecting Cross Stitching and Needlepoint

Do your hobbies include cross stitching, needlepoint, or crewel? Then check out Cross Stitches Auction (www.xstitches.com), an auction site devoted solely to these arts.

Collecting Vintage Clothing

If you like to collect vintage clothing, check out VintageUSA Direct Auction (www.vintageusa.com/auction.htm). This site features auctions for vintage clothing—including Levis—and collectible shoes, such as Air Jordans.

Collecting Buttons

Pinback buttons (the type of political or advertising or "statement" buttons you pin on your lapel) are a fairly recent collectible, popular only in the last thirty years or so. One of the best auction sites for buttons is Pinbacks.com (www.pinbacks.com), specializing in pinback buttons of all forms, sizes, and nationalities.

The Least You Need to Know

➤ Collecting can be an enjoyable hobby, or a profitable investment.

➤ Although eBay and the other big auction sites often have robust collectibles sections, there are many auctions dedicated just to collectible items.

➤ Many auction sites exist just for specific types of collectibles, such as Beanie Babies or coins or vintage radios.

Chapter 8

Antique Auctions: Furniture, Jewelry, and Other Old Stuff

OOH!

In This Chapter

➤ Discover the many antique auctions available on the Web

➤ Find out which general auction contains more antiques listings than any specialist site (hint: it starts with an "e")

➤ Learn which sites to visit if you want to buy or sell jewelry and gemstones

The Internet has many sites dedicated to auctions of antiques, jewelry, and gemstones. In addition to the specialist sites discussed in this chapter, many more listings are available on the Big Five auction sites—particularly on eBay, Auction Universe, and Amazon.com Auctions.

If you're looking for an antique to bid on, it's often better to browse than to search. Given the wide variety of items called "antiques," browsing through the Antiques category on a general auction site is the online equivalent of wandering the aisles of a flea market or antique store—you never know what you'll stumble across!

How to List and Search for Antiques

If you're looking for something specific, go ahead and use the site's search engine, but be precise about the keywords you use for your query. Your query should probably include the type of antique (painting, chair, and so on), the manufacturer of the antique, the material from which it was made, the year or period in which it was produced, and so on. Leaving out any of this information is likely to result in too many (and too imprecise) matches. But also remember that different people will describe

Buy, Not Bid

If you would rather just shop for antiques outright and skip the whole auction process, check out the list of almost 200 stores at the Internet Antique Shop (www.tias.com/stores/).

and list the same items differently—so you may need to perform several searches, each worded with a slightly different description of what you're looking for. (This is why browsing the Antiques category is often a better way to go!)

If you're listing an antique for sale, you have a wide variety of options, especially on eBay and the other large sites. On eBay, for example, you can choose to list an item by age, material, maker, or merchandise category. If you're not sure which category is best, I recommend that you search for antiques similar to yours, and then list your item in the same category.

In your listing's title, include as much relevant information as possible. Try to include the area where the item was made, the material it was made from, the date or period of the item, the type of merchandise it is, and the item's manufacturer. Then, within the item's description, go into even more detail—include an accurate description of the item's condition. The more you say about the item, the better. Naturally, including a picture of the antique will help bidders better determine their interest level.

Angling for Antiques

Obviously, eBay, Auction Universe, Yahoo! Auctions, and other general auction sites contain a ton of listings for antiques of various shapes and sizes. But don't overlook the sites that specialize in antiques; they're often run by large antique dealers, and sometimes contain items that are hard to find elsewhere.

A good general antique auction has items available in most if not all of the following categories:

➤ Ancient World
➤ Architectural
➤ Books/Manuscripts/Maps
➤ Folk Art
➤ Furniture
➤ Metalware
➤ Musical Instruments
➤ Prints
➤ Scientific Instruments
➤ Textiles
➤ Post-1900 Antiques

Obviously, some of the smaller antique auctions might not fill out all these categories—or might specialize in just one or two specific categories.

Table 8.1 lists the major antiques-specific auctions on the Web.

Table 8.1   General Antique Auctions

Site	URL	Comments
Ampersand Antiques	www.qwikhomes.com/antiques/	Antiques and collectibles from around the North Texas area as well as items found throughout the rest of the country; offers a locator service for hard-to-find items.
Antique Canada/Antiques Ontario	www.antique-canada.com	Antiques and collectibles from Canada.
Antique Country	www.antiquecountry.com	General antiques auction; very few listings.
Antique Trails	www.utrade.com/index.htm?MID=64656	General antiques, jewelry, vintage clothing, collectibles, and memorabilia.
Auction Works	www.auctionworks.com	General antiques, porcelain, Royal Doulton, jewelry, and collectibles; very few listings.
AuctionPort	www.auctionport.com	General antiques and collectibles; includes an Appraisal Wizard to appraise the value of your items.
Biddington's Art & Antiques Online Auctions	www.biddingtons.com	Up-market antique auction and information, featuring higher-priced items for the serious bidder; categories include architecture, art, Asian, books, furnishings, glass, historical, jewelry, metal and silver, porcelain, sports, and textiles—recommended.
Boxlot Online Auction	www.boxlot.com	Easy-to-use auction of general antiques, books/prints, jewelry, and collectibles.
Dargate Auction Galleries	www.dargate.com	Fine estate property from Pittsburgh's premier auction gallery; includes both daily auction and a monthly gallery.
Fainco Auction	www.faincoauction.com	General antiques, jewelry, and collectibles.

continues

Table 8.1   Continued

Site	URL	Comments
Golden Age Antiques and Collectibles	www.goldnage.com	General antiques and collectibles.
Interactive Collector	auction.icollector.com	General antiques, books/manuscripts, and collectibles.
John Morelli Auctioneers	www.abcliveauction.com	Weekly live online auctions of antiques and collectibles.
LUNDS Auctioneers & Appraisers Ltd.	www.lunds.com	Canadian antiques auction, in a variety of categories.
Palm Beach Auctions	www.palmbeachauctions.com	From the collected galleries of Palm Beach, FL, antique furniture, lithographs, photographs, gems, and collectibles.
Past's Presents	www.auction-land.com/antiques/	Categories include Ancient World, Books/Manuscripts, Folk Art, Metalware, Prints; very few listings.
Phoebus Auction Gallery On-Line	www.phoebusauction.com	Virginia company offering periodic estate auctions Auction online.
Popula	www.popula.com	Offers first editions, vintage clothing, jewelry, furniture, and antique photos.
Sotheby's	www.Sothebys.com	Coming soon—high-priced antiques, jewelry, and art.
Up4Auction	www.up4auction.com	Good selection of antiques of all types, from furniture to curios to lamps to metalware.
Waverly's Online Antique Auction	www.waverlys.com	General antiques and collectibles; very few listings.

These sites vary tremendously in terms of approach and items listed; many have very few listings at any given time. The sites that consistently have the most listings include Antique Trails (via Utrade), Biddington's, Boxlot, and Up4Auction. All pale, of course, to the 50,000 items listed in eBay's Antiques category—which is the site I recommend you visit first.

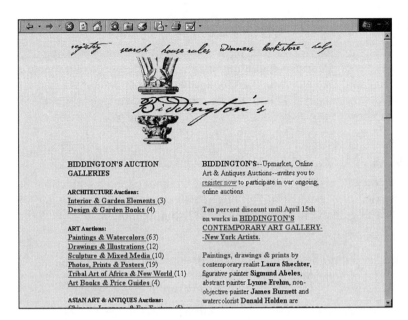

Bidding for upscale antiques at Biddington's.

Reading Up on Rare Books, Manuscripts, and Maps

Although most of the general antique auctions also deal in rare books, manuscripts, and maps (as does eBay, of course), a handful of sites specialize in these historical paper collectibles. The best of the bunch include

➤ **EworldAuction (www.eworldauction.com)**   Offering a monthly online auction of old books, maps, prints, medieval manuscripts, and other works on paper.

➤ **Jim's Historic Collectibles (www.ica-ark.com/jimhistoricpage.htm)** Offering old newspapers, documents, prints, maps, books, magazines, and other paper items (contains very few listings, unfortunately).

➤ **Paulus Swaen Old Maps and Prints Internet Auction (www.swaen.com)** Offering a weekly auction of antique maps, views, prints, atlases, globes, and medieval manuscripts.

➤ **Popula (www.popula.com/categories/current/book/)**   Offering first editions, paperbacks, religious, sci-fi, children's, comics, magazines, and Americana.

Getting Fired Up About Antique Firearms

Not all antiques sites offer firearms, for various legal reasons. In fact, eBay recently banned auctions of all types of firearms—including antique firearms—from its site. This leaves AntiqueGuns.com (`206.151.91.7/antiqueguns/html/categories.htm`) as the premiere specialist in this category. This site offers antique and restored guns from pre-1750 through the Revolutionary and Civil Wars up to WWI and WWII weapons.

Looking Pretty with Jewelry and Gem Auctions

If you're looking to buy or sell jewelry and gems, almost every general or collectible auction site offers some degree of selection. You might also want to check out some of the specialty jewelry and gem auctions, such as those listed in Table 8.2.

Table 8.2   Jewelry and Gem Auction Sites

Site	URL	Comments
Antique Trails	`www.utrade.com/index.htm?MID=64656`	Offering antique jewelry, beads, costume, gold, loose stones, silver, and watches.
Gemtraders.com	`www.gemtraders.com/auction/`	Gem categories from Amethyst to Zircon, including both natural and laboratory-grown gems—recommended.
Jewelnet Auctions	`www.jewelnetauctions.com`	Offers the following jewelry categories: antique/estate, costume, diamonds, gemstones, gold, silver, and watches.
New Age Auction	`www.newageauction.com`	Unusual auction offering oddities, crystals, jewelry magnets, staffs and wands, new age books, and "alien items."
New Spirit	`www.wehug.com`	Bimonthly gem auction; very few auction items on an otherwise content-rich site.
RMG Auction Services	`www.binary.net/treasure/AuctionInfo.html`	Categories include fossils, gold and silver, jewelry, minerals, and rocks.
Royal Auction	`www.royalauction.com`	Jewelry categories include gold, silver, watches, beads, gemstones, and vintage.

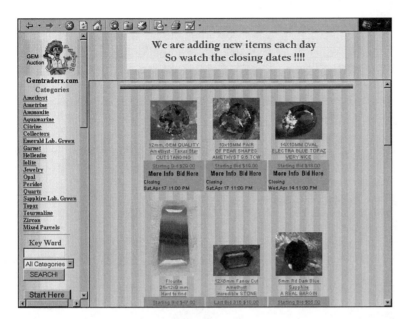

Gemtraders.com—more rocks than you can shake a stick at.

For gems, the best site around is Gemtraders.com—it's a true gem trader's delight. For jewelry, I have to go with eBay—more than 70,000 items listed, when I last looked. And for sheer weirdness, check out the New Age Auction; I really want to know if the "Genuine Stardust from Between Jupiter and Saturn" (bidding starts at just $1.00) is the real deal or not!

The Least You Need to Know

➤ The best auction site for antiques and jewelry is eBay.

➤ Of the specialized antiques auctions, Biddington's is good for upscale items.

➤ Several sites specialize in rare books, manuscripts, and maps.

➤ Gemtraders.com is a good site for auctions of gems and other minerals.

Chapter 9

Art Auctions: Sotheby's and Other Dealers Online

In This Chapter

➤ Discover where to find the largest quantities of art for auction on the Web

➤ Find out where to find the best quality art auctions on the Web

➤ Learn why the world's largest art auction house doesn't do online auctions—yet

---

Collectors traditionally have bought works of art at fine art galleries. Many of these galleries sell their art via live auctions; it's only natural that art auctions eventually move onto the Internet.

Now, I'll grant you that it's hard to fully examine and appreciate a piece of art just by looking at a tiny JPG image on your computer screen. However, by putting art on the Web, millions of potential customers can see and bid on pieces of art that formerly only a select handful had access to. In a way, the Internet is bringing art to the masses—if, in fact, the masses want it!

The Biggest Art Auction on the Internet: eBay, Of Course

As is true with most other types of auctions, the biggest art auction on the Internet can be found at eBay.

To find eBay's art auctions, click the **Collectibles** category and scroll down the page a bit. eBay includes the following categories of art and fine art items:

Other Online Art Resources

For a listing of real-world art auctions, check out The Auctiongoer's Guide (www.auctiongoer.com). You can go to Art Library Online (www.artlibrary.com) to search for auctions by artist, or to access a database of more than a million auction sales since 1987. And for a good general art site, try Art on the Net (www.art.net).

➤ Amateur Art
➤ Artist Offerings
➤ Calendars
➤ Decorator/Designer
➤ Drawings
➤ General
➤ Multiple Techniques
➤ Nudes
➤ Painting
➤ Posters
➤ Prints
➤ Sculptures
➤ Supplies

All total, eBay has over 20,000 works of art listed on any given day—more than every other art-related site on the Internet combined, and then some. If you're looking for art, it's a good place to start.

Finding the Finest Fine Art Auctions on the Web

eBay doesn't have all the art in the world, however—and especially doesn't have some of the best fine art. For more exclusive and expensive works of art, you need to go to a fine art gallery—or to a fine art gallery online auction.

Table 9.1 lists some of the top auction sites on the Web for works of fine art.

Table 9.1   Fine Arts Auction Sites

Site	URL	Comments
A J Fine Arts Silent auctions	www.ajarts.com/ajarts/ auctnhp.html	30-day Auction, typically a dozen or so items listed
Art and Fine Art Sales	www.art4sale.com	Full-service fine arts site, always has art for sale, occasionally runs online auctions
Art Auction International	www.art-auction-intl.com	High-stakes art auction; only a few high-priced items listed at a time

Site	URL	Comments
Art Planet: List of Traditional Auctions Houses and Online Auctions	`www.artplanet.com/search-category.html?category= Auction+Houses`	List of traditional art and antiques houses which have online displays of their real-world auctions
Artists Online Silent Auction	`www.onlineart.com/ auction.htm`	More than 150 pieces of art available for bidding
artnet. com Auctions	`www.auction1.artnet.com`	One of the best art auctions on the Web; works in Impressionist, Modern, Contemporary, Photography, and American categories; recommended
Biddington's Art & Antiques Online Auctions	`www.biddingtons.com`	High-priced art auction for the serious collector; categories include paintings, watercolors, drawings, illustrations, sculpture, mixed media, photos, prints, posters, and tribal art of Africa; recommended
Dargate Auction Galleries	`www.dargate.com`	Fine estate property from Pittsburgh's premier auction gallery; includes both daily auctions and a monthly gallery
France Auction Web	`www.auction-fr.com`	French auction site, lets you search by artist and category
Global Auctions	`www.globalauctions.com`	Limited number of items, not always running
Heidelberg Editions International	`www.hei-art.com`	Monthly online auctions featuring California artists
Martin Lawrence Galleries	`martinlawrence.com/ auction.html`	Weekly auctions of works by contemporary artists
Palm Beach Auctions	`www.palmbeachauctions.com`	From the collected galleries of Palm Beach, FL, lithographs, photographs, and other fine art
Sloan's Auctions	`www.sloansauction.com`	Various pieces of art from Sloan's Miami and Washington, D.C., galleries
Sotheby's	`www.Sothebys.com`	Soon, but not yet—high-priced art from the granddaddy of all auction houses
Wcollect.com	`www.wcollect.com`	Art created by celebrities, including Tony Bennett, Charles Bronson, and John Lennon

All these sites have their merits, and they're all worth checking out—after all, no two pieces of art are alike! My favorite of these is artnet.com, because of its large selection and top-notch site design. While you're at it, go to artnet.com's main site (www.artnet.com) for some of the best art information on the entire Internet.

Pick up an Andy Warhol at artnet.com—one of the best art auctions on the Web.

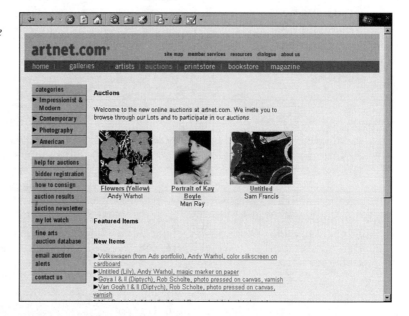

Waiting for Sotheby's

The biggest art auction house in the world is Sotheby's. Although Sotheby's has had a Web site for some time (at www.Sothebys.com), it's mainly been informational, offering details about upcoming real-world auctions and such. However, Sotheby's has not allowed any online bidding in its auctions, nor has it offered online auctions period.

That is about to change.

Sotheby's has signed up 1,500 art dealers in the United States and Europe for a new online auction site that is set to launch in mid-1999—and will probably be up and running by the time you read this book. The new Sotheby's site will offer an online platform for auctioning art, antiques, and jewelry and is aimed at complementing Sotheby's core live auction business. This won't be a run-of-the-mill auction site, either; the company plans to make an initial investment of more than $25 million for the site's first year of operation.

If you're a serious art or antiques collector, this promises to be a site worth waiting for. Look for it!

Another Famous Auction House Without Online Auctions—And One That Will Have Them, Soon

Sotheby's isn't the only world-famous international auction house that doesn't yet offer online auctions. Christie's also has a Web site (www.christies.com) that offers a lot of information about its operation and auctions, but doesn't (yet) offer online bidding. (Rumor has it this could change before the end of 1999, however...)

One of the other major "live" auction houses, Butterfield & Butterfield (www.butterfields.com), was recently acquired by eBay. Expect to see B&B online with their high-end auctions in short order.

The Least You Need to Know

➤ If you want a good selection of affordable art, check out eBay.

➤ If you want higher-priced, more exclusive works of fine art, go to one of the fine arts gallery auction sites, such as artnet.com.

➤ Sotheby's, the world's largest art auction house, is preparing to launch its own online auction site, later in 1999.

Chapter 10

Sports Auctions: Bats, Balls, and Memorabilia for Sale

In This Chapter

➤ Discover the best auction sites on the Web for sports cards and memorabilia

➤ Find out which sites are best for buying and selling golf clubs and accessories

➤ Uncover the best auction sites for general sporting goods

Whether you're collecting baseball cards or autographed jerseys, you know how addictive your hobby can be. It should come as no surprise, then, to discover that sports memorabilia—especially trading cards—is one of the largest categories in many online auction sites. Literally hundreds of thousands of different sports items are listed each day on the Web; it can be a full-time job sorting through all these listings to find that one item you need to complete your collection!

Online auctions are also great places to find sporting equipment. Several sites are dedicated to auctioning either discounted merchandise or items from other sports buffs—with golf clubs and gear being the most in-demand category.

Capture the Past with Sports Cards and Other Memorabilia

A mind-boggling number of auction sites offer sports cards for trade—almost as many as there are dealing in Beanie Babies! Although this chapter talks about sports-dedicated auctions, you shouldn't neglect the general auction sites when you're on a quest for items to bid on.

Among the general auction sites, eBay and Auction Universe have the largest selections of sports cards and related memorabilia—eBay alone has almost a quarter-million sports memorabilia items listed on any given day! It pays to check eBay and the other Big Five sites when you're looking to buy merchandise in this category.

Although dedicated sports auctions might not have as many items listed as does eBay, they're sometimes better places to find more rare and exclusive items. Table 10.1 lists some of the leading sports memorabilia auctions on the Web.

Table 10.1 Sports Cards and Memorabilia Auctions

Site	URL	Comments
Andy Pak's Sports Card Auction	`www.azww.com/apak/auction.shtml`	Individual collector; typical items include rookies, inserts, and team assortments cards
Basketball Bonanza	`www.basketballbonanza.com`	Online auction and store featuring the world's largest collection of autographed basketball memorabilia, including sports cards, photos, programs, balls, and uniforms
Bill Henderson's Sports Card Auction	`www.azww.com/hendo/auction.shtml`	Individual collector; typical auctions include baseball, football, and basketball cards
Boekhout's Collectibles Mall	`www.azww.com/mall`	"Mall" with more than 30 individual auctions, each with 100–700 lots; sports cards and memorabilia—recommended
Boxlot Online Auction	`www.boxlot.com/tradingcards.shtml`	Good selection of baseball, basketball, football, hockey, and racing cards
Collectit.net	`www.collectit.net`	Good collection of baseball, basketball, football, and hockey cards
Collectors Universe.com	`www.collectorsauction.com`	Good collection of baseball, basketball, football, and hockey cards, plus sports action figures and other memorabilia
Curran's Cards and Auctions	`www.curranscards.com`	Huge collection of baseball, basketball, football, and hockey cards; more than 23,000 sports cards for auction every month—recommended

Site	URL	Comments
fan2fan	www.fan2fan.com/html/categories.htm	Small collection of sports cards
K&B Sports Cards Auction	www.kbsportscards.com	Good collection of sports cards and other memorabilia, including autographed basketballs, baseballs, and jerseys
Mid-Atlantic Sports Cards Baseball Auction On-Line	www.azww.com/midatlantic/auction.shtml	Continually changing lots of sports cards from an established dealer
New Age Sportscards & Autographs Auction	www.newagecards.com	Small collection of sports cards
Peggy's Baseball Cards	www.erols.com/pegbbcds/	Baseball cards and only baseball cards!
Rotman Collectibles	www.wwcd.com/rotman/	Over 1,200 sports-related items for auction, including sports cards, memorabilia, and autographs
SoldUSA	www.sportauction.com	Small selection of sports cards and memorabilia
Sporting News Auction House	www.auctions.sportingnews.com	Links to Auction Universe's collectibles category; huge selection of sports cards and memorabilia, including lots of NASCAR items
Sports Collectors Universe	auctions.sports-universe.com	Offers a consignment auction of PSA-graded sports cards ending every Thursday and Monday, as well as daily dealer auctions of sports cards and memorabilia; very large selection—recommended
SportsAuction	www.sportsauction.com	Tons of autographed sports memorabilia plus collectibles and sports cards
SportsTrade	www.sportstrade.com	Rare sports memorabilia, including autographed bats and game-used jerseys, plus sports cards
Strickler's Sports Den	sportsden.hypermart.net	Email bidding on sports cards and memorabilia
Teletrade Auctions	www.teletrade.com/teletrade/	Four auctions every week of memorabilia and sports cards

continues

Table 10.1 Continued

Site	URL	Comments
Vintage Sports Auctions	`www.davidrudd.com`	From David Rudd's Sports Cards, Seattle's largest vintage sports dealership; okay selection of baseball, basketball, and football cards
Yong & Dell's Sports Cards Auction On-Line	`www.azww.com/yong/auction.shtml`	Lots of sports cards from an established dealer

Auctions of sports cards, memorabilia, and more at Sports Collectors Universe.

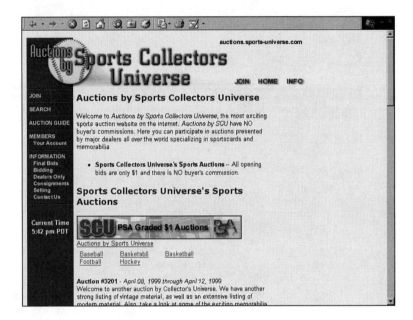

The biggest selection of sports cards (outside of eBay, of course) can be found at either Curran's Cards Auctions or Sports Collectors Universe. You should also check out the individual auctions at Boekhout's Collectibles Mall—they sometimes contain some rare and unique items.

Be a Good Sport with Sporting Goods Auctions

If you're more of a participant than a collector, you can also use the Web to find and bid on affordable sporting equipment. From golf clubs to skateboards, you can buy and sell all sorts of sports gear on the auction sites listed in Table 10.2.

Table 10.2 Sporting Goods Auctions

Site	URL	Comments
Cheap Snowboards	www.cheapsnowboards.com/base.htm	Offering snowboards, boots, bindings, and accessories
DiversCasino	www.diverscasino.com	Offering scuba equipment and dive tour packages
eGolf.com	www.egolf.com	Small selection of irons, woods, and wedges
Golf Auction USA	www.golfauctionusa.com	Small selection of clubs and accessories
Golf Club Exchange.com	www.golfclubexchange.com	Very large selection of clubs and accessories; features unique Personal ClubFinder service, club-specific searching (search by manufacturer, shaft type, price, and so on), and BlueBook Price Guide—recommended
golfbids.com	www.golfbids.com	Small selection of golf equipment, accessories, and memorabilia
Golfpeddler. com	www.golfpeddler.com	Very large selection of individual clubs, sets, and accessories—recommended
LiveToPlay	www.livetoplay.com	Offering outdoor gear, including bikes, camping gear, climbing equipment, inline skates, skateboards, skiing gear, snowboards, and snowshoes
Mountain Zone	auctions.mountainzone.com	Offering mountain sports products, including snowboards, skis, bikes, and backpacking gear
OnlyGolfAuction	www.robotica-inc.com/quickauction/golf/index.asp	Small selection of golf clubs and gear
SportingAuction	www.sportingauction.com	Small selection of general sporting goods

If you're looking for golf clubs, the best site on the Net is the Golf Club Exchange.com—big selection and wonderful club-finding tools. If you can get by without all the bells and whistles, Golfpeddler.com also has a large selection of clubs and gear.

For general sporting goods, the two sites to check out are LiveToPlay and Mountain Zone. Both offer a wide variety of gear and a decent number of listings.

The best place to buy and sell golf clubs on the Web—Golf Club Exchange.com.

The Least You Need to Know

➤ eBay has the most listings of sports cards and memorabilia—more than 250,000 items.

➤ There are many dedicated auctions for sports cards and memorabilia; two of the best are Curran's Cards Auctions and Sports Collectors Universe.

➤ If you're looking for golf clubs, try the Golf Club Exchange.com or Golfpeddler.com.

➤ The best auctions for general sporting goods are LiveToPlay and Mountain Zone.

Chapter 11

PC Auctions: Computer Hardware and Software at a Great Price

In This Chapter

➤ Find out which auctions have the most listings from individuals selling PC equipment

➤ Learn how to bid in a merchant computer auction

➤ Discover which merchant-run PC auctions are the biggest—and offer the best deals

Because you have to use a computer to access the Internet (WebTV excepted), it makes sense that the Internet would develop as a trading place for new and used computer equipment. As it now stands, computers represent one of the biggest categories of auctioned merchandise, and dozens of sites have been created that focus on nothing but computer auctions.

Today, buying a new PC or accessory from an online auction site is a viable alternative to buying from a traditional retail store. In most cases you find brand-new (albeit close-out or surplus) merchandise online, but at lower prices than you find at retail. Of course, you can also find used PCs from other users at some of the sites—which can also be a good deal, if that's what you need.

The bottom line—if you need new PC equipment, prepare to spend some time searching the online auctions!

Buying Computers at the Big Five Sites

Computers are big categories at each of the Big Five auction sites, which makes them logical places to look if you're buying or selling anything PC-related. Most of the listings here are from individuals or small retailers, and are primarily used merchandise.

Here's what you'll find at each site:

➤ **eBay** The biggest PC auction site, period, with more than 30,000 listings for all types of PC hardware and accessories, over 30,000 listings for software items, and almost 500 listings for computer-related services.

Name That Auction—And Auction That Name!

If you want to buy or sell a Web site domain name (the bit of the URL between the www. and the .com), check out Domains Auction (www.domainsauction.com). It's the first place to look if your chosen name isn't available through normal means.

➤ **Amazon.com Auctions** Not a lot of listings yet on this relatively new site; hardware, especially, is not one of Amazon's strengths.

➤ **Auction Universe** Not a strong player in PC hardware and software, with fewer than 1,000 total listings.

➤ **Classifieds 2000 Auctions** Kind of middle-of-the-pack, with around 3,000 computer-related listings—one-third of which are for PC software items.

➤ **Yahoo! Auctions** This category is one of Yahoo!'s strengths, with over 12,000 listings for computer hardware and software—plus 500 domain name auctions!

The top two sites to check out are eBay (of course...) and Yahoo! Auctions (surprise!). These two sites are also my recommended sites if you need to list PC equipment for sale.

Managing Merchant Auctions of Computer Hardware and Software

A large number of auction sites are dedicated to PC hardware and software. Unlike the general auction sites, most of these sites are run by merchants or liquidators—and do *not* include listings from individuals. (Go to eBay if you want to buy used equipment from regular folks.)

There are too many sites available to provide detailed comments across the board, but Table 11.1 gives you a little information on some of the more popular sites.

Table 11.1   Computer Hardware and Software Auctions

Site	URL	Comments
1st Class Auction	www.1stclassauction.com	New equipment
3D Auction	www.3dauction.com	New equipment
Affiliated Computer Auction	www.remarketing.com /auction/index.html	New, used, and refurbished Sun Microsystems, SGI, DEC Alpha, and Cisco equipment
Affiliated ReMarketing Web	www.remarketing.com	Refurbished equipment; over 30,000 listings for PCs, routers, workstations, midrange, and mainframe systems
At-Auction	www.at-auction.com	Small selection of listings from individuals
Auction Bidding	www.auction-bidding.com	Small selection of listings from individuals
Auction Depot	www.auctiondepot.com	From Toronto, Canada; small selection of merchant listings
Auction Floor	www.auctionfloor.com	New equipment
Auction House	www.unclebob.com/main.htm	New equipment
Auction IT	www.auction-it.net	Auction computer hardware to 185 dealers at once
Auction Sales	www.auction-sales.com	New, refurbished, and close-out equipment
Auction Watchers	www.auctionwatchers.com	Search engine that lets you comparison shop various online auctions for PC hardware and software
Auction World	www.a-world.com	New equipment
AuctionBox Computer Auction	www.auctionbox.com	New equipment
AuctioNet.com	www.auctionet.com	New equipment
AuctionGate Interactive	www.auctiongate.com	New equipment; owned by CNET
AuctionMax	www.auctionmax.com	New equipment
Auction-Warehouse.com	www.auction-warehouse.com	New equipment
Bid.com	www.bid.com	U.S. and Canadian sites; new equipment
Bid-4-It	www.bid4it.com	New and refurbished equipment
Biddernet Online Auctions	www.biddernet.com	New and refurbished equipment

continues

Table 11.1 Continued

Site	URL	Comments
Bidnask.com	www.bidnask.com	New, close-out, and liquidated equipment
BidnBuy	www.bidnbuy.com	New, refurbished, and close-out equipment
BidsWanted	www.bidswanted.com	New and refurbished PCs, electronics, and home office products
Bullnet Online Auctions	www.bullnet.co.uk/auctions	U.K.-based, new and surplus equipment
Computer Paradise Unlimited	www.cpu2000.com	New equipment
CyberSWAP	www.cyberswap.com	New equipment
DealDeal	www.dealdeal.com	New equipment
Digital Auction	www.digital-auction.com	New equipment
Egghead.com Surplus Auction	www.surplusauction.com	From Egghead, previous-version hardware, software, and accessories—recommended
emarketlive	www.emarketlive.com	Liquidated equipment
Encore Auction	www.encoreauction.com	Overstock, end-of-life, liquidated, and refurbished equipment
EZBid.com	www.ezbid.com	New equipment
Fair Auction	www.fairauction.com	New and surplus equipment
First Auction	www.firstauction.com	New equipment from the Internet Shopping Network (part of TV's Home Shopping Network)—recommended
Global Auction Club	www.gaci.net	New equipment
Going Once	www.goingonce.net	New equipment
Haggle Online	www.haggle.com	New and used equipment, including individual listings
Hardware Canada	www.hardwarecanada.com	Canadian site; small selection of individual listings
Infinite Auction	www.sweetdeal.com	New equipment
Innovative Auctions	www.innauction.com	New equipment
Interactive Auction Online	www.iaoauction.com	New equipment
Keybuy Auction House	www.keybuy.com	New and used equipment; small selection of individual listings

Site	URL	Comments
OnSale	`www.onsale.com`	Close-out and refurbished equipment; associated with Yahoo!; one of the first and the biggest PC auctions on the Web—recommended
Outpost Auctions	`www.outpostauctions.com`	New equipment; part of the Cyberian Outpost site
PCAuctioneer	`www.pcauctioneer.com`	New and used equipment
Quixell	`www.qxl.com`	European site; new equipment
RightAuction.com	`www.rightauction.com`	New and used equipment
Robotica Computer Products Auction	`www.robotica-inc.com/ quickauction/robotica/`	Small selection of individual listings
SellAll	`www.sellall.com`	New and used equipment
Shop4u.com	`www.shop4u.com`	New PC, electronics, and home office products
ShopZone	`www.shopzone.co.nz`	New Zealand site; new equipment
Software Auction Online	`www.gosao.com/door11.asp`	Software auction—new and used
ThinkBID	`www.thinkbid.com`	New and used equipment
Tradehall Global Trading Network	`www.tradehall.com`	Small selection of individual listings
uBid	`www.ubid.com`	Excess, refurbished, and limited-availability equipment; one of the larger PC auctions on the Web—recommended
UBID4IT	`www.ubid4it.com`	New, refurbished, liquidated, and close-out equipment
USAuctions	`www.usauctions.com`	New and liquidated equipment
WebAuction	`www.webauction.com`	New and refurbished equipment

It's hard to pick one of these sites over another; many are similar in the type of close-out merchandise they offer. With those similarities in mind, it's sometimes better to go with one of the bigger sites, with a good reputation and established customer service policies.

Of the bigger auctions, First Auction, OnSale, Egghead.com Surplus Auction, and uBid are my recommended sites. All are established and reputable and offer lots of stuff at good prices. You can't go wrong with any of these four.

uBid—one of the best PC auction sites on the Web.

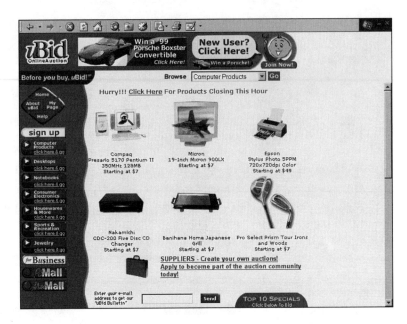

The Art of the Deal—Bidding for PC Equipment at a Typical Merchant Auction

Since merchant auctions are different from person-to-person auctions—and since most computer auctions are merchant auctions—I thought this would be a good place to walk you through how a typical merchant auction works.

You Gotta Have Credit

On Egghead.com, as on most merchant auction sites, you can't bid unless you place your credit card on file. This is because the site automatically charges your card when you win an auction.

For our example, let's use Egghead.com's Surplus Auction (www.surplusauction.com). Here's how you sign up and start bidding at this particular site:

1. Before you can place your initial bid, you first have to register with Egghead.com. To do this, click the **Sign Up to Bid** button on the home page. Fill in all the pertinent information (including your name, shipping address, and credit card number) and click the **Submit** button.

2. Return to the home page and browse through the item categories. Click on any item name to view the complete listing.

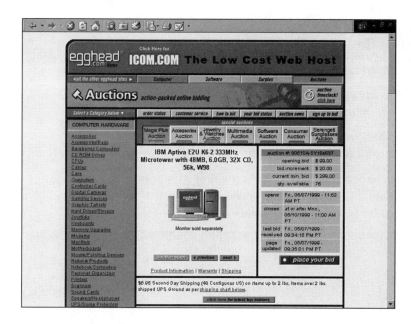

*A typical item listing at Egghead.com's Surplus Auction—click the **Place Your Bid** button to start bidding.*

3. When you find an item you want to buy, click the **Place Your Bid** button. When the next page appears, enter your Account Number and Password and click **Go!**.

4. Once you've been verified, you'll see the Place a Bid page. Enter your bid amount in the **Enter Your Bid** box; make sure your bid is equal to or higher than the Current Minimum Bid Required number. Click the **Submit Bid** button to register your bid.

5. When the auction is over, you will be notified via email if you hold a winning bid. You don't have to do anything else at this point, because winning a merchant auction essentially equates to placing an order for that piece of merchandise. Your credit card will automatically be charged within 12 hours of the auction close, and the merchandise will be shipped to you within 24–48 hours.

So now you see the big difference between a merchant auction and a person-to-person auction—after you win, everything else happens automatically. You don't have to worry about contacting the seller or arranging payment or arguing about shipping costs; the merchant behind the merchant auction just charges your credit card and ships the merchandise out as soon as possible.

The Least You Need to Know

➤ Used PCs from individuals can be found on eBay and Yahoo! Auctions.

➤ New, close-out, surplus, and refurbished equipment can be found at literally dozens of different merchant-run auction sites.

➤ The biggest merchant-run PC auction sites are First Auction, OnSale, Egghead.com, Surplus Auction, and uBid.

➤ Bidding at a merchant auction is a lot like bidding at a person-to-person auction; if you have a winning bid, however, the post-auction activity is just like placing an order at a traditional online retailer.

Chapter 12

Travel Auctions: Bidding Your Way to the Perfect Vacation

In This Chapter

➤ Discover how to lower the cost of your next vacation by bidding in online travel auctions

➤ Learn how you can name your own price for airline tickets and hotel rooms through priceline.com

When you travel, do you always accept the first price quoted for your tickets or lodging? Or do you check around, from agent to agent, to try to find the best possible deal?

If you're a deal hunter and a traveler, you should experiment with some of the Internet's online travel auctions. These sites, while somewhat limited, let you bid on packaged vacations and cruises—and, in some cases, hotel reservations, car rentals, and plane tickets. After checking the prices at some of these auctions, you'll be loathe to pay normal rates the next time you travel!

Bidding and Booking with Online Travel Auctions

Believe it or not, travel is one auction area where eBay hasn't really penetrated. Last I looked, eBay had fewer than 300 listings in its Travel category, and most were for luggage or travel-related memorabilia. No, if you want to bid on a trip, eBay *isn't* the place to go.

The place to go is to one of the dedicated travel auction sites on the Web. Here are some of the major ones:

➤ **Bid 4 Vacations** (`www.bid4vacations.com`)   Features beach vacations, spa and fitness getaways, family fun trips, cruises, vacation rentals, golf packages, guest and dude ranches, and ski trips.

➤ **First Internet Travel Auction** (`www.4a.com/auction/`)   Specializes in airline tickets, lodging facilities, car rentals, and cruise ships in the Colorado and Florida markets.

➤ **GoingGoingGone Travel Auctions** (`www.goinggoinggone.com/going/ homego.htm`)   Offers cruises and complete vacations.

➤ **lastminute.com** (`www.lastminute.com`)   Offers a U.K. travel and tickets auction.

➤ **Onsale Vacations & Travel** (`www.onsale.com/departments/vacations.htm`) Offers cruises and pre-packaged vacations.

➤ **TravelBids Travel Discount Auction** (`www.TravelBids.com`)   Offers air travel, resorts, and cruises—you enter the trip you want to take and travel agents bid on your business.

➤ **Travelfacts Auction** (`www.bid4travel.com`)   Offers cruises, hotel rooms, travel packages, airline tickets, and other travel services and products.

Bid on your next vacation at TravelBids Travel Discount Auction.

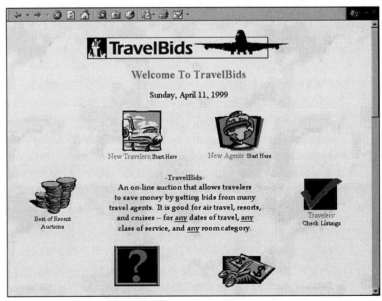

I'll be honest: None of these sites really do a great job. Most deal with "surplus inventory" of vacation packages or hotel rooms, which means you don't always get a great selection to choose from. But if you can work within these limitations, the price is right—online travel auctions *will* save you money on your next vacation!

Almost Like an Auction: priceline.com

Okay, so priceline.com (www.priceline.com) isn't technically an auction, and therefore shouldn't be included in this book. But priceline.com kind of looks and feels like an auction—and it's definitely a site you want to check out if you're interested in getting the best bang for your travel bucks.

In essence, priceline.com lets you name your own price for airline tickets and hotel rooms. Then they try to find an airline or hotel to accept your offer. No supplier is obligated to accept, so you can always end up out in the cold. But if your offer is matched, you'll get some of the best prices available in the travel business.

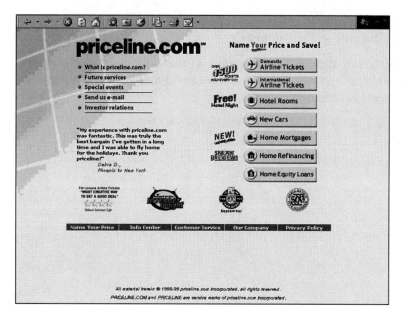

Not quite an auction, but darned close—name your own price for airline tickets and hotel rooms at priceline.com.

Let's take a look at the airline ticket example. You click one of the **Airline Tickets** buttons, and then select your destination and travel dates. Then you name the price you want to pay, and priceline.com searches for a major airline willing to release seats on flights with unsold space. Within one hour, priceline.com tells you whether any airline agreed to release the seats, and if so, which flights you're scheduled on. After you've accepted the deal, your tickets are non-refundable, non-changeable, and do not earn frequent flyer miles.

You don't have a lot of control over the time of your departure or arrival, either, which means priceline.com isn't great for business travelers or people on a tight schedule. But if you don't mind flying at odd hours—and, in many cases, making some unusual connections—you can save some bucks by scheduling through priceline.com.

In the case of hotel rooms, priceline.com offers lodging in 26 U.S. cities—including New York, Los Angeles, Las Vegas, San Francisco, Chicago, and the other biggies. You can specify the quality of hotel you're looking for, as well as the price, and priceline.com does the rest—within an hour!

For leisure travelers, priceline.com could be better than auctions, in that you call more (but not all) of the shots. In any case, the service is revolutionizing the travel industry, and it's probably worth checking out.

The Least You Need to Know

➤ Online travel auctions let you bid on packaged vacations and cruises—and, in some cases, hotel rooms and airline tickets.

➤ priceline.com functions sort of like an auction, in that you name your own price for airline tickets and hotel rooms; major carriers and hotels have the option of accepting or refusing your offer.

Other Auctions: Odds and Ends and Bits and Pieces

In This Chapter

➤ Learn when to use a local auction site

➤ Discover where to buy and sell cars, horses, and bicycles online

➤ Uncover the best wine auctions on the Web

➤ Find out how your bidding can support a good cause at online charity auctions

In writing this book, I found more than 300 different auction sites on the Internet. Granted, a lot of them were general auctions (like eBay), a lot more focused on collectibles or sports cards or computer equipment, but a surprising number of sites were dedicated to...well, to *other* stuff.

This chapter looks at what I like to call the "odds and ends" of the online auction world.

Keep Your Bidding Close to Home with Local Auctions

The one problem with most auction sites is that anyone in the world can put something up for bid, or become a bidder. This is fine if the item being sold is something small and easily shipped; it really stinks if you have something larger or perishable.

When you have something to sell that only local users will be interested in, it's time to search out a local auction site. There's not a whole lot of them yet, but expect this to be a growing trend.

Today, most of the local auctions are part of the Auction Universe Network (www.aun.com). This network contains a group of local newspaper and television/radio sites, affiliated with the larger Auction Universe site.

Another batch of local auctions comes under the heading of CityAuction (www.cityauction.com), owned by TicketMaster Online, and partnered with CNET's Snap portal. CityAuction allows users to search for an item within only a local auction site, or nationally.

Up in Canada, Bargoon (www.bargoon.com) is building a series of local auction sites for selected Canadian cities; Halifax and Toronto are first off the block. Like the other local site networks, the goal here is to facilitate the auctioning of products that have local appeal—furniture, automobiles, homes, and real estate.

None of these large-ticket items really makes a lot of sense on a site like eBay—unless, of course, eBay figures out how to do local auctions. And they're working on it.

As I write this, eBay is testing local auctions with an eBay LA site. Key to this local auction initiative is the ability to search for items by zip code; once this is implemented systemwide, it will be easier for users to list and bid on items within a specific geographic region. In addition, eBay's $75M deal with America Online suggests that eBay's local auctions-to-come can be marketed by and accessed through the local sites of AOL's Digital City subsidiary. It's certainly something for eBay users to look forward to.

All that said, Table 13.1 lists the major local auction sites in existence today.

Table 13.1   Local Auction Sites

Region	Site	URL
Network of local sites	CityAuction	www.cityauction.com
Arizona	AZ Auctions	www.azauctions.com
California: Los Angeles	Los Angeles Times Auctions	www.laauctions.com
Connecticut: Hartford	Courant CTAuctions	www.ctauctions.com
Florida	Florida Auctions Online	www.comspec-marketing.com/auction/
Florida: Orlando	Auctions Orlando	www.auctionsorlando.com

Region	Site	URL
Florida: South Florida	AuctionsSouthFlorida	www.auctionssouthflorida.com
Florida: St. Lucie County	St. Lucie Marketplace	www.stluciemarketplace.com
Maine	Maine Market Auctions	www.maineauctions.com
Michigan: Lansing	WLAJ Auction	www.wlajauction.com
Michigan: Western Michigan	WWMT Auction	www.wwmtauction.com
Minnesota: Minneapolis /St. Paul	Minneapolis Star Tribune Strib Auctions.com	www.stribauctions.com
Missouri: St. Louis	Postnet Auctions	www.postnetauctions.com
North Carolina	Triangle Auction	www.triangleauction.com
Ohio: Cleveland	NewsNet 5 Auctions	www.newsnet5auctions.com
Oklahoma	Auction OK	www.auctionok.com
Oklahoma	NeedFulThings	www.needfulthings.net/auction.shtm
Oregon: Portland	Channel 6000 Auctions	www.channel6000auctions.com
Pennsylvania: Allentown	Morning Call Penn Auctions	www.pennauctions.com
Pennsylvania: Lancaster	LancAuctions	www.lancauctions.com
Pennsylvania: Philadelphia	Philadelphia Online Philly Auctions	www.phillyauctions.com
Texas: McAllen	Monitor Auctions	www.monitorauctions.com
Vermont	VermontAuctions	www.vermontauctions.com
Virginia: Richmond	Auctions VA	www.auctionsva.com
Washington, D.C.	DC Values	www.dcvalues.com
Washington: Southwest Washington state	Columbian.com Auctions NW	www.auctionsnw.com
Wisconsin: Madison	Channel 3000 Auctions	www.channel3000auctions.com
Midwest U.S.	MFCP Auctions Midwest	www.auctionsmidwest.com
Canadian communities (Halifax, Toronto, more)	Bargoon	www.bargoon.com

Auctions Outside the United States

Online auctions aren't just a U.S. phenomenon. Online consumers all around the world are bidding and selling items on global auction sites such as eBay, as well as on auction sites native to their own countries. Here are just a few of the non-U.S. auctions on the World Wide Web today, by country/region:

➤ **Canada**   Antique Canada/Antiques Ontario (www.antique-canada.com), AB!C (www.auctionsbyabc.com), Auction Depot (www.auctiondepot.com), Bargoon (www.bargoon.com), Bid.com (www.bid.com), CanAuction (www.canauction.com), Graham Auctions (www.grahamauctions.com), Hardware Canada (www.hardwarecanada.com), and Trader's Cove Online Auction (www.niximage.com/auction/)

➤ **Europe**   Quixell (www.qxl.com)

➤ **France**   France Auction Web (www.auction-fr.com)

➤ **Germany**   Jordan & Jordan Online Wine Auction (www.saarwein.com/auktion.htm)

➤ **Netherlands**   Auction Online De Veiling (www.auction-online.com)

➤ **New Zealand**   ShopZone (www.shopzone.co.nz)

➤ **Russia**   Russian Auction (www.russianauction.com)

➤ **U.K.**   Auction Hunter (www.auctionhunter.co.uk), AuctionsUK (guestservices.hypermart.net/uk.htm), Auctionuniverse.co.uk (www.auctionuniverse.co.uk), Bullnet Online Auctions (www.bullnet.co.uk/auctions), eBid (www.ebid.co.uk), lastminute.com (www.lastminute.com), Online Auctions UK (www.onlineauctions.co.uk), and SPEEDBID (www.speedbid.com).

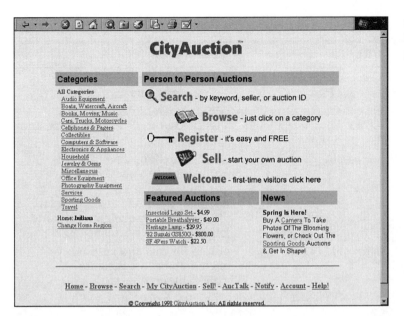

CityAuction—specify your home region, and search for items available locally.

Better Than Scalping: Online Ticket Auctions

Whether you're looking for tickets to sporting events, theater productions, or concerts, two sites on the Web let you buy and sell tickets in an online auction format. Check out Pick Your Seat (www.pickyourseat.com) or Tickets.com (www.auction.tickets.com), the next time you need tickets to that special event!

Bidding in Stereo: Consumer Electronics Auctions

Although many of the PC auctions (discussed in Chapter 11, "PC Auctions: Computer Hardware and Software at a Great Price") and liquidation/surplus auctions (discussed later in this chapter) sell consumer electronics goods, a handful of other sites also specialize in home and business electronics. The sites to go to are EZBid.com (www.ezbid.com), First Auction (www.firstauction.com), Going Once (www.goingonce.net), and Interactive Auction Online (www.iaoauction.com).

So if you're looking for a VCR, home stereo, car audio system, camcorder, or camera, these are the sites to check out! (And don't forget eBay—which probably has the most listings for consumer electronics goods of any online auction site.)

Going Mobile with Automotive Auctions

Did you know you could buy a car via an online auction—not to mention automotive parts and memorabilia? Well, you can—at one of the sites listed in Table 13.2.

119

Table 13.2   Automotive Auctions

Site	URL	Comments
Automobile Auctions Online	www.dealerschoice.com/conauc.htm	Listing of automobile auctions accessible online
Cycle Auction Online	ep.com/ep/csp.html?csp=3758	Motorcycle-only auction and classifieds, offering bikes, parts, and accessories
Manheim Online	www.manheim.com	Online auctions from the king of real-world auto auctions; view pre-sale inventories by auction or consignor/manufacturer, and sort lists by make/model, mileage, and other criteria
Mobilia	www.mobilia.com	A hub for cars and automotive memorabilia, for the auto collectibles enthusiast
National Corvette Museum Auction	auction.corvettemuseum.com	Corvette-related auctions
RacersAuction	www.racersauction.com/auction	Featuring new and used racing parts—from complete race cars to engine parts to tow trucks and trailers

In addition, eBay recently acquired Kruse International, a major real-world auctioneer of classic and collectible automobiles. This acquisition lets eBay expand the range of cars offered for auction on its site—and gives car collectors one more auction site to monitor!

Rental Cars for Auction

Budget Rent a Car lets users bid on car rentals at their BidBudget (www.bidbudget.com) site. No, you're not bidding on used cars from their fleet—you're actually bidding on local rental contracts!

Do a Little Horse Trading with Equine Auctions

If internal combustion isn't your style, get a horse! There are two major equine auctions on the Web, where you can buy and sell horses and horse-related

items. Both Cyber Horse Auction (www.
cyberhorseauction.com) and OnLine Equine
Sales Company (www.online-equine.com) are
worth checking out if you're a horse enthusiast.

Playing Around with Musical Equipment and Pro Audio Auctions

Want to buy or sell a musical instrument? How
about some pro audio equipment? Check out
these music/audio-related auction sites:

Another Mode of Auctionable Transportation: Bicycles!

PlanetBike (www.auction-land
.com/planetbike/) auctions new
and used bicycles, as well as bicycle-
related parts and accessories. You
don't need a motor to get around
on this auction site!

➤ **Digibid (www.digibid.com)**   Offering
secondhand and new pro audio and
video equipment, plus musical instruments, recording gear, and more.

➤ **Gibson Musical Instruments (www.auction.gibson.com)**   The premiere
instrument maker offers high-integrity instrument auctions, verifying the
model, year, condition, and originality of every instrument up for bid.

➤ **Guitarauction (www.guitarauction.com)**   A guitar-only auction open to both
dealers and individuals.

➤ **Rock Auction (www.rockauction.com)**   From Daddy's Junky Music Stores,
more than 10,000 pieces of used musical gear for auction.

A Bottle of Red, a Bottle of White, Time for a Wine Auction Tonight

I was surprised to find so many dedicated wine auction sites available. Suffice to say,
wine connoisseurs go out of their way to find a fine vintage, and the sites in Table
13.3 offer numerous opportunities to enlarge and enhance a collection.

Table 13.3   Wine Auctions

Site	URL
AuctionVine	www.auctionvine.com
Brentwood Wine Company	www.brentwoodwine.com
International Wine Exchange	www.wine-exchange.com
Jordan & Jordan Online Wine Auction	www.saarwein.com/auktion.htm

continues

Table 13.3   Continued

Site	URL
Mid-Atlantic Wine Auction Company	www.midatlanticwine.com
Wine Online	www.winecollector.com
Wine.Com Auction	www.wine.com/bidwine/auction.cgi
WineBid.com	www.winebid.com

Vintage bidding at the Web's top online wine auction house, WineBid.com.

Put Some Magic Back into Your Life with Magic Supplies Auctions

Magic Auction (www.magicauction.com) has to be the most specialized auction I've stumbled across. This site holds weekly online auctions for magician supplies. So if you want to bid on a hat full of rabbits, this is the site to visit!

Doing Business on the Cheap with Business-to-Business Auctions and Liquidations

Many manufacturers, distributors, and retailers use online auctions to get rid of excess inventory. Some of these auctions are industry specific, but many include merchandise of interest to the general public. Note that a few of these "business-to-business" auctions are sometimes restricted to known partners or customers.

Table 13.4   Business–Related Auctions

Site	URL	Comments
emarketlive	www.emarketlive.com	Liquidations of computer equipment
Encore Auction	www.encoreauction.com	Overstock, end-of-life, and refurbished computers, electronics, and office equipment
Hybrid Liquidation	www.liquidation.com	Business-to-business liquidation auctions; listings cover the gamut from toothpicks to airplanes to industrial equipment to real estate
Intermodal Equipment Exchange	www.intermodalex.com	Auctions of marine and domestic cargo containers
PIRSS On-Line A/E/C Auctions	www.insa.com/auction/	For architecture/ engineering/ construction professionals, featuring building materials, products, and services
SellAll	www.sellall.com	Business-to-business sales of telephone, datacom, and other industrial and electronic surplus merchandise
U.S. Government FinanceNet Auctions	www.financenet.gov/sales.htm	The Federal government's FinanceNet Project provides information on government asset sales, surplus, and auctions

Doing a Good Deed with Charity Auctions

Real-world auctions are often used to benefit various charities; why shouldn't online auctions do the same? If you're in a charitable mood, check out these charity auctions on the Web:

➤ **AFundRaiser.Com (www.afundraiser .com)**   Provides online fundraiser auctions for non-profit organizations.

➤ **Hollywood Auction (www.travel.to/ Hollywood/)**   From Broadcaster.com, a monthly online Hollywood charity auction, featuring items such as movie premier packages, signed movie posters, walk-on roles, signed scripts, and VIP TV show tickets. Proceeds provide training

Getting Religion with Christian Auctions

The JC Shopping Club Auction (www.jcshopping.com) lets you buy and sell collectibles, antiques, and religious items in a Christian environment. (This site is a division of the JC Book Club.)

opportunities to minority college graduates in radio/television news reporting and management.

➤ **Stardoodles for Kids** (www.stardoodle.com)   Auctions celebrity doodles, with the proceeds going to the Champions for Children Foundation.

➤ **WebCharity.com** (www.webcharity.com)   Provides online auctions and a Virtual Thrift Shop whose proceeds benefit various charities.

Find some neat movie memorabilia and support a good cause at the Broadcaster.com Hollywood Auction.

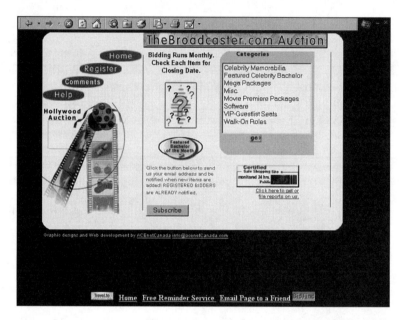

The Least You Need to Know

➤ Beyond the general auction sites, there are a number of very specialized online auctions.

➤ Local auctions are a way to buy and sell larger or perishable merchandise; CityAuction and the Auction Universe Network are two good sources of local auctions.

➤ Other specialized auctions feature automobiles, horses, musical instruments, and wine.

Part 3

Essential eBay: Buying and Selling on the Internet's Largest Auction Site

If you're really serious about online auctions, eBay is the place to be! With more than 1.5 million individual auctions every day, eBay is the biggest auction site on the Internet—and one of the most popular Web sites, period! Read the chapters in this section to learn how to use eBay—how to search for items, how to bid on items, how to sell items, how to use HTML in your item listings, and how to personalize your experience with My eBay. You'll even discover some of the secrets that eBay doesn't want you to know—but could give you a hidden advantage over other eBay users!

eBay Wants You: Joining Up and Getting Started

In This Chapter

➤ Uncover eBay's "hidden" features, services, and contacts—and how to access them directly

➤ Find out when you have to register—and how to do it

➤ Discover when you have to pay eBay—and when you don't

You read all about eBay in Chapter 6, "General Auctions: A Little Bit of Everything, All in One Place." Or you've read a news article or two about eBay or observed eBay's high-flying stock price over time. Or maybe you have friends or family who use eBay to buy and sell a few items now and then. You might have even visited the eBay site, curious about all the buzz.

Whatever the case, you're now interested enough to actually try a little trading on eBay. How do you get started?

This chapter presents a guided tour of eBay and shows you how to register so you can buy and sell items online. The next seven chapters in this section tell you everything else you need to know to successfully bid, buy, and sell items on the eBay site. Think of this section of *The Complete Idiot's Guide to Online Auctions* as a book-within-a-book that serves as your complete guide to the most popular online auction on the Internet!

Getting Around eBay

Not even counting the millions of individual auction listings, eBay has a ton of content and community on its site—if you know where to find it. To be honest, aside from the item lists, eBay's site is so poorly organized that most users never find some of eBay's most interesting and useful features.

I tell you where they are.

The Place to Start: eBay's Home Page

When you go to www.ebay.com, you see eBay's home page. From here, you can access a handful of eBay's features and services, as shown in the following figure.

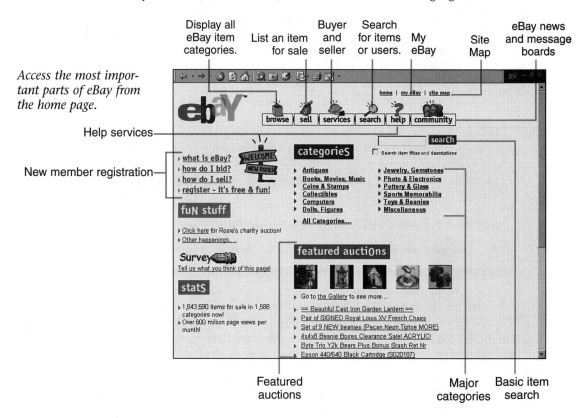

Access the most important parts of eBay from the home page.

Probably the most important links on eBay's home page are

➤ **Site Map** This link takes you to a page listing *all* of eBay's features and services—which is where you'll really find things.

➤ **Search** This takes you to eBay's advanced search page— a *better* way to search for items.

➤ **Sell Your Item** This links directly to a form that lets you list a new item for sale.

➤ **Listings** This displays all of eBay's item categories, as well as featured auctions.

➤ **Register** Click this first if you're a new user and need to become an eBay member.

The Weird and the Wonderful on eBay

With close to two million individual items on auction every single day of the year, you're bound to come across some, shall we say, *unusual* items for sale on eBay's site. Here are just a few of the stranger items I've found on eBay:

➤ 1954 Chevrolet Bel Air convertible (red)

➤ 1969 newspaper advertisement for Holiday Inn ("You're No. 1")

➤ 500 billion Dinar banknote from the Republic of Yugoslavia (with the most zeros of any currency ever issued)

➤ *Action Comics* #1 (fine/very fine condition)

➤ Assorted small old keys (four, unmarked)

➤ Beef jerky (1 lb., fresh)

➤ Cigar condoms (for those with executive privileges)

➤ Fully equipped physician's office/clinic (includes six examination rooms and in-office laboratory)

➤ High-quality lawnmower mufflers (a lot of three)

➤ Life-size crystal skull (asking price: $6,500)

➤ "Polka Lovers Parking Only" metal sign (suitable for indoor or outdoor display)

➤ Quicksilver MXII Sprint home-built airplane (seats two)

➤ Software that turns your Windows cursors into exploding pigs

➤ Team of Internet service provider engineers (one director, three managers, seven senior engineers, and five administrators)

➤ Title to a British manor (includes automatic lordship)

➤ Toyota propane forklift (3,500-lb. capacity)

➤ Turn-key publishing business: *Impression* Webzine (founded at the University of Missouri)

➤ Vincent Van Gogh's last painting (value: $5 million)

Where can you find some of these eclectic items? Try eBay's Big-Ticket Items lists (www.pages.ebay.com/aw/big-ticket.html) for starters; after that, you'll just have to stumble over them.

Where to Find Everything Else: eBay's Site Map

Even if you can't get to a particular feature or service from eBay's minimalist home page, you can link to it from eBay's Site Map. Although eBay's home page suffers from a dearth of links (which, on the plus side, gives it a very clean design), eBay's Site Map serves as the true access point to the site's numerous and diverse features. If you've never visited the Site Map page, I guarantee you'll be surprised at everything you'll find there—including a lot of features and services that you didn't even know existed!

(Why eBay hides all these features is beyond me, but that's one of the reasons I'm writing this book—to show you all the good stuff you would have missed otherwise.)

Discover parts of eBay that you didn't even know existed via the Site Map.

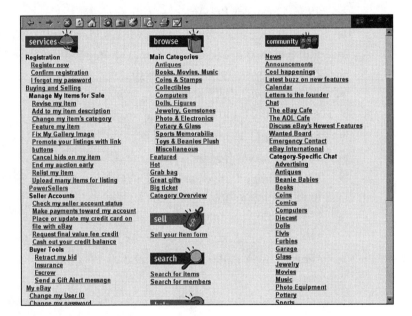

Here's some of what you'll find on the Site Map page:

➤ **Welcome**   Links to information of value for newer eBay users, including tutorials on how to use key features.

➤ **Quick Links**   A link to a page that duplicates the links on eBay's home page—useless, unfortunately.

➤ **Current Listings**   Links to various listings of eBay categories and special auctions. My favorite link here is eBay Category Overview, a simple list of eBay item categories without the massive featured auction listings that typically slow down the loading for the listings page.

➤ **Buyer Services**   Information and services for eBay buyers.

➤ **Seller Services**   Information and services for eBay sellers.

➤ **Registered User Services**   Information and services for all eBay members.

➤ **Information**   General help information and FAQs.

➤ **eBay Bulletin Boards**   Message boards where you can talk to other users—and to eBay staff.

Find Out What's New and Happening

With so much going on—and new stuff being added almost daily—how do you keep up with all the events and happenings on eBay? Here are some links on the Site Map page you might find of value:

➤ If you're relatively new to eBay, you might want to check out eBay's Welcome and Community pages.

➤ If you want to learn how to use various site features, try the Tutorial links or click the Help link at the top of any eBay page.

➤ To find out about any technical system updates (or planned outages), click the Announcements link.

➤ Announcements about eBay's newest features, enhancements, and promotions appear when you click the News/Chat link at the top of any eBay page.

➤ Finally, don't neglect eBay's home page. Although a lot of users tend to rush by this opening page on their way to specific auctions, take the time to scroll down and see what's new; any big events and promotions are displayed here.

How to Go Directly to the Most Important Stuff

Tired of clicking to eBay's site map and then clicking to another link (and maybe another after that) to access a specific eBay feature? Don't despair; just about every part of eBay's site has its own unique Web address. Just reference Table 14.1 to find the direct URLs for eBay's most important features.

Table 14.1   Direct Access Information for eBay Services

Feature/Area	URL
Home page	www.ebay.com
About Me personal Web pages	members.ebay.com/aw/aboutme-login.html
Account status	pages.ebay.com/aw/account-status.html
Announcements	calculus.ebay.com/aw/announce.shtml
Auctions ending today	listings.ebay.com/aw/listings/endtoday/index.html
Big ticket items	pages.ebay.com/aw/big-ticket.html
Canceling a bid (seller)	pages.ebay.com/aw/seller-cancel-bid.html
Category list (simple)	listings.ebay.com/aw/listings/overview.html
Category list (including featured auctions)	listings.ebay.com/aw/listings/list
Community Center	pages.ebay.com/aw/community.html
Completed auctions	cayman.ebay.com/aw/listings/completed/index.html
Contacting eBay	pages.ebay.com/aw/help/help-support.html
Contacting other users	pages.ebay.com/aw/user-query.html
Current listings	listings.ebay.com/aw/listings/list
eBay Cafe	cgi3.ebay.com/aw-cgi/eBayISAPI.dll?ViewBoard&name=cafe
eBay community guidelines	pages.ebay.com/aw/guidelines.html
eBay Life	pages.ebay.com/aw/ebay-life-pA1.html
Ending auction early	pages.ebay.com/aw/end-auction.html
Extending auction	pages.ebay.com/aw/autoextension.html
Fee list	pages.ebay.com/aw/agreement-fees.html
Feedback Forum	pages.ebay.com/aw/feedback.html
Forgot password	pages.ebay.com/aw/reqpass.html
Frequently asked questions (FAQ)	pages.ebay.com/aw/faq.html
Gallery	pages.ebay.com/aw/gallery.html
Gifts	pages.ebay.com/aw/gift-section.html
Help	pages.ebay.com/aw/help/help-start.html
Listing an item for sale	pages.ebay.com/aw/newitem.html
My eBay	pages.ebay.com/aw/myebay.html
New auctions today	listings.ebay.com/aw/listings/newtoday/index.html
News and chat	pages.ebay.com/aw/newschat.html
Personal Shopper	cgi6.ebay.com/aw-cgi/eBayISAPI.dll?PersonalShopperViewSearches

Feature/Area	URL
Registering	pages.ebay.com/aw/registration-show.html
Requesting another user's email address	cgi3.ebay.com/aw-cgi/eBayISAPI.dll?GetUserEmail
Retracting a bid (buyer)	pages.ebay.com/aw/retract-bid.html
Searching	pages.ebay.com/aw/search.html

Before You Buy or Sell—Register!

Anyone can browse through the listings on eBay. To bid on an item—or to list an item for sale—you have to be a registered user.

Registration Required for the Adult Stuff

As a means of verifying legal age, eBay restricts access to its Erotica, Adults Only, category to registered users only. (Remember, you need to be 18 to register...which is old enough to see the dirty pictures!) You'll need a credit card on file with eBay to both view and bid on these items.

Everybody Does It: Fill Out eBay's Registration Form

Registration is free, easy, and relatively quick. All you have to do is click the **Register** link on eBay's home page, which takes you to the initial eBay Registration page. Select which country you're from, and click the **Begin the Registration Process Now** button to access the main eBay Registration page.

Fill out the form on this page by entering the following information:

➤ Your email address.

➤ Your name, address, and phone number.

➤ Optional personal information about yourself. (You don't have to complete this part; it's just for eBay's marketing department.)

Click the **Continue** button to finalize your registration. Shortly after you submit this form, you will receive an email from eBay with a temporary password. Follow the directions in this email to confirm your new registration, and then, you're ready to start trading.

How Private Is Your Private Information?

eBay asks all members to supply a valid physical address and telephone number. They don't disclose this info to anyone outside eBay, although they will supply your data to other eBay users on their request. (It's how they try to contact deadbeat bidders and sellers.)

Handling Change

If you move, you'll need to change the address and phone number information eBay has on file. Just go to the Site Map page and click **Change Registered Information** (in the Registered User Services section).

The Costs of Using eBay

You don't have to pay eBay anything to browse through items on its site. You don't have to pay eBay anything to bid on an item. You don't even have to pay eBay anything if you actually buy an item (although you will be paying the seller directly, of course). But if you're listing an item for sale, you gotta pay.

There's No Free Lunch

eBay charges two main types of fees:

➤ **Insertion fees** (I prefer to call them *listing* fees) are what you pay every time you list an item for sale on eBay. These fees are based on the minimum bid or reserve price of the item listed.

➤ **Final value fees** (I prefer to call them *selling* fees, or *commissions*) are what you pay when an item is actually sold to a buyer. These fees are based on the item's final selling price (the highest bid).

eBay also charges a variety of fees for different types of listing enhancements. Table 14.2 lists all the fees eBay charges, current as of Spring 1999.

Table 14.2   eBay Fees

Type of Fee	Explanation	Fee
Insertion fee	In a regular auction, based on the opening value or minimum bid. In a reserve price auction, based on the reserve price of the item. In a Dutch auction, based on the opening value or minimum bid—multiplied by the number of items offered.	For items priced at $9.99 or less, $0.25; for items priced from $10.00 to $24.99, $0.50; for items priced from $25.00 to $49.99, $1.00; for items priced at $50.00 or more, $2.00.
Final value fee	In regular and reserve price auctions, based on the closing (high) bid. In Dutch auctions, based on the lowest successful bid—multiplied by the number of items sold.	5% of the amount of the high bid up to $25, plus 2.5% of that part of the high bid from $25.01 up to $1,000, plus 1.25% of the remaining amount of current high bid that is greater than $1000. For example, if the item sold for $1500, you'd pay 5% of the first $25 ($1.25) plus 2.5% of the next $975 ($24.38) plus 1.25% of the remaining $500 ($6.25), for a total fee of $31.88.
Bold text	Boldfaces the title of your item on the listing pages.	$2.00
Category featured auction	Puts your listing at the top of the listings pages for that category and also displays your listing (randomly) in the Featured Items section of the related category home page.	$14.95
Featured auction	Puts your listing at the top of the main Listings page and also displays your listing (randomly) in the Featured area on eBay's home page and on the Featured Items section of the related category home page.	$99.95
Gift icon	Displays a special icon next to your listing, indicating that your item would make a great gift; also displays your listing in eBay's Gift section.	$1.00
Gallery listing	Allows the picture of your item to be presented as a thumbnail in the Gallery section.	$0.25

continues

Table 14.2   Continued

Type of Fee	Explanation	Fee
Featured gallery	Randomly displays your Gallery listing at the top of the category, in a larger size.	$19.95

There's all manner of fine print associated with these fees. Here are some of the more important points to keep in mind:

➤ Insertion fees are nonrefundable.

➤ You will not be charged a final value fee if there were no bids on your item or (in a reserve price auction) if there were no bids that met the reserve price.

➤ It doesn't matter whether the buyer actually pays you (or how much he or she actually pays); you still owe eBay the full final value fee.

Invoicing on your account occurs on the first day of each month for the previous month's activity. You'll get an invoice via email detailing your charges for the month; if you've set up your account for automatic credit card billing (see the next section), your credit card will be charged at that time. (If you prefer to pay via check, now's the time to get out the old checkbook.)

Credit Line

eBay automatically assigns all new users a $10 "credit line." That means that you can immediately start listing items for sale, as long as the listing fees total less than your $10 limit. If you want to list more items, then you'll either need to prepay your account via check or money order (very inconvenient) or set up automatic billing via credit card.

Painless Payment: Automatic Credit Card Billing

To set up credit card billing (which I recommend), go to the Site Map page and click **Place or Update Your Credit Card** (in the Seller Services section) to access the Credit Card Submission form. Enter your user ID or email address, password, and credit card billing information, and click the **Submit** button. Your credit card information will be applied to your eBay account within 24 hours—at which time you'll be able to participate fully in everything eBay has to offer.

Credit Cards for Bidders?

By the way, if you're a buyer, you might also want to register your credit card—not that eBay requires it, or will charge anything against it. Registering your card allows you access to eBay's adult areas and sets everything in place in case you do want to list items for sale in the future.

Handling Change

If you want to change or update your credit card information, go to the Site Map page and click **Place or Update Your Credit Card** (in the Seller Services section).

Sometimes You Get a Second Chance...

What do you owe if you put an item up for auction, and it doesn't sell?

Obviously, you *don't* owe a final value (selling) fee because you didn't actually sell your item.

But you do owe eBay the insertion (listing) fee because you did list your item. (In other words, eBay doesn't care whether you actually sell your item; it collects its listing fees either way.)

Under certain conditions, however, eBay gives you the option of relisting your item in a new auction. If you do this, eBay waives the initial insertion fees—so you only pay for one insertion, even though you received two listings (in two separate auctions).

Here are eBay's parameters for a relist:

➤ The original auction was *not* a Dutch auction.

➤ If the original auction was a regular auction, you didn't receive *any* bids on the item.

137

➤ If the original auction was a reserve price auction, you didn't receive any bids that met or exceeded your reserve price.

➤ You choose to relist your item with 30 days of the closing date of your initial auction.

To relist an item, go to the Completed Auction Item page, click the **Relist** link, and follow the instructions on the Relist Item page.

When you relist an item, you can't change the item itself, although you can revise your listing slightly. On the Relist Item page, eBay lets you revise the title, price, and description for your item. (In fact, I recommend you *do* change your listing on a relist because there was *something* about the listing that turned off potential bidders. Examine the price, title, and so on to see whether you can't put together a more compelling offer.)

If your item sells the second time, the insertion fee for the relisted item will be refunded at the end of the billing cycle.

No Third Chances

eBay lets you relist your item *once*. That means if it doesn't sell the second time, any additional listings come out of your pocket, not eBay's. (By the way, you can only relist regular or reserve price auctions; you *can't* relist items sold via Dutch auction.)

Getting a Refund on Final Value Fees

In a handful of other situations, you can obtain a refund of your final value fees. (eBay never refunds insertion fees, so don't even bother asking.) Here are the circumstances under which you can ask eBay for a full or partial refund:

➤ The high bidder did not respond after you attempted to contact him or her or backed out and did not buy item.

➤ The high bidder's check bounced or a stop payment was placed on it.

➤ The high bidder returned the item, and you issued a refund.

➤ The high bidder claimed the payment or shipping terms were unacceptable and refused to complete the transaction.

➤ The sale price was actually lower than the highest bid.

> ➤ The high bidder backed out, but you sold the item to another bidder at a lower price.

> ➤ One or more of the bidders in a Dutch auction backed out of the sale.

To request a final value fee credit, go to the Site Map page and click **Final Value Fee Credit Request** (in the Seller Services section).

Contacting eBay—*Directly!*

While you *could* use eBay's bulletin boards and the links at www.pages.ebay.com/ aw/help/help-support.html to try to contact eBay, you'll quickly discover that these methods of communication often leave something to be desired—like a fast response! Instead, try contacting eBay staff *directly* via the following email addresses—addresses, by the way, that eBay does a good job of hiding from its user base.

Table 14.3 lists eBay's some eBay email addresses to contact for specific problems and issue:

Table 14.3 "Secret" eBay Contact Addresses

Issue	Contact
Questions of an urgent nature	timesensitive@ebay.com
Questions of a general and non-urgent nature	support@ebay.com
Questions about user agreement	agree-questions@ebay.com
Questions about why an auction ended early	whyended@ebay.com
Questions about buying and selling outside the U.S.	goglobal@ebay.com
Questions about finding a job working for eBay	jobs@ebay.com
Questions about the Mister Lister bulk listing service	misterlister@ebay.com
Questions about eBay's privacy policy	privacy@ebay.com
Questions about account status & credit cards	billing@ebay.com
Request merging of two accounts into a single account	e-merge@ebay.com
Remove your credit card from your account	ccard@ebay.com
Report bidding offenses, selling offenses, and other potential abuses	safeharbor@ebay.com
Report suspected pirated items	buddyitems@ebay.com
Report suspected illegal items	ctywatch@ebay.com
Report problems with the Gallery	gallery@ebay.com
Make a suggestion to eBay	suggest@ebay.com

What's Next for eBay?

eBay is constantly adding new features and services for its current and future users. Here are just a few new things to look forward to:

➤ **Local auctions**   As I write this, eBay is testing the market for local auctions. This will let eBay auction items—such as automobiles, furniture, and real estate—that need to be seen and purchased locally.

➤ **Fixed-price auctions**   Following Auction Universe's lead, eBay is mulling the possibility offering classified ad–like fixed-priced auctions, in which the first bidder to offer a minimum price wins and closes the auction.

➤ **Higher-priced items**   eBay recently acquired Butterfield & Butterfield—the third-largest traditional auction house in the U.S.—and announced plans to offer Butterfield's antiques and fine arts items via eBay's online auctions. This will help move eBay's listings a tad more upscale and compete to some degree with Sotheby's upcoming online auction launch. Another recent acquisition—of Kruse International—moves eBay into the high-priced collector car market. The end result of these and other potential moves? More higher-priced auctions, resulting in higher revenues for eBay!

➤ **Live auctions**   With Amazon.com acquiring LiveBid.com, look for eBay to follow suit to offer real-time bidding on larger, more exclusive items (such as those offered by Butterfield & Butterfield, for example).

➤ **Merchant auctions**   Don't be surprised to see eBay pursue the lucrative merchant auctions category, probably in a similar fashion to the way Amazon.com is doing it—by partnering with hundreds of merchants to provide new and surplus items within eBay's standard category listings.

➤ **Easier payment—and more protection**   eBay recently acquired Billpoint, an online credit-card processing company. By integrating Billpoint's services into eBay's operations, eBay will be able to offer users the convenience (and security) of paying for items by credit card. I also look for eBay to expand its insurance and escrow protection. The trend is to offer more consumer protection, and eBay will be forced to follow other online auctions in this direction.

eBay wants to be your one-stop-shop for all types of auctions and appears to be doing whatever it takes to achieve that goal.

The Least You Need to Know

➤ Use eBay's Site Map to access all of its "hidden" features and services.

➤ To bid on items, or to list items for sale, you first have to register (for free) as an eBay member.

➤ Browsing, bidding, and buying on eBay are free.

➤ eBay charges sellers fees for listing (insertion fees) and selling (final value fees) items.

➤ Insertion fees are nonrefundable; under specific circumstances, you can obtain a refund of final value fees or relist an unsold item.

Chapter 15

Searching for Items and People on eBay

In This Chapter

➤ Learn how to browse for items in eBay's 1,500+ categories

➤ Find out how to effectively and efficiently search for specific items on eBay

➤ Discover how the Personal Shopper service can notify you when desired items are put on auction

Let's get right down to it: eBay is the largest auction site on the Web, no questions asked. It's big. It's bigger than big. It's, like, really incredibly massively big. Think of the biggest thing you've ever seen, and eBay is bigger than that.

If you want to browse through the largest selection of merchandise for sale on the Internet, this is the place to go.

However, eBay's size (it's big, remember?) sometimes makes it difficult to find that *one* item you're looking for. How do you search through the two million or so items that are up for bid on eBay on any given day?

Browsing or Searching—Which One Is for You?

There are two main ways to locate items to bid on and buy on eBay. You can browse through eBay's 1,500+ categories, or you can search for specific items.

Table 15.1 shows you what's good and what's bad about both browsing and searching.

Table 15.1   Browsing Versus Searching—Strengths and Weaknesses

	Browsing	Searching
How easy is it to do?	Easy	Not as easy
How quickly can you find a specific item?	Slow	Fast
How many items will you find?	A lot	Not quite as many
Will you find the specific item you're looking for?	Not always	Yes
Can you find other bidders and sellers?	No	Yes

The bottom line: If you're not sure what you're looking for (or if you're looking for all types of items within a general category), then you should browse. If you're looking for a specific item or type of item, then you should search.

Browsing: The Easy Way to Find Things

eBay has more than 1,500 different categories, listing all sorts of items—antiques, Beanie Babies, books, coins, collectibles, comics, computers, dolls, electronics, figures, gemstones, glass, jewelry, magazines, music, photography, pottery, sports memorabilia, stamps, toys, and many, many more. To view all the items within a specific category or subcategory, you need to browse through eBay's category listings.

eBay's main categories are listed on its home page. You can also access a complete list of eBay's 1,500+ categories and subcategories by going to the Site Map page and clicking eBay Category Overview.

eBay's major categories are divided into a hierarchy of subcategories. For example, if you click the Antiques link, you'll see General, Ancient World, Architectural, and a dozen other subcategories. In fact, many of eBay's subcategories have their own subcategories (which makes them sub-subcategories, I guess!).

When you access a main category page, you see a list of subcategories. Click any subcategory link, and you'll see the following:

> ➤ **Any additional subcategories within this subcategory**   Click a subcategory link to display listings for that subcategory only.

> ➤ **Featured Auctions**   These are auctions where sellers have paid to receive special placement.

> ➤ **All Items**   This is the complete list of all items for sale in this category. There are typically many, many pages of listings; click the Next Page link to display

the next page of listings, or click a page number to access a specific page of listings directly.

➤ **Hot Items**   These are items (excluding reserve price auctions) that have received more than 30 bids to date.

You'll see some special icons next to selected listings. The PIC icon indicates that the listing includes a picture of the item; the NEW icon indicates that the item was listed within the past 24 hours; and the GIFT icon indicates that the seller thinks the item might make a good gift. Just click a listing's link to display the entire listing for that item.

Additional subcategories   When the auction ends

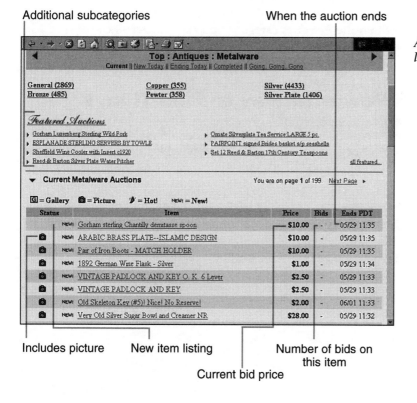

A typical eBay category listing.

Includes picture   New item listing   Number of bids on
                                                        this item

Current bid price

Restrict Your Listings

Within any category or subcategory listing, you can restrict the items listed within certain parameters. New Today displays items posted in the last 24 hours; Ending Today displays auctions ending within the next 24 hours; Going, Going, Gone displays auctions ending in the next 3 hours; and Completed displays auctions that have recently ended. Within the Antiques category, you can also access the Gallery, which includes featured items (with pictures) for sale.

Searching: The Powerful Way to Find Things

You could browse through the merchandise categories on eBay's home page, as I just described, but given the huge number of categories, this could take forever—and, besides, you're never quite sure whether all sellers have picked the right categories for their merchandise. No, in most cases, a better solution is to use eBay's built-in search engine.

Using eBay's Search Page

eBay's home page has a simple search box, but I prefer to use the more powerful Search page displayed when you click the Search link.

Use this search form to search for items for sale on eBay.

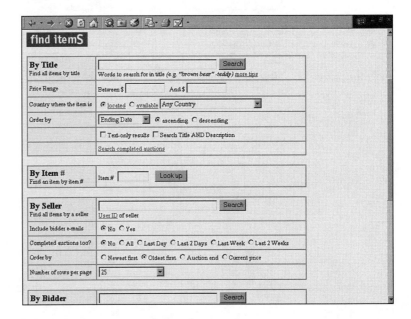

eBay's search page lets you search by the following criteria:

➤ **Title**   This is the best place to start searching; enter words describing the item you're looking for.

➤ **Price range**

➤ **Country**   Indicate where the item is either located or available (good for bidders outside the U.S.).

➤ **Item number**   All eBay items are assigned a unique number; if you know the item's number, this is the best way to go directly to the listing.

➤ **Seller ID**   This option lists all items from a given seller.

➤ **Bidder ID**   This lists all items bid on by a given bidder.

➤ **Completed searches**   This lists only those auctions that are already over.

In addition, this form lets you sort your results by either ascending or descending auction ending date, starting date, bid price, or search ranking (how well the item matched your query). I like to display my results by ending date, with expiring auctions listed first; that way, I know what items have to take priority in my bidding activities.

eBay is also adding regional search capabilities to this page on a city-by-city basis. When you click the Regional Search link, you'll be able to search for local auctions in your city or region.

Complex Searches—For Simpler Results

To get the best results from your eBay searches, you need to know which commands and operators you can use in the various search boxes. These commands are used almost exclusively in the Title box, to help modify your keywords and fine-tune your searches. Table 15.2 lists the commands you can use when searching on eBay.

Table 15.2   eBay Search Commands

To Do This	Use This Command	Example
Search for part of a word.	*	bat*
Search for either word.	(*word1, word2*)	(batman,robin) (NOTE: Do not include spaces after the comma.)
Search for either word.	@0	@0 batman robin (NOTE: No comma in between words.)

continues

Table 15.2 CONTINUED

To Do This	Use This Command	Example
Include at least two of the words.	@1	@1 pez furbie plate (NOTE: No comma in between words.)
Search for an exact phrase.	" "	"batman pez dispenser"
Must include a word.	+	batman +pez
Must exclude a word.	-	batman -pez
Include a year or number.	#	#1972

No Boolean

If you're an experienced searcher, you're probably used to using Boolean operators (AND, OR, NOT, and so on) to fine-tune your query. Well, forget your ANDs and NOTs; eBay doesn't permit the use of Boolean operators in its search function. In fact, if you enter Boolean operators in your query, eBay will treat them as keywords—and search for them!

Note that eBay automatically assumes that you want to search for items that match all the words in your query. This is the equivalent of inserting a Boolean AND in between all the words in your query; a query for **batman robin** essentially looks for items that match "batman AND robin."

Get Wild!

What if you're not quite sure which form of a word to search for? For example, would the best results come from looking for *auto, automobile,* or *automotive*? With eBay, you can use a wildcard (in the form of the * character) to "stand in" for parts of a word that you're not quite sure about. A wildcard will match any character or group of characters from its specific position in the word to the end of that word. In the preceding example, entering **auto*** would return all three words—auto, automobile, *and* automotive.

Practice Makes Perfect: Some Sample Searches

Let's quickly put together a few sample searches using some of these commands.

First, say you want to look for all Batman-related merchandise. The search is simple; enter this query in the **Title Search** box:

batman

That's too simple. What if you want to search not only for Batman, but also for Batgirl or Batmobile or Batplane or Bat*anything*? For this task, you apply the * wildcard to create this query:

bat*

Good enough. Now, let's make it more complex. You want to search for Batstuff, but not *all* Batstuff—just PEZ dispensers or costumes. For this search, enter this query:

bat* (pez,costume)

What if you want to look for something by title—such as the title of a movie? This is where you use quotation marks to surround the exact phrase you're searching for. If you want to search for anything associated with the movie *Batman Forever*, you enter this query:

"batman forever"

What if you want to search for Batman stuff but don't want anything related to Adam West? In this case, you use the exclude operator, in the form of a – sign, to automatically exclude any listings that include the designated word. The query looks like this:

batman –west

Conversely, if you only want to look at Batman items that had something to do with George Clooney, you use the include operator, in the form of a + sign, to search only for items that include that specific word. The query looks like this:

batman +clooney

You can also search for items where the date of production is important. If you put a # in front of a number, eBay knows you're searching for a particular year. For example, assume you want to search for all rare coins issued in 1955. You use this query:

coin #1955

Finally, don't be afraid to string several of these commands together to create a more complex query—which will return more targeted results. Let's do a hypothetical search for all *Batman Forever* props and comics featuring George Clooney but not including Jim Carrey. (Whew!) Here's the query:

"batman forever" (prop,comic) +clooney –carrey

See how it works? It's a little like constructing an algebraic equation; you just have to think it through, logically, and use all the tools you have at hand.

By the Way...

Don't be surprised if you enter that complex sample query into eBay's search engine and end up with zero results. The more targeted the query you enter, the fewer results will be returned—and some queries can be so targeted that nothing matches at all.

Secrets for Successful Searching

Here are a few tips to keep in mind when using eBay's search function:

➤ **Use nouns as keywords.** Verbs and conjunctions are either ignored by the search engine or are too common to be useful. Just remember—search for specific things.

➤ **Use descriptive or specific words to narrow your search.** Using multiple words helps eBay's search engine get a handle on the concept you're looking for; the more words, the better. Instead of searching for a **model**, search for a **Captain America aurora model**.

➤ **3Search for specific phrases.** Use quotes to search for exact phrases. If you want to search for the movie *Heavy Metal*, search for **"heavy metal"**; searching for **heavy metal** (without the quotation marks) will return a lot of listings for lead, the heavy metal!

➤ **4Use wildcards.** If you want to pick up both singular and plural versions of your keywords, don't search for the plural. Searching for **trucks** (plural) won't return any listings for a **truck** (singular); instead, search for **truck*** to pick up both.

Want More Help on Searching? Read the Book!

Searching is such an important topic—not just on eBay, but across the entire Internet—that I wrote an entire book about it. Look for *The Complete Idiot's Guide to Online Search Secrets* from Que at a bookseller near you—or search for it online.

Let eBay Do the Searching for You with Personal Shopper

Tired of searching for the same items every time you log on to eBay? You can let eBay do the searching for you, automatically, with its Personal Shopper service.

Personal Shopper (`www.cgi6.ebay.com/aw-cgi/eBayISAPI.dll?PersonalShopperViewSearches`, also accessible by clicking the Personal Shopper link on many eBay pages) is a free service that keeps track of your favorite item searches and notifies you via email when items you're looking for come up for auction.

The first time you access Personal Shopper, you need to click the Add a New Search button to add a new search. You can specify the Search query (which searches the item's title only or the title and description), the desired price range (optional), how often you want to receive notification emails, and how long you want to keep this search active. The next time you visit the Personal Shopper page, you'll see a list of all your active searches; click the **Search** link to view the results of a search online.

Fill in this form, and eBay's Personal Shopper will notify you when similar items are put on auction.

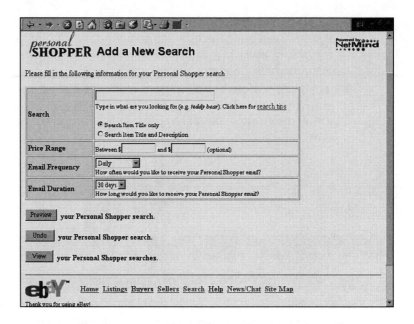

You can create up to three active searches at any given time. To add a fourth search, you must first delete one of your first three; that's three total searches, remember.

Personal Shopper is a great tool for active eBay bidders or for anyone searching for that elusive item. I love having eBay tell me when it has something for me, rather than having to log on and do a manual search every day. I highly recommend the Personal Shopper service.

The Least You Need to Know

➤ Browse through eBay's 1,500+ categories when you're not sure of the exact item you're looking for.

➤ Use eBay's search page to track down specific items for sale.

➤ Activate the Personal Shopper service to have eBay notify you when desired items come up for sale.

Chapter 16

Protecting Yourself on eBay

In This Chapter

➤ Discover how to protect yourself against deadbeat bidders and unscrupulous sellers

➤ Find out about eBay's SafeHarbor insurance program

➤ Learn what kind of feedback to leave about other users you deal with

eBay is an exciting new way to engage in person-to-person sales. Although it uses an auction format, remember that you're dealing with an individual—*not* eBay—when it comes down to making the financial transaction, and everyone is going to behave differently and expect different behavior of you. In the course of your eBay dealings, it's possible that you'll run into a shady seller who never sends you the item you purchased or a buyer who never sends you a check. What can you do to protect yourself against other users who aren't as honest as you are?

Fortunately, you can do several things to protect yourself on eBay. This chapter details some of the standard guidelines and procedures you can follow to ensure that your eBay buying and selling experience is not only successful, but profitable and enjoyable as well.

Safer Bidding with SafeHarbor

eBay has recently implemented a number of features intended to provide a safer auction experience for its users. These features, collectively called *SafeHarbor*, include eBay's customer support and customer information, as well as a new insurance program for buyers.

What's So Safe About SafeHarbor?

You access SafeHarbor by clicking the **SafeHarbor** link on eBay's home page or going directly to www.pages.ebay.com/aw/safeharbor-index.html. You'll see immediately that SafeHarbor is actually a collection of seven different features:

➤ **Feedback Forum** This is where you leave feedback about the users you transact with—and where they leave feedback about you. If you have a positive transaction, leave positive feedback; if you have a bad transaction, leave negative feedback. To determine the honesty and the quality of any users you might deal with, just look at their feedback profiles. You can generally trust users with positive overall feedback—and you might want to avoid dealing with users who have overwhelmingly negative feedback.

➤ **Customer Support** Having trouble with another user? Suspect the use of questionable or disallowed techniques (such as those described in Chapter 21, "Undercover eBay: The Secrets That eBay Doesn't Want You to Know")? Then, notify eBay through its SafeHarbor Customer Support Investigations services.

➤ **Understanding eBay Auctions** New to eBay? Not sure about how something works? Then, access this section for tips on conducting safe online auctions, protecting your privacy, and other important issues.

➤ **Escrow** Sometimes, it pays to put a third party in between the buyer and the seller to ensure each party performs as contracted and gets what's due. This feature links to several third-party escrow services who act as the "middleman" in complex or high-priced transactions.

➤ **Verified eBay User** This service enables you to be verified by Equifax (a noted credit check service) as a trustworthy user. After you present a fair amount of personal information and are verified by Equifax, you'll receive an onscreen icon that will follow you everywhere on eBay's site, letting other users know that you're who you say you are.

➤ **Authentication and Grading** Here, you find information on how to grade and evaluate items you have for sale, with a focus on collectibles (coins, trading cards, Beanie Babies, and so on).

➤ **Insurance** Even though eBay says the Feedback Forum is the most important feature, I disagree; I think it's the insurance. This insurance, provided by Lloyds of London, is provided free of charge to any eBay user in good standing. You get coverage for up to $200, with a $25 deductible.

Get the Straight Poop with eBay's Bulletin Boards

eBay provides a number of bulletin boards where you can converse with other eBay users on relevant topics—and, in some instances, leave "live" feedback with eBay staffers. Often, these lively discussion forums are the only places to find out what's *really* going on behind the screens at eBay. They're also kind of a first alert to any big-time cheats operating on eBay at the moment. The key bulletin boards are the Q&A Board and the Support Q&A Board, both accessible from eBay's Site Map page.

Insuring Your Transactions with SafeHarbor Insurance

eBay's SafeHarbor insurance is a big deal and a good deal. If you have a feedback rating that isn't negative, you qualify for free insurance on just about any item you buy through eBay. If, for any reason, you're shafted by a seller, you can get reimbursed (up to a point) via this insurance program.

Here are some of the details you need to know:

➤ Insurance is provided by Lloyds of London.

➤ You're insured on items with a final value between $25 and $200. If the item is priced under $25, you're on your own. (No big loss.) If the item is priced over $200, you probably should be using an escrow service.

➤ There's a $25 deductible on each claim. If you submit a claim for a $35 item, you'll get $10 back ($35 minus the $25 deductible). If you submit a claim for $200, you'll get $175 back.

➤ You'll only be reimbursed for the final bid price, not for any other fees (such as shipping, handling, or escrow fees).

➤ To qualify, your feedback rating has to be either positive or neutral. You can't be insured if you have a negative feedback rating. Also, the personal information you supplied to eBay must be accurate.

➤ All items that meet eBay's user agreement are covered; items that violate the user agreement (firearms, illegal items, and so on) aren't covered.

➤ You aren't covered if you knowingly purchase something from a seller with a negative feedback rating. (You should know better!)

➤ You can get reimbursed if you send money to a seller and you don't receive the item. You can also get reimbursed if you receive the item, but it's significantly different than described in the auction listing.

➤ You won't be reimbursed if something happens to the item in transit. If the shipping company loses or damages the item, that's its problem to fix.

➤ All claims must be filed within 30 days of the end of the auction.

➤ You can only file a maximum of one claim per month.

How do you file an insurance claim? First, you have to register a complaint in eBay's Fraud Reporting System. (Click the **SafeHarbor** link from eBay's home page, then click **Insurance**, and then click **Fraud Reporting Process**—or go directly to www.crs.ebay.com/frs/start.asp.)

If your complaint meets the guidelines for insurance, the Fraud Reporting System will provide you with an online insurance form. Fill out the insurance form and mail the form to the Lloyds claim administrators. (The address is on the form.) It will contact you within 45 days after filing to let you know the results of its investigation. If your claim is approved, you should receive payment within 45 days of filing the claim.

I hope you'll never have to use eBay's insurance program. But if you are the unfortunate recipient of an unscrupulous seller, it's good to know that eBay is looking out for you.

Employing Escrow: Protection for Larger Items

SafeHarbor insurance is great for items under $200, but what if you're buying a more expensive item? How do you protect yourself?

A good course of action is to employ an escrow service. An escrow service acts as a neutral third party between the buyer and seller, holding the buyer's money until the seller's goods are delivered. (Escrow services also allow you to pay by credit card when you're dealing with individuals who can't otherwise accept credit card transactions.)

Here's how a typical escrow transaction works:

1. At the end of an auction, the buyer and seller contact each other and agree to use an escrow service. The escrow service's fees can be split between the two parties or (more typically) paid by the buyer.

2. The buyer sends payment (by check, money order, cashier's check, or credit card) to the escrow service.

3. After the buyer's payment clears, the escrow service instructs the seller to ship the item.

4. The buyer receives the item, verifies its acceptability, and notifies the escrow service as such.

5. The escrow service pays the seller.

If anything goes wrong at any point, the escrow service steps in. If the buyer doesn't pay, the seller doesn't ship. If the buyer doesn't receive or accept the merchandise, the seller doesn't get paid. It's a great way to insert a neutral "middleman" between the two interested parties in the transaction.

Although eBay doesn't offer escrow services itself, a number of recommended third-party escrow services are available:

➤ i-Escrow (`www.iescrow.com`)

➤ Internet Clearing Corporation (`www.internetclearing.com`)

➤ SecureTrades (`www.securetrades.com`)

➤ TradeSafe (`www.tradesafe.com`)

When should you use an escrow service? I recommend escrow services when you have really high-priced transactions, when you just don't trust the seller (or buyer), or when you want to use a credit card when purchasing from a nonmerchant seller.

Dealing with Deadbeat Bidders

A deadbeat bidder is someone who wins an auction but never follows through with the transaction. Not only should you leave negative feedback about these deadbeats, but you should also request a credit from eBay for your final value fee. (See Chapter 14, "eBay Wants You: Joining Up and Getting Started" for more details.)

When eBay receives a credit request pertaining to a deadbeat bidder, the service automatically sends a warning to the user in question. If the alleged deadbeat receives three such warnings, he or she will be suspended from eBay for 30 days. Once the bidder returns to the service, the next offense will get him or her kicked off eBay permanently.

eBay Feedback: Finding Out Who You're Dealing with Before You Deal with Them

eBay regards its Feedback Forum as the best protection against fraudulent transactions. I certainly recommend that, whether a transaction went swell or went south, you leave feedback about your partner in every transaction. I know that I check the feedback rating of every seller I choose to deal with; it really is a good way to judge the quality of the other party in your eBay transactions.

What Do All Those Stars and Numbers Mean?

Next to every buyer and seller's name on eBay is a number and (more often than not) a colored star. These numbers and stars represent that user's feedback rating. The larger the number, the better the feedback (and the more transactions that user has participated in).

How are feedback ratings calculated?

First, every new user starts with 0 points. (A clean slate!) For every positive feedback received, you add 1 point to your feedback rating. For every negative feedback received, you subtract 1 point. Neutral comments add 0 points to your rating.

Let's say you're a new user, starting with a 0 rating. On the first two items you buy, the sellers like the fact that you paid quickly and give you positive feedback. On the third transaction, however, you forgot to mail the check for a few weeks, and the seller left you a negative feedback. After these three transactions, your feedback rating would be 1. (That's $0 + 1 + 1 - 1 = 1$.)

If you build up a lot of positive feedback, you qualify for a star next to your name. Different colored stars represent different levels of positive feedback:

➤ Yellow star: 10–99 points
➤ Turquoise star: 100–499
➤ Purple star: 500–999
➤ Red star: 1,000–9,999
➤ Shooting star: 10,000 or more

Obviously, heavy users can build up positive feedback faster than occasional users. If you're dealing with a shooting star user, you know you're dealing with a trustworthy eBay pro.

You can also read the individual comments left by other users by going to the user's Feedback Profile page. To access this page, just click the number (feedback profile) next to a user's name.

How to Leave Feedback

There are a number of ways to leave feedback about other users, but here's the simplest method:

1. First, go directly to the auction page for the item that was part of the transaction.
2. Then, click the number (feedback rating) next to the buyer or seller name.
3. When the Feedback Profile page appears, click the **Leave Feedback** link and fill in the resulting form.

Just make sure your feedback is accurate before you click the **Leave Comment** button; you can't change your comments after they've been registered.

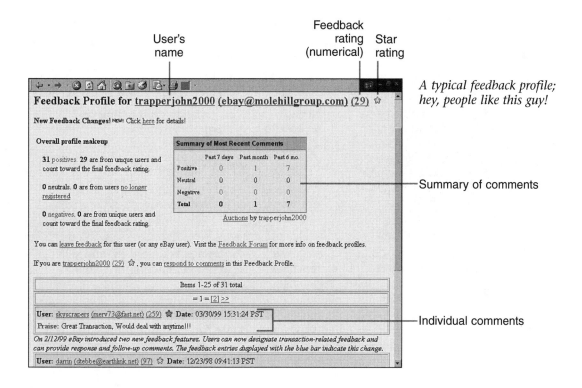

User's name — Feedback rating (numerical) — Star rating

A typical feedback profile; hey, people like this guy!

Summary of comments

Individual comments

Figuring Out What Kind of Feedback to Leave

You should leave feedback at the end of every auction—whether it was a positive or a negative experience for you. Don't miss your chance to inform other eBay users about the quality of the person you just got done dealing with.

Table 16.1 offers some guidelines on when you should leave positive or negative feedback—and the types of comments you might use to embellish your feedback.

Table 16.1   Recommended eBay Feedback

Transaction	Feedback	Comments
Transaction transpires in a timely fashion.	Positive feedback	"Great transaction. Fast payment/ shipment. Recommended."
Transaction goes through, but buyer/seller is slow or you have to pester the other user.	Positive feedback	"Item received as described" or "Payment received," accompanied by "a little slow, but otherwise a good seller/buyer."
Transaction is very slow (over a month to completion).	Neutral feedback	"Very slow payment/shipment;" if you're buying, followed by "item received as described."

continues

Table 16.1   Continued

Transaction	Feedback	Comments
Other user backs out of transaction, with a good excuse.	Neutral feedback	"Buyer/seller didn't follow through on sale but had a reasonable excuse."
Other user backs out of transaction without a good excuse, disappears off the face of the earth before paying/shipping, or bounces a check.	Negative feedback	"Buyer/seller didn't complete transaction; avoid!"
Transaction goes through, but item isn't what you expected or was damaged in transit; seller refunds your money.	Positive feedback	"Inaccurate description of item; seller refunded money."
Transaction goes through, but item isn't what you expected or was damaged in transit; seller won't refund your money.	Negative feedback	"Item not as described, and seller ignored my complaint; avoid!"

As you can see, there's a proper feedback and response for every situation. Just make sure you think twice before leaving *any* feedback (particularly negative feedback). Once you submit your feedback, you can't retract it.

No Business, No Feedback

You should only leave feedback for users that you actually deal with. If you weren't in an auction with someone, keep out of his feedback file!

Tips for Protecting Yourself on eBay

When all is said and done, eBay is a fairly safe environment to conduct person-to-person transactions. The vast majority of eBay users are honest individuals, and you'll no doubt enjoy hundreds of good transactions before you hit your first bad one.

That said, here are some tips on how to better protect yourself when you're dealing on eBay:

➤ Remember that you're dealing with human beings. Be nice, be polite, and, above all, *communicate!* Send emails confirming receipt of payment or shipment of merchandise. Say "please" and "thank you." And don't send short, snippy emails in the heat of the moment. Be tolerant and friendly, and you'll be a better eBay citizen.

➤ Realize that, in most cases, you're dealing with individuals, not businesses. Keep that in mind if things don't go quite as smoothly as they would if you ordered from Amazon.com or L.L. Bean. Most folks don't have automated shipping systems installed in their living rooms!

➤ Know that experienced eBay users take the feedback system very seriously—if not obsessively. Positive feedback is expected for every successful transaction, and negative feedback should only be used in the most dire of circumstances. When in doubt, just don't leave any feedback at all.

➤ When you're listing an item for sale, be honest and be descriptive. Don't leave out details that could surprise a reasonable buyer. If the item isn't in tip-top shape, say so. If you can make a fair valuation or grading of the item, so do. Include payment and shipping details in your description, and include a picture of the item when possible. Above all, don't lie—and don't leave out important details. The cardinal rule is *no surprises*.

➤ If you have questions about an item for sale, or about any part of the transaction, ask! Email the seller if you're not sure about payment or shipping terms. Good communication eliminates surprises and misinterpretations; don't assume anything.

➤ If you're a seller and you receive an email from a potential bidder, answer it promptly and accurately. Better to weed out dissatisfied bidders before they buy than afterwards.

➤ When an auction closes, send an email to the seller or buyer as soon as possible. If you're selling, inform the buyer about payment and shipping options. If you're buying, inform the seller when she should expect payment. If you haven't heard from the seller/buyer within three days of the close of the auction, send another email.

➤ When the item you purchased arrives, inspect it thoroughly and confirm that it's as described. If you feel you were misled, contact the seller immediately, explain the situation, and see what you can work out. (You'd be surprised how many sellers will go out of their way to make their customers happy.)

➤ If the merchandise doesn't arrive in a timely fashion, contact the seller immediately. If the item appears to be lost in transit, track down the letter/package via the shipping service. If the item never arrives, it's the seller's responsibility to file an insurance claim with the carrier, and you should receive a refund from the seller.

➤ If a buyer has a complaint, handle it quickly, gracefully, and to the best of your abilities—but don't do anything you honestly don't feel is fair. Remember that the customer is always right, most of the time.

161

The Least You Need to Know

➤ Most eBay buyers and sellers are honest and trustworthy.

➤ For those who aren't, eBay offers its SafeHarbor program, which includes $200 worth of insurance per transaction for aggrieved buyers.

➤ For larger transactions, engage an escrow service to serve as a "middleman" and protect both parties.

➤ You should always leave feedback about the people you deal with—whether positive or negative.

Chapter 17

Personalizing Your Page with My eBay

In This Chapter

➤ Discover eBay's "best-kept secret": My eBay

➤ Learn how to customize My eBay for your own personal preferences

➤ Find out how to use My eBay to track all your auction activity on a single page

---

If you're a buyer or a seller, how do you keep track of all the auctions you're currently participating in?

The standard method is to go to eBay's Search page, enter your user ID in either the Seller Search or Bidder Search boxes (depending on whether you're selling or buying), and click the Search button. You can select whether you just want to check your active auctions or whether you want to look at closed auctions as well. If you're checking on items you have for sale, you can even choose to sort your auctions in a variety of ways (by age, by end time, or by current bid price).

Frankly, it's a real pain to go to the Search page and reenter your personal search parameters every time you want to check all your auctions. There has to be a better way to do this.

Fortunately, there is. It's called *My eBay*, and eBay calls it its "best-kept secret."

Creating Your First My eBay Page

My eBay is a way to personalize your eBay experience. It's a page that you customize to your own personal preferences to track your own bidding and selling activities in your own way. I highly recommend you avail yourself of this useful feature.

You access My eBay by going to the Site Map and clicking My eBay or going directly to pages.ebay.com/aw/myebay.html. (Don't bookmark this page yet; I'll tell you why shortly.)

When you access My eBay this way, you see the following page.

Getting ready to customize your My eBay page.

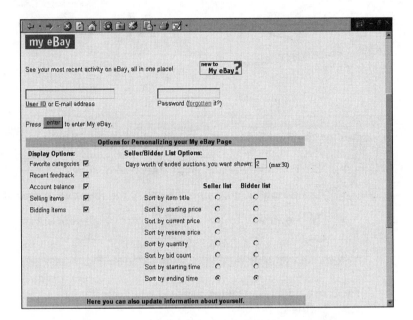

This is not My eBay; it's merely the page that sets up your own personal My eBay page (which is why you don't want to bookmark it).

The first things you can personalize are the particular items that My eBay displays. You can choose to have your My eBay page display (or not display) the following:

- ➤ **Favorite categories** Displays the eBay item categories you browse most often.
- ➤ **Recent feedback** Displays the most recent feedback comments about you from other eBay members.
- ➤ **Account balance** Displays the current balance of your eBay account.
- ➤ **Selling items** Displays items you currently have on auction at eBay.
- ➤ **Bidding items** Displays items you're currently bidding on.

Next, you get to pick how you want your auction listings displayed. You can choose to sort your listings in one of the following ways:

- ➤ Item title
- ➤ Starting price

➤ Current price

➤ Reserve price (only available for sellers)

➤ Quantity

➤ Bid count

➤ Starting time

➤ Ending time

You can also determine how many days of ended auctions you want displayed in your listings. The default value is 2 days; you can display up to 30 days' worth of ended auctions if you so desire.

Once you make all your selections, click the **Enter** button to display your personalized My eBay page.

The first time you see your page, you need to select which auction categories you want to display in the My Favorites section. Click the **Click Here to Change Your Favorite Categories** link to display the Changing Your User Preferences page. You can choose to display up to four favorite categories; pick them one at a time from the four Favorite Category lists and then click the **Submit** button. (You can change your My Favorites selections at any time by returning to this page.)

Exploring My eBay

Let's take a minute and look at the My eBay page because a lot of the items here will be useful to you.

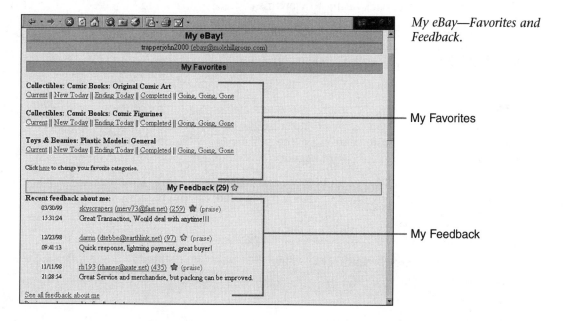

My eBay—Favorites and Feedback.

My Favorites

My Feedback

My Favorites

The first section of the page is the My Favorites section. Here, the auction categories you selected are displayed in the order you selected.

Underneath each category head are links to five different lists of items within the category:

➤ **Current**   Displays all current auctions in this category.

➤ **New Today**   Displays auctions just started today.

➤ **Ending Today**   Displays all auctions ending today.

➤ **Completed**   Displays recently ended auctions.

➤ **Going, Going, Gone**   Displays auctions that will be ending in the next three hours.

Click a link to display the desired item list.

My Feedback

Next, you have the My Feedback section. The header of this section displays your current feedback rating and star rating. Underneath them are the three most recent feedback comments left about you by fellow users.

You can click a user's user ID to display his or her User ID History (which shows all the different IDs used by this user over time); click his or her email address to send an email; or click the feedback rating to view his or her Feedback Profile page.

If you want to display your entire Feedback Profile, click the **See All Feedback About Me** link. You can also choose to review and respond to your feedback, as well as display all feedback you've left about other users.

My Account

This short section lets you see your current eBay account balance. You can also display your full account information for the past two months or for the life of your full eBay membership (with the Entire Account link).

This section is particularly useful because it contains direct links to some of eBay's normally well-hidden customer service features. Here are the sections you can access:

➤ Fees and credits.

➤ Payment terms.

➤ Use a credit card for automatic billing.

➤ Credit request.

➤ Refunds.

➤ Make a one-time payment.

166

It's easier to click them here than to hunt them down on eBay's Site Map page.

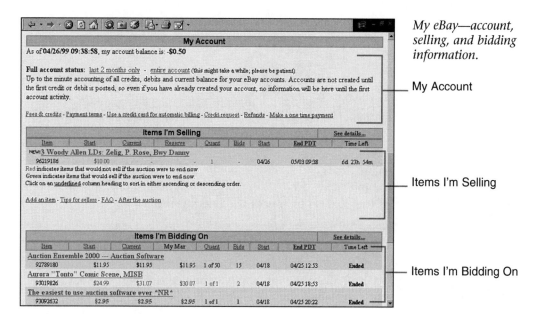

My eBay—account, selling, and bidding information.

— My Account

— Items I'm Selling

— Items I'm Bidding On

Items I'm Selling

Now, you get to the really good part. All your current or most recent auctions (depending on what you selected on the setup page) are listed in the order you selected.

For each auction listed, you see the following information:

➤ **Item** The item number of this auction item.

➤ **Start** The initial bid price.

➤ **Current** The current bid price.

➤ **Reserve** The item's reserve price if this is a reserve price auction.

➤ **Quant** How many items are being sold if this is a Dutch auction.

➤ **Bids** The number of bids on this item so far.

➤ **Start** The day the auction started.

➤ **End PDT** The time the auction ends in Pacific Daylight Time.

➤ **Time Left** The precise days, hours, and minutes left in this auction.

To view a complete item listing, click the link for that specific auction. To view the item listing for all your auctions on a single page, click the **See Details** link.

All items that currently have a high bid higher than your minimum or reserve price are listed in green. All items that haven't yet reached the minimum bid level are listed in red.

167

This is a great way to see, in a single glance, the status of everything you're currently selling on eBay. I love it!

Sort Your Results

In both the Items I'm Selling Items and Items I'm Bidding On sections, you can re-sort the results by any column (Item, Start time, Current bid, and so on). Just click on the link at the top of the column to re-sort the entire section.

Items I'm Bidding On

This final section is pretty much like the Items I'm Selling section, except that it displays all items you've recently placed bids on.

For each auction listed, you see the following information:

➤ **Item**   The item number of this auction item.

➤ **Start**   The initial bid price.

➤ **Current**   The current high bid—whether it's your bid or someone else's.

➤ **My Max**   Your specified maximum bid price.

➤ **Quant**   How many items are being sold if this is a Dutch auction.

➤ **Bids**   The number of bids on this item so far.

➤ **Start**   The day the auction started.

➤ **End PDT**   The time the auction ends in Pacific Daylight Time.

➤ **Time Left**   The precise days, hours, and minutes left in this auction.

To view a complete item listing, click the link for that specific auction. To view the item listing for all your auctions on a single page, click the **See Details** link.

All auctions that you're currently winning are in green; all auctions that you're currently losing are in red. (Dutch auctions don't display in color, whatever your bid is.)

Like the Items I'm Selling list, this is a great way to display all your bidding activity at a glance. This feature is why you need to use My eBay!

Keep It Handy: Bookmark My eBay

Now, let's talk about bookmarking this page (in Netscape Navigator) or adding it your favorites list (in Internet Explorer). You see, if you don't bookmark the page, you have to go through that annoying setup procedure every time you click the My eBay link within eBay. If you bookmark the page—after you've customized it to your preferences—then you never have to bother with customizing it again.

Let's get down to it. First, make sure you've got My eBay set up exactly as you want it—with the right auction categories listed, the number of old auctions displayed, and the item listings sorted in the manner that you like best. Once it's all set up, just follow the procedure in your own specific Web browser to create a bookmark or favorite, and that's that. Every time you access that bookmark or favorite, you'll go directly to your personally customized version of My eBay.

The Least You Need to Know

➤ My eBay lets you track all your personal information on one page—including your favorite auction categories, your feedback, your eBay account status, all the items you're selling, and all the items you're bidding on.

➤ You can customize My eBay for your own personal preferences.

➤ Once you get My eBay customized, you should save it as a bookmark or favorite in your Web browser.

Chapter 18

A Tutorial for Sellers: How to Put an Item Up for Bid

In This Chapter

➤ Learn how to sell an item on eBay

➤ Uncover the secrets of successful item listings

➤ Discover how to edit, amend, or cancel an auction in progress

➤ Find out what to do after the auction is over

You've poked around eBay some. Maybe you've bid on an item or two; maybe you've even been the high bidder in an auction. Now, you're looking at your collection of...well, whatever it is you collect and thinking that maybe you ought to be getting some of that online auction action.

In other words, you're ready to put your first item up for bid on eBay.

Getting Started: Basic Steps for Listing an Item for Sale

Before you list an item for sale, you have to be a registered user. It also helps to have your credit card on file. If you need to do either of these things, turn immediately to Chapter 14, "eBay Wants You: Joining Up and Getting Started," for more information.

Assuming you're registered and filed, now what do you do? Well, listing an item for sale on eBay is pretty simple, if you follow these steps:

1. From eBay's home page, click the **Sell Your Item** link; this takes you to the Sell Your Item form.

Fill in all the blanks in the Sell Your Item form, and you'll have your item listed in no time.

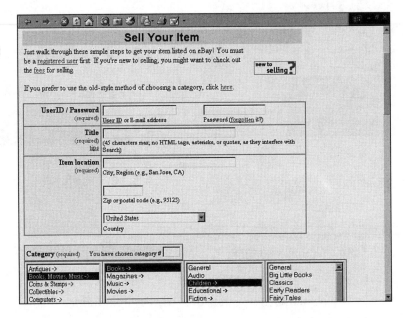

2. Enter your user ID (or email address) and password.

3. Create a short title for your item, and enter it in the **Title** box. *Short* is the operative word here; your title can include only 45 total characters. (Important: Do not include any HTML code in your title.)

4. Enter the city and state where you (and presumably your item) are located.

5. Enter your zip code.

6. Select your country from the pull-down box.

7. Select the category where your item is to be listed. Within the category, pull down the list to select the appropriate subcategory for listing. (For example, you could pull down the **Antiques** list and select **European**; your item would be listed in the Antiques category under the European subcategory.)

8. Check which methods of payment you will accept.

9. Check the appropriate payment terms for this auction.

10. Check the appropriate shipping terms for this auction (domestic or international).

11. Enter a description for your item. (More on this later in this chapter—and note that you can use HTML code in this description.)

12. If you want to include a picture of your item, enter the Web page address (URL) where the picture is located. (More on pictures later in this chapter.)

13. Enter your desired minimum bid for this item. The minimum bid will be the starting bid in this auction.

14. Enter the desired duration for this auction; you can choose from 3, 5, 7, or 10 days. Unless you're in a rush for cash (or have an extremely hot item), pick a longer time frame; it exposes your auction to more potential bidders, and the more potential bidders, the higher your potential selling price.

15. If you want this to be a reserve price auction (discussed later in this chapter), enter your desired reserve price. Remember, of course, that the reserve price must be higher than the minimum bid price.

16. If you want to boldface your title, make this a featured auction, feature your item in its category, or add a Gift icon, check the appropriate boxes. You can use these options to make your listing stand out from other ads or to gain special placement for your listing.

Buy a Better Listing

To learn more about boldfacing, featured auctions, and other listing enhancements, see the fee list in Chapter 14.

17. If you want to make this a private auction (where bidders' identities are kept secret), check that box.

18. If you're selling an antique, you can choose to include your item in the Gallery; if you do, you'll need to include a URL for a picture of your item.

19. When you're done filling out the form, click the **Review** button to see a preview of your item listing. If you like what you see (and agree with the fees listed at the bottom of the preview page), click the **Submit My Listing** button.

20. You're shown a confirmation screen, which presents you with important details about your auction—including your item listing's URL, in case you want to publicize your auction elsewhere on the Internet.

Once you see the confirmation screen, your completed ad will appear on the eBay Web site sometime within the next hour.

What's It Cost?

eBay charges a small fee (called an *insertion fee*) for every item you list, as well as a commission (called a *final value fee*) for every item you actually sell. See Chapter 14, for more details about eBay's fees.

Dealing with Different Types of Auctions

The preceding steps apply specifically to creating a listing for a regular auction. However, eBay has three other, slightly irregular auctions:

➤ Reserve price auctions

➤ Dutch auctions

➤ Private auctions

All three types of auctions are discussed in more detail in Chapter 3, "Those Other Types of Auctions: Dutch and Reserve."

Set a Higher Minimum with a Reserve Price Auction

A reserve price auction is one in which your initial bid price really isn't the minimum price you'll accept. Even though bids might exceed the initial bid price, if they don't hit your reserve price, you don't have to sell.

Most buyers don't like reserve price auctions because the reserve price is never disclosed to bidders. Let's say you set a minimum price of $5 for an item (really low, to get a buzz going and attract some early bidders) but a reserve price of $50 (because that's what you believe the item is really worth). If the high bidder bid $25, that bid doesn't win (because it's less than the $50 reserve), and the bidder has no idea how much more to bid to hit the undisclosed reserve price. Messy and confusing, eh?

If you insist on running a reserve price auction, it's easy enough to do. On the Sell Your Item form, just make sure you enter a price (higher than your Minimum Bid price) in the Reserve Price box. That's all you have to do; after that, the auction runs as normal—or as normal as a reserve price auction gets.

Remember, if no one bids the reserve price or higher, no one wins.

Sell Larger Quantities with a Dutch Auction

Dutch auctions are those in which you have more than one quantity of an identical item to sell. It's great if you have a dozen Scooby Doo PEZ dispensers, 10 copies of *Titanic* on videocassette, or a hundred units of white extra-large BVDs to sell.

To set up a Dutch auction, all you have to do is enter a quantity greater than **1** in the **Quantity** box in the Sell This Item form. When you do this, eBay automatically registers your auction as a Dutch auction.

The way Dutch auctions work is a little complicated, so I'll refer you to the explanation in Chapter 3. Suffice it to say that the highest bidder always wins something but doesn't always have to pay the highest price. (To be precise, all bidders pay the lowest winning price, even if they bid higher; I told you it was complicated!)

In any case, eBay handles all the details automatically as long as you specify multiple quantities.

Keep it Anonymous with a Private Auction

The final oddball auction type is simple. If you're auctioning off something that is a little delicate, sensitive, or downright embarrassing, choose a Private auction and none of the bidders' names will ever be revealed publicly. It's great for items in the Adult category, although some bidders on ultra-high-priced items might also want to remain anonymous.

To activate a Private auction, all you have to do is check the box next to the **Private Auction** option on the Sell Your Item form. (One caveat: You can't make a Dutch auction private.)

Tips for a More Effective Ad

Did you know that only about half the items listed on eBay at any given time actually sell during the current auction? That's right; in about half the current auctions, no one meets the minimum bid.

How do you increase the odds of *your* item selling? It's all about creating a powerful, effective item listing.

Write a Title That SELLS!

You need to accomplish two things with the title of your listing:

➤ You have to include the appropriate information so that anyone searching for a similar item will find your item in his search results.

➤ You have to make your title stand out from all the other titles on those long listing pages.

Do those two things, and you significantly increase your chances of getting your item noticed and sold.

Let's tackle the first point first. You have to think like the people who will be looking for your item. As an example, let's say you have an original 1964 Superman model kit, manufactured by Aurora, still in its shrink-wrapped box. How do you list this item?

You have to make sure you get all the right keywords in your title. For this example, it's obvious that **Superman** should be a keyword, as should **Aurora** and maybe **1964**. Then, it gets iffy-er. Should you call it a **model kit** or a **plastic model kit** or a **plastic model**? Should you call it **unassembled** or **still in box** or **original condition**?

When dealing with collectibles, you often can use accepted abbreviations and acronyms. In this case, you could use the abbreviation **MISB**, which stands for *mint in sealed box*. True collectors will know what this means, and it saves precious "real estate" in your title. (By the way, if this model wasn't in the box but was instead already assembled, you could use the abbreviation **BU**, for *built-up*.) Continuing this example, a title that included all the keywords users might search on would be **1964 Superman Aurora Plastic Model Kit MISB**. (This comes in just under 45 characters!)

Beyond including as many relevant facts as possible in your title, how do you make your title POP off the page and STAND OUT from all the other boring listings? Obviously, one technique is to employ the judicious use of CAPITAL LETTERS. The operative word here is *judicious*; titles with ALL capital letters step over the line into overkill.

You can also try a lot of nonalphanumeric characters, such as !!! or ### or *** at the beginning of your title. The only problem with this technique is that eBay's search engine might totally ignore titles that include too many of these nonsense characters—which is the exact opposite of what you want to accomplish.

Instead, I advise you to think like an advertising copywriter. What words almost always stop consumers in their tracks? Use attention-getting words such as FREE and NEW and BONUS and EXTRA and DELUXE and RARE—as long as these words truly describe the item you're selling and don't mislead the potential bidder.

Try this one on for size: Which would you rather bid on, a **1964 Superman Model Kit** or a **RARE 1964 Superman Model Kit**? I'm betting you go for the second one—and mentally prepare yourself to pay more for it, too!

In short, use your title to both inform and attract attention—and include as many potential search keywords as possible.

Make the Grade

Grading is a way of noting the condition of an item, according to a predetermined standard. Collectors use these grading scales to help evaluate and price items within a category.

Different types of collectibles have their own unique grading systems. For example, trading cards are graded from A1 to F1; coins are graded from Poor to Perfect Uncirculated.

One of the most common grading systems is the Fair-to-Mint system:

➤ Mint (MT or M)

➤ Near Mint (NM)

➤ Excellent (EX)

➤ Very Good (VG or G)

➤ Good (GD)

➤ Fair (F)

Degrees between grade levels are indicated with a + or -. Naturally, the definition of a Mint or Fair item differs by item type.

In addition, there are some other grading-related abbreviations you might run across in eBay's item listings, including

➤ BU: Built Up

➤ CC: Cut Corner

➤ CO: Cut Out

➤ COH: Cut Out Hole

➤ HC: Hard Cover

➤ MIB: Mint In Box

➤ MIP: Mint In Package

➤ MISB: Mint In Sealed Box

➤ MOC: Mint On Card

➤ NRFB: Never Removed From Box

➤ RR: Re-Release

➤ SC: Soft Cover

➤ SS: Still Sealed

If you run across an abbreviation that you can't figure out, email the seller and ask what it means!

Write the Right Description

If the listing title is the headline of your ad, the listing description is your ad's body copy.

What makes for good copy? First, you have all the space you need, so say as much as you need to say. You don't have to scrimp on words or leave anything out. If you can describe your item adequately in a sentence, great; if it takes three paragraphs, that's okay, too.

Be Up Front About *Everything*

When you're writing the description for your ad, make sure you mention anything and everything that a potential bidder might need to know. Note any defects or imperfections of the item. Include your desired payment terms and your preferred shipping methods. If the object is graded or evaluated in any way, include that assessment in your description. In other words, include everything you can think of that will eliminate any surprises for the buyer.

However, you should probably put the most important and motivating information in your initial paragraph because a lot of folks won't read any farther than that. Think of your first paragraph like a lead paragraph in a newspaper story; grab 'em with something catchy, give them the gist of the story, and lead them onto reading the next paragraph and the one after that.

Although you need to be descriptive (and in some collectibles categories, you need to be *obsessively* so), it doesn't hurt to employ a little marketing savvy and salesmanship. Yes, you should talk about the features of your item, but it's even better if you can talk about your product's *benefits* to the potential buyer.

Let's say you're selling a used cordless phone, and the phone has a 50-number memory. Saying "50-number memory" is stating a feature; saying instead that the phone "lets you recall your 50 most-called phone numbers at the press of a button" is describing a benefit. Remember, a feature is something your item has; a benefit is something your item does for the user.

Include as much descriptive copy as you need to, but make sure that every sentence sells your item.

Your Boring Description Doesn't Have to *Look* Boring

When you enter plain text into the Description box, eBay formats it as plain text on your item listing page. However, you can enter HTML code as part of your description, and make your listing look as lively as a page on the World Wide Web. To learn more about using HTML to spice up your otherwise-boring listings, turn to Chapter 20, "Pretty Up Your eBay Ads with HTML."

Pick the Right Category

This one sounds simple. You have a thing, you find the category that describe the thing, and you're done with it. To be fair, sometimes it is that simple. If you have a retired Beanie Baby, you put it in the Toys & Beanies: Beanies: Retired category, no questions asked.

What if you have a Batman action figure? Does it go in the Toys & Beanies: Action Figures: Super Hero category or the Collectibles: Comic Books: Comic Figurines category?

Where you put your item should be dictated by where the highest number of potential bidders will look for it. In the Batman action figure example, if there are more bidders traipsing through the Action Figures category, put it there; if there are more potential buyers who think of this as a Batman thing, then put it in the Comic Books category. (In reality, you'll find listings for this sort of item in both categories.) Think like your potential buyers, and put it where you would look for it if you were them.

(eBay won't let you list your item in two different categories; thanks for asking.)

Set the Right Price

How should you price your item? If you set your minimum price too high, you might scare off potential buyers. If you set your minimum price too low, you'll probably get more interested bidders, but you might end up selling your item for less than you want or than what it's worth.

So what's the right starting price?

I like setting a price that's low enough to get some interested initial bidding going, but not so low that it won't get up to the price I think the item can really sell for. As a rule of thumb, 10 percent of what I think the final selling price will be is a good place to start.

Of course, you can always go the reserve price auction route—where you get to set a low initial price and a high selling floor.

What's the Real Secret?

Do you want to know how I go about setting prices when I personally put items up for sale on eBay? Do you want to learn selling strategies that will virtually guarantee you selling your item for the highest possible price? Then, you'll need to turn to Chapter 23, "How to Get the Most for Your Merchandise: Strategies for Sellers." That's where the real good stuff is!

Show Them What's What: Add a Photo to Your Ad

A picture in your listing greatly increases the chances of actually selling your item—and also increases the average price you will receive.

Knowing that, you'd think more eBay ads would include pictures. The fact that they don't is because adding a picture to an eBay listing is a little less than easy.

Basically, you have to do five things to put a picture in your ad:

1. Take a picture of your item.
2. Convert that picture to a digital graphics file.
3. Edit the image file (so that it looks pretty).
4. Upload your image file to a server somewhere on the Internet.
5. Point to the location of the image file from your item description.

Let's look at each of these steps individually.

Take a Picture

Look, I'm not going to tell you how to take a picture. If you can't aim, focus, and shoot (with appropriate lighting and composition), you're beyond my help. Just make sure you take a clean, uncluttered, *centered*, well-lit picture of your item. In fact, take a few pictures from a few different angles. And get close enough so users can tell what it is you took a picture of.

Convert a Picture to a Digital Graphics File

Now that you have a pretty photograph, how do you turn it into a digital graphics file (preferably in JPG format)?

Assuming that you didn't use one of those expensive new digital cameras (which actually capture images in digital format), you have a number of options, all involving *scanning*. Basically, you run your photograph (or negative) through a computer scanner, which digitizes the image and stores it in a graphics file. You can buy your own flatbed scanner for under $150 or so, you can ask a friend with a scanner to scan your photo for you, or you can pay around $10 to have Kinko's or some similar establishment do the job professionally.

eBay and Kodak: A Picture-Perfect Match

It might get a little easier to create and store a digital image for use in your eBay listings. eBay has announced that it will be partnering with Kodak to enable its users to add photographs to their auction listings without scanners or other equipment. When this feature is up and running, all you'll have to do is take your film to a Kodak photo processor, who will scan the images and put them on a special Kodak Internet site. When you're ready to create your item listing, you go to the Kodak site, enter a personal access code, view your entire roll of film, and choose the images you want to insert in your auction listing—and then the selected images get added to your ad, automatically. Look for this feature to debut sometime in the near future.

Edit the Image File

Once your photograph has been converted to a JPG file (the graphics file type of choice on the Internet), you can then do a little editing to "clean it up" for eBay use. You can crop the image to focus only on the subject at hand, resize the image so it fits better in your eBay listing, and even lighten it up, make it darker, or color-correct it so it looks better.

How do you do this? You need an image-editing program, such as Adobe Photoshop, Adobe PhotoDeluxe, PaintShop Pro, or Microsoft Picture It!—or access to a friend who has some of this software. If all else fails, have Kinko's do it for you.

While you're resizing, eBay recommends that you size your image to no more than 300×300 pixels and keep the file size to 50KB or less. This makes for the best fit on your listing page—and keeps the loading time down to a reasonable level.

Upload Your Image File to the Internet

Here's the irritating part: You go to all this trouble of taking a photo, scanning it in, and editing it down to a small JPG file—and then eBay won't let you upload it to its site. No, you can upload it anyplace else on the Web, but don't even think about storing your files on eBay's servers.

Okay, enough complaining.

What you have to do is find a Web server that will host your files. Fortunately, this isn't a tough search.

If you have your own personal page on the Web, you can upload your picture to that Web server. For example, if you have a personal page on GeoCities or Tripod, upload your images to that site.

If you don't have a personal page but *could* have a personal page (via America Online or your Internet service provider), that's a potential place for you to upload picture files. If your company has a Web server, there's a chance it'll let you use a little space there.

If you don't have any other options, you can go to a site that specializes in storing image files for eBay users. Some of these sites include:

- ➤ AuctionDesigner.com (www.auctiondesigner.com)
- ➤ AuctionWatch Image Hosting (www.auctionwatch.com/ihost/)
- ➤ imagehost (www.imagehost.com)
- ➤ ImageHosting.com (www.imagehosting.com/auction.shtml)
- ➤ MyItem.com (www.myitem.com)
- ➤ PhotoPoint (www.photopoint.com)
- ➤ picturebay (www.pbay.com)
- ➤ PixHost (www.pixhost.com)
- ➤ Pongo WebWorks (pongohost.com)
- ➤ Scan 'N Stor (solo3.abac.com/scanman/)

Note that you might have to pay a fee for this service at some of these sites.

Point to the Image File

Once your image is on the Web, you need to add the exact address (URL) of your image file. Once you have the URL, enter it into the **Picture URL** box on the Sell Your Item form, in the form of *www.webserver.com/picture.jpg*. (eBay automatically inserts the http://.)

If you don't get your picture scanned and uploaded until *after* you've created your eBay item listing, you can add the picture to your ad at a later date. All you have to do is go to eBay's Site Map and click the **Add to Your Item's Description** link (or go directly to `pages.ebay.com/aw/add-to-item.html`). When the next page appears, enter your User ID and password and then enter the URL for your picture into the **Description** box in the form of

```
<img src="http://www.webserver.com/picture.jpg">
```

Just replace *www.webserver.com/picture.jpg* with the correct URL for your picture. (Remember—when you add your picture *after* you create your initial listing, you have to use the full HTML tag as shown.)

Managing Your Auction

Once your listing is complete, the auction itself begins. What happens during the long days of an eBay auction?

One thing that happens is that eBay helps you out by sending you a daily email about all your open auctions. This email details the status of all your auctions, including the current high bid and high bidder. It's a good way to keep track of what's happening, on a daily basis.

What *you* do during the course of the auction, of course, depends on you.

Adding to and Editing Your Listing

One thing I heartily recommend doing is to look at your ad again. Maybe you like it—great. Maybe you don't—not so great. If you don't like your listing, there are two things you can do:

➤ If you haven't received any bids yet, you can edit your title, description, and pictures. Go to your item listing page and click the **Revise** link (located directly underneath the seller/high bidder information). This opens an editing screen where you can change whatever information you want.

➤ Once that first bid is in, you can't change a thing. What you can do, however, is add more information to your description. When you do this, know that your original description remains as is; the addition does not change or delete anything you've done previously.

To add to your description, go to eBay's Site Map and click the **Add to Your Item's Description** link (or go directly to `pages.ebay.com/aw/add-to-item.html`). When the next page appears, enter your user ID and password, and then enter the text you want to add. As with any description text, you can enter plain text or HTML-coded text—or URLs for additional pictures for your listing.

183

Canceling an Auction

What if your auction starts and you decide you really don't want to sell that item? You need a good excuse, but you can cancel eBay auctions.

Canceling an auction is a two-step process:

1. Cancel any existing bids on your item. Go to the Canceling Bids page (pages.ebay.com/aw/seller-cancel-bid.html) and cancel the first bid on your item. Then, return to this page as many times as necessary to cancel all the outstanding bids.

2. Officially end your auction. (You can't end an auction that has open bids, hence the reason you had to cancel all the bids first.) Go to the Ending Your Auction page (pages.ebay.com/aw/end-auction.html), enter your user ID, password, and auction item number. When you click the **End Auction** button, your auction is automatically cancelled.

Answering Bidder Questions

Over the course of a popular auction, chances are a few potential bidders will ask questions about your item or your auction. eBay lets bidders email sellers directly, so don't be surprised if you get a few emails from strangers asking unusual questions.

When you receive a question from a potential bidder, answer that question promptly, courteously, and accurately. It's in your best interest to make the questioner happy; after all, that person could turn out to be your high bidder.

Don't Keep It a Secret!

Here's something else you can do to improve your chances of selling your item: Tell people about your auction!

You can drop notes about the item you're selling in Usenet newsgroups and email mailing lists, and you can email your friends and family and colleagues and let them know about your auction. When you mention your auction, make sure you include the URL for your item listing page. It should look like this:

```
http://cgi.ebay.com/aw-cgi/eBayISAPI.dll?ViewItem&item=xx
```

All you have to do is replace xx with the actual auction item number for your particular item, and you've created a direct link to your auction page.

The Auction's Over—Now What?

The days go by, and finally, your auction is over. If you're fortunate, you've received a high bid that far exceeds your opening bid or reserve price—which means that you have a buyer.

The question is, now what do you do?

Contacting the Winning Bidder

eBay will notify you via email when your auction is over and include the user ID and email of your auction's high bidder. It is now your responsibility to contact that high bidder to arrange payment and shipping.

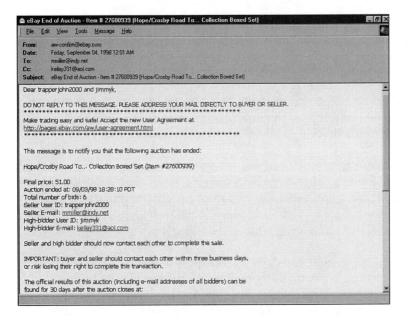

A typical eBay email notifying you of the end of your auction.

What you need to do, as soon as possible, is to email the high bidder with the following information:

➤ Your name and address so the buyer will know where to send the payment

➤ Your email address so the buyer can contact you with any questions or problems

➤ The total amount the buyer owes you—which will be the final auction price plus a reasonable shipping and handling fee

➤ Your preferred method of payment or payment options (check, cashier's check, money order, credit card, and so on)

Some sellers even go to the extreme of emailing the buyer a preformatted form (either as part of the email message or attached in a Word document) that the buyer can print, fill out, and include with the payment. (That's a nice touch; I like it.)

If you haven't heard back from the buyer in a day or two, send another email. If you still can't contact the buyer, go to eBay's Site Map and click the **Contact Other Registered User** link (or go directly to `pages.ebay.com/aw/user-query.html`), request full contact information for that user—which should include their email address, street address, and phone number—and try contacting him or her again.

If, after three days, you still haven't been able to contact the buyer, you can consider that person a *deadbeat bidder* (see the next section), and if you want, you can contact the second-highest bidder to see whether that person still wants to buy your item. Note, however, that at this juncture, you are no longer obligated to sell the item, and the second-highest bidder is not obligated to buy it.

Dealing with Deadbeat Bidders

If you are unfortunate enough to get stuck with a deadbeat bidder, you have a few options:

➤ First, go directly to the Feedback Forum and leave negative feedback against that user.

➤ Second, go to eBay's Site Map and click the **Final Value Fee Request** link (in the Seller Services section). Follow the instructions there to receive a credit for the final value fee normally charged by eBay when an item is sold.

Per eBay's Deadbeat Bidder Policy, any time you request a final value fee credit due to a deadbeat bidder, that slimebucket will receive a warning from eBay. After the second warning, temporary and then permanent suspension of his eBay account will occur.

Shipping It Out

Let's assume you didn't get left high and dry by a deadbeat bidder, but rather, you received payment in a prompt fashion. Now you have to ship your item to the buyer—in a prompt yet cost-effective fashion. See Chapter 27, "Shipping It Out— Without Spending a Fortune," for more information on the best ways to ship eBay auction items.

Finishing Things Up and Leaving Feedback

As you ship the sold item, there are two more things you need to do:

➤ First, send an email to the buyer, letting him or her know that the item is on its way. (You should note in your message when and by which method the item was shipped.)

➤ Second, you need to leave feedback about the buyer. Whether it was a good transaction or a bad transaction, you need to let your fellow eBay members know how things turned out.

To leave feedback, go to the listing page for the item you just sold and click the number (feedback rating) next to the high bidder's user ID. When the Feedback Profile page appears, click the **Leave Feedback** link and fill in the resulting form. Make sure you really want to leave the comments you've written, and then click the **Leave Comment** button. Your feedback will be registered and added into the buyer's other feedback comments.

See Chapter 16, "Protecting Yourself on eBay," for more information about the type of feedback to leave in different situations.

Managing Multiple Auctions: Advice for High-Volume Sellers

If you're a high-volume individual seller, or a merchant selling a lot of stuff on eBay, it gets real tedious real fast handling each and every auction—the listing, the ad creation, the auction management, the email notifications—one auction at a time. Automating some of your auction-management tasks would make the process easier.

One way to do this is through the use of commercial auction-management software. For a list of these programs, see Chapter 24, "Tracking Your Auctions with Auction Management Software."

eBay also includes its own built-in utility to help sellers create large quantities of item listings. The Mister Lister bulk upload feature lets you enter listings for multiple auctions all at one time.

The way Mister Lister works is that you use a separate software program to prepare a text file (formatted to eBay's specifications) to use as your eBay item listing. You then transmit the formatted text file to eBay within the body of a plain-text (that is, non-HTML) email message. After eBay confirms receipt of your file (via email), you go to the Mister Lister page, review and edit your batch of listings, and then activate your auctions.

To learn more about Mister Lister, send an email with the words "Software Design Specifications" in the subject line to misterlister@ebay.com. In your message, include your eBay user ID and the email address you registered with eBay; you should hear back from eBay within two business days.

The Least You Need to Know

➤ Before you sell an item, you have to be a registered eBay user and have a credit card on file.

➤ To start an auction for an item, click the **Sell Your Item** link on eBay's home page, and completely fill out the resulting form.

➤ Improve the chances of selling your item by writing a descriptive yet punchy title (headline) and an item description that includes all the pertinent details in a positive fashion.

➤ Further increase your item's chances by adding a picture to your listing.

➤ When the auction is over, you'll be notified by eBay; you then should contact the buyer and communicate payment and shipping terms and information.

➤ After you've received payment, ship the item and leave feedback about the buyer.

Chapter 19

A Tutorial for Buyers: How to Make a Winning Bid

In This Chapter

➤ Learn how to bid on any item listed on eBay

➤ Discover how to retract any bid you've made in error

➤ Find out what to do when you win an auction

You've browsed through listings or searched for an item and actually found something you're interested in. Now, it's time to pony up and make a bid.

How does bidding work? In a nutshell, it's pretty much as simple as telling eBay how much you'd be willing to pay for an item—and then finding out whether anyone else is willing to pay more than you. If not, you win—and you have to buy the item.

It's important to remember that it doesn't cost you anything to bid. You only have to pay if you win—and even then, you don't have to pay eBay anything. (All eBay fees are charged to the seller.) You'll have to pay the seller the amount of your winning bid, plus any reasonable shipping and handling costs to get the item to you.

Sounds easy enough, doesn't it?

Before You Bid...

Although anybody can browse on eBay, to bid you have to be a registered user. If you haven't registered yet, now's the time. (For information on registering, see Chapter 14, "eBay Wants You: Joining Up and Getting Started.")

With registering out of the way, look at a typical listing page to see what you can find out about an item and a seller. Each listing page includes three sections:

➤ **Auction details**   This is where you find all the details about the current auction, including the current bid, the time left in the auction, the seller's ID, and so on.

➤ **Description**   This is the description of the item written by the seller. This section is normally plain text but sometimes includes a picture of the item.

➤ **Bidding form**   This is where you enter your user ID, password, and bid.

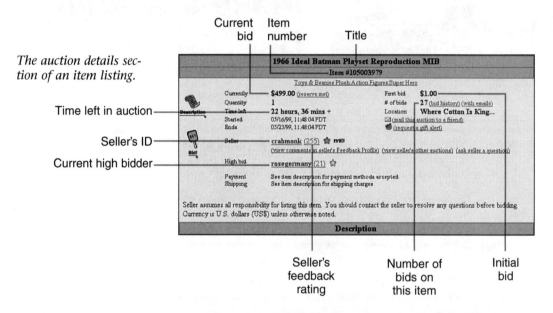

The auction details section of an item listing.

The item description section of an item listing.

Before you place your bid, make sure you read all the details of the item you're interested in. Look at the seller's feedback rating; is it positive? You might even want to click the number next to the seller's name to view his or her feedback profile; this is where you can read the individual comments about this person left by other users.

In other words, take your time and get comfortable with both the item and the seller before you place your bid. If you find anything—anything at all—that makes you uncomfortable, then don't bid.

190

Enter your user ID.   Item title and number   Current bid

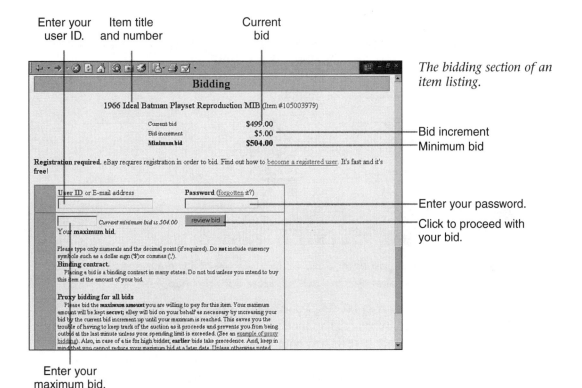

The bidding section of an item listing.

Bid increment
Minimum bid

Enter your password.

Click to proceed with your bid.

Enter your maximum bid.

How Much Should I Bid?

Want to know how much you should bid? Want to know when you should bid? Want to learn bidding strategies that will virtually guarantee a winning bid at minimal cost? Then, you'll need to turn to Chapter 22, "Winning an Auction: Strategies for Buyers." That's where the real good stuff is!

Just Do It—Placing a Bid

You've waited long enough. Now, it's time to finally place your bid.

Here's what you do:

1. Scroll down to the bidding section of the listing page, and enter your user ID, password, and maximum bid amount.

2. Click the **Review Bid** button.

3. Check the information on the review page—especially your bid amount. If everything is correct, click the **Place Bid** button.

4. Your bid is officially entered, and eBay indicates whether you're the current high bidder or you've already been outbid.

How Can I Be Immediately Outbid?

It might seem fishy if you enter a bid a few dollars above the current bid, only to discover that you've already been outbid. How does this happen?

It's all related to the proxy bidding I discussed in Chapter 4, "Bidding by Proxy: Robot Bidders Rule!" What has happened in this instance is that the previous high bidder (previous to you, that is) had entered a maximum bid amount higher than your maximum bid amount. As soon as you entered your bid, this increased the current bid to the level of your maximum bid, which triggered the proxy bidding agent to raise his bid even higher than your highest bid. And it all happened instantaneously!

If this happens to you—and you really, really want that item—then return to the item listing page and enter a new bid, this time with a higher maximum bid amount.

Remember, eBay's proxy bidding system will automatically place your bids for you, up to but not exceeding your specified maximum bid amount. If the minimum bid is currently $10, and you entered a maximum bid of $20, eBay enters your bid as $10. Your bid will get raised automatically if and when other bidders enter their (higher) bids. (For more information on how proxy bidding works, see Chapter 4.

Remember this simple bit of advice: Enter the highest amount that you're willing to pay for that item, no matter what the current bid level. If you think an item is worth $40, enter $40 as you maximum bid—and don't worry if the current bid is half that amount. But also, don't get upset if the bidding goes higher than your specified maximum; have the discipline to bid only as high as you initially thought the item was worth.

How *Not* to Bid by Proxy

What if you don't want to use the proxy bidding system? After all, if your robot bidder gets involved in a bidding war with another robot bidder, the price can go up and up and up very fast, without any human interaction whatsoever!

You can't disable eBay's proxy software, but you can manually defeat it by making your maximum bid equal to the current bid amount. That leaves no room for eBay's proxy to increase your bid automatically—but it also means that you have to constantly monitor your auction, because any new bids will have to be placed manually.

What to Do After You've Bid

What do you do after you've entered a high bid for an item? The answer is a four-letter word: *Wait*. As Tom Petty says, the waiting is the hardest part. That's certainly true with online auctions.

Immediately after you place a high bid, eBay automatically sends you an email notifying you of your bid status. You'll also receive an email once a day from eBay, notifying you of your status in any and all auctions in which you're the highest bidder. In addition, if you get outbid on an item, eBay sends you an immediate email informing you of such.

Otherwise, feel free to check in on all of your auctions in progress, just to see how things are proceeding. Remember that a watched kettle never boils—and constantly tracking your auctions doesn't make the time go any faster, either.

You can search for all the auctions that you've recently bid on by clicking the **Search** link at the top of eBay's home page to display the Search page. Enter your own user ID or email address in the **Bidder Search** box and then click the **Search** button; eBay will list all the active auctions in which you're a bidder.

You can also use My eBay to automatically track all your auctions. See Chapter 17, "Personalizing Your Page with My eBay," for more details.

Increasing Your Bid Amount

As you get further along in a particular auction, you might suddenly realize that your maximum bid isn't going to hold, and you want to ensure a large enough bid to win a long, hard-fought auction. How can you increase your bid—even though you're currently the high bidder?

It's really easy. Just return to the item listing page and place a new bid, making sure that your new maximum bid is higher than your old maximum bid. (You can't decrease your maximum bid!) When you enter this new bid, it supplants your previous bid.

Pretty easy, isn't it?

Oh, No! You've Been Outbid!

It happens. Your auction is progressing, and then, you get that dreaded email from eBay informing you that you've been outbid.

What do you do?

First, you have to decide whether you want to continue to play in this auction. If you decided up front that an item was only worth, let's say, $10, and the bidding has progressed to $15, you might want to let this one go.

On the other hand, if you hedged your bets with the earlier bid, you might want to jump back into the fray with a new bid. If so, return to the item's listing page and make a new bid. Maybe your new bid will be higher than the current high bidder's maximum bid.

Or maybe not. You don't know until you try!

Don't Wait for the Email

During the last hour of most auctions, the bidding really heats up. If you wait for an email to inform you when you've been outbid during an auction's final minutes, you might not have enough time to log onto eBay and make a new bid. For that reason, many bidders will log onto eBay (and onto the individual auction about to end) and manually monitor the auction's closing minutes. Just remember to hit the "reload" button on your browser frequently, to keep the item listing page up-to-date with the latest bids!

Retracting a Bad Bid

Everybody makes a mistake sometime. What happens if you place a bid in an auction that you shouldn't have placed?

Fortunately—but reluctantly—eBay lets you retract bids under certain circumstances.

When does eBay allow you to retract your bid? Well, if the seller has substantively changed the description of the item after you bid, you're free to change your mind, too. You can also retract your bid if you made a "clear error" in the amount of your bid. What's a "clear error?" Well, bidding $100 when you meant to bid $10 is clearly an error; other circumstances are left up to your judgment.

The thing is, you can always retract a bid (because you can always claim a "clear error"), but you won't win any friends doing so. In fact, if you retract too many bids, eBay will come after you and possibly kick you off the site. So retract a bid if you have to, but don't make a habit of it.

How do you retract a bid? It's actually fairly easy. Go to eBay's Site Map and click the **Retract a Bid** link (in the Buyer Services section). You'll need to fill out an online form and give a reason for your retraction. When you click the Retract Bid button, your bid will be deleted from the auction in progress.

Beware, of course, that you're apt to generate negative feedback from the item's seller if you retract a bid. It's common courtesy—and common sense—to email the seller before you retract a bid, explaining the circumstances and begging forgiveness.

You Won! Now What?

You've somehow waited patiently (or not) throughout the entire progress. As the clock ticked down to zero, no other viable competitors entered the arena, and your high bid stood. You won!

Now things *really* start to happen.

First, you should receive an email from eBay notifying you that you won the afore-mentioned auction. You'll probably receive an email from the item's seller, as well, telling you how much you need to pay (your high bid amount plus shipping and handling) and where to send the payment.

If you don't hear from the seller within 24 hours, then you should take the initiative and send your own email. Click the seller's name on the listing page to generate an email message, introduce yourself, and gently inquire about shipping and handling costs and where you should send your payment.

Arranging Payment

Once you've heard from the seller, it's time to pay. In most cases, the price you pay will include your high bid and a reasonable amount of shipping and handling fees.

Don't be surprised if the shipping/handling actually runs a little more than what you might know the actual shipping to be; remember, the seller has to cover the costs of packaging and (in some sellers' minds) the cost of listing the item on eBay. If shipping/handling runs a few bucks more than actual shipping, don't sweat it.

Many sellers offer several different shipping options (insurance versus no insurance, UPS versus FedEx versus USPS Priority Mail, and so on), at different costs to you. Others only ship one way. If given the choice, pick the best compromise between cost and speed. If not given the choice, live with it. If you have special shipping concerns (FedEx doesn't deliver to your address), now is the time to raise them with the seller and reach some sort of agreement on how you'll get the goods and who'll absorb the costs. (That would be you, the buyer.)

Also, find out what kind of payment the seller wants. Short of receiving cash in the mail (never a good idea), most sellers prefer to be paid as fast and as securely as possible. If you're buying from a merchant seller, you might have the option of paying by credit card; if you're buying from an individual seller, you probably don't. Most sellers profess their preferences for cashier's checks and money orders, but these methods might be impractical or not cost-effective for lower-priced items. If you pay by personal check, many sellers will hold the item you bought for 10–14 days (until the check clears the bank) before they ship.

In any case, verify the method of payment before you send the payment so there are no surprises. Figure out when you should receive the item shipped, and make a note to email the seller if you don't receive it by that time. (Allow a few extra days of wiggle room just to be fair.)

When all the details are taken care of, send your payment and wait for your merchandise.

Receiving the Goods

Once your item arrives, check it out immediately. Don't wait a month before determining that there's something wrong; find out now whether the item is in good shape and delivers on what was promised.

If all is fine, email the seller to say that you received the merchandise and that you're happy. If all isn't fine, then email the seller and let him or her know that you have a problem.

If you have a problem—or if you didn't receive the merchandise at all after a reasonable amount of time—you should first try to work out a compromise with the seller. Most sellers will bend over backwards to make you happy; some won't.

If you can't work out anything with the seller, then turn to eBay. See Chapter 16, "Protecting Yourself on eBay," for instructions on what to do when a deal goes bad.

Finishing Things Up and Leaving Feedback

You've made your bid, won the auction, paid the seller, and received the merchandise. Now, you're done, right? Wrong.

You need to leave feedback about the seller. Whether it was a good transaction or a bad transaction, you need to let your fellow eBay members know how things turned out.

To leave feedback, go to the listing page for the item you just bought and click the number (feedback rating) next to the seller's user ID. When the Feedback Profile page appears, click the **Leave Feedback** link and fill in the resulting form. Make sure you really want to leave the comments you've written, and then click the **Leave Comment** button. Your feedback will be registered and added to the seller's other feedback comments.

See Chapter 16 for more information about the type of feedback to leave in different situations.

The Least You Need to Know

➤ Before you place a bid, you have to be a registered eBay member—and you should check out the feedback rating and comments of the item's seller.

➤ You place your bid in the Bidding section of the item listing page; enter your user ID, password, and the maximum bid you're willing to make.

➤ eBay's proxy bidding software manages your bidding, raising your bid as necessary up to but not exceeding your specified maximum bid amount.

➤ When you win an auction, you'll be notified by eBay; you then should contact the seller and arrange payment and shipping terms.

➤ After you've received the item, don't forget to leave feedback about the seller.

Chapter 20

Pretty Up Your eBay Ads with HTML

In This Chapter

➤ Discover how the eBay pros create attention-getting item listings

➤ Learn just enough HTML coding to create a great-looking listing

➤ Find out how you can create HTML listings without doing the coding yourself

Most of the item listings on eBay look the same—a paragraph or two of plain text, maybe a picture unceremoniously dropped in after the text. That's how a listing looks when you enter a normal, plain-text description on eBay's Sell Your Item page.

But then there are those ads that shout at you with colored text and different font faces and sizes and multiple columns and sizzling graphics and...well, you know the ones I'm talking about. How do you go about creating a dynamic listing like that?

Those colorful, eye-catching listings are created with HTML. HTML is the engine behind every Web page you've ever viewed, the coding language that lets you turn on and off all sorts of different text and graphic effects.

Here's a secret known to successful sellers: eBay lets you use HTML in your item listings; all you have to do is know which HTML codes to enter in the Description box on the Sell Your Item page.

Crack the Code: An HTML Primer

HTML—which stands for Hypertext Markup Language—is really nothing more than a series of codes. These codes tell a Web browser how to display different types of text and graphics. The codes are embedded in a document, so you can't see them; they're only visible to your Web browser.

Any document created with HTML can have all the fancy features you find on the Web: different font sizes, hyperlinks to other Web pages, graphics, sound, video, and even embedded applets. HTML documents aren't limited to the Web, of course; many email programs let you send and receive HTML email, and Microsoft Word even lets you save its word processing documents in HTML format.

HTML coding might sound difficult, but it's really pretty easy. First, know that HTML is nothing more than text surrounded by instructions, in the form of simple codes. Codes are distinguished from normal text by the fact that they're enclosed within angle brackets. Each particular code turns on or off a particular attribute, such as boldface or italic text. Most codes are in sets of "on/off" pairs; you turn "on" the code before the text you want to affect and then turn "off" the code after the text.

For example, the code **<h1>** turns specified type into a level-one headline; the code **</h1>** turns off the headline type. The code **<i>** is used to italicize text; **</i>** turns off the italics. (As you can see, an "off" code is merely the "on" code with a slash before it, **</like this>**.)

Any text not surrounded by code uses HTML's default formatting—normal Times Roman text. It's the same with tables and other elements; if no code is applied, they default to standard formatting.

To create state-of-the-art item listings, then, you need to learn some of the basic HTML codes. Although I can't teach you all there is to know about HTML in a single chapter, I can show you enough basic HTML to help you create some stunning eBay ads.

That's Not All, Folks

I present only a handful of the huge number of HTML codes available to you. If you want to learn more about these and other HTML codes, I recommend that you go to The HTML Tutor (`html.cavalcade-whimsey.com`) or HTML Goodies (`www.htmlgoodies.com`) Web sites. You can also pick up a copy of *The Complete Idiot's Guide Creating an HTML 4 Web Page* wherever good books are sold, which is a great primer for creating your own Web pages with HTML.

Codes for Text Formatting

Using HTML formatting codes is the fastest and easiest way to add spice to your item listings. If you do nothing else, boldfacing important words in your description will add selling power to your ad—and you can do that with a pair of simple HTML codes.

Here are some of the common HTML codes that format the way selected text looks in your listing:

```
<h1>formats text as the largest headline</h1>

<h2>formats text as the second-largest headline</h2>

<h3>formats text as the third-largest headline</h3>

<b>boldfaces text</b>

<i>italicizes text</i>

<u>underlines text</u>

<tt>creates monospaced, or typewriter-style text</tt>

<blink>creates blinking text</blink>

<center>centers text</center>

<pre>displays "preformatted" text to preserve line breaks and
such</pre>
```

Insert the "on" code right before the text you want formatted, and insert the "off" code right after the selected text. For example, if you want to boldface a single word in a sentence, make it look just like this:

```
This is the sentence with the highlighted word.
```

It's really that simple; just add the **<b>** and **</b>** codes around the text you want boldfaced. The rest of your item description looks as normal as it did before.

One common design technique is to use the **<h1>** code for any major headings within your listing and then use **<b>** and/or **<i>** to highlight important words or phrases within your description. You can also use the **<center>** code for any text or graphics you want centered in your description.

An eBay ad with head-line, boldface, and italic text.

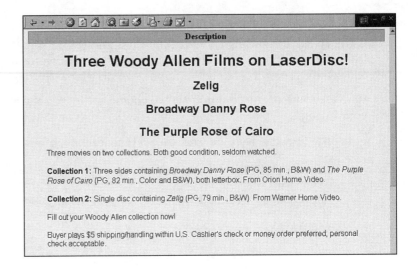

Codes for Fonts

You don't have to settle for the standard Times Roman font used on every other eBay page; you can make your ad stand out with your own choice of font.

To specify a different font for a piece of text, use the following code:

```
<font face="xxxx">text</font>
```

Replace *xxxx* with the name of the font you want. For example, if you want to change the font to Arial, enter this code:

```
<font face="Arial">text</font>
```

Use Common Fonts, Please

Just because you have a specific font installed on your computer doesn't necessarily mean that all the other Web users who'll be viewing your ad have the same font installed on their PCs. If you change fonts in your listing, change to a common font, one of those preinstalled on all Windows computers. Arial and Times Roman are always safe bets; choosing something more obscure could ensure an unpredictable display for your listing on many computers around the world.

If you want to change the size of your text, use this code:

```
<font size="xx">text</font>
```

Replace the **xx** with the size you want, from -6 to +6, with -6 being the smallest, +6 being the biggest, and 0 (or no size specified) being "normal" size type.

That's right—you don't specify the exact point size, just the *relative* size displayed onscreen. For example, if you want really tiny type, you'd go with size -1 and enter this code:

```
<font size="-1">text</font>
```

You can also string these font codes together. Let's say you want to change your text to the largest possible Times Roman; you enter this code:

```
<font face="Times Roman" size=6>text</font>
```

Be careful about changing fonts within your description. Too many different fonts look garish. This might be something you want to set at the beginning of your description and leave the same throughout the entire listing. (If so, just remember to put the **</font>** code at the very end of your description.)

Codes for Color

Adding color to your text works pretty much the same as changing the font or size. The code you use looks like this:

```
<font color="#xxxxxx">text</font>
```

Replace the six *x*s with the code for a specific color. Table 20.1 lists some basic color codes.

Table 20.1   Common Color Codes

Color	Code
White	FFFFFF
Red	FF0000
Green	00FF00
Blue	0000FF
Magenta	FF00FF
Cyan	00FFFF
Yellow	FFFF00
Black	000000
Light gray	DDDDDD

As an example, then, suppose you want to color some text red. You use this code:

```
<font color="#FF0000">red text</font>
```

Color is a good way to highlight important parts of your listing. You can put headings or subheadings in a different color or highlight selected words or phrases in the same manner. Don't use too many colors, however; if your ad looks like a rainbow, the color loses its ability to impact.

Codes That Insert Things

So far, I've shown you codes that format text. Other codes insert items into your document. These codes don't have "on/off" pairs; they're freestanding. These types of codes include

> ➤ **<p>** inserts a paragraph break

> ➤ **
** inserts a line break

> ➤ **<hr>** inserts a horizontal rule

Get the Codes—in Color!

For a complete list of the literally hundreds of different HTML color codes, go to The HTML Tutor: RGB Color Codes (`html.cavalcade-whimsey.com/rgb.html`).

If you want to separate two paragraphs, you insert a **<p>** between the two blocks of text. If you want to put a line between the two paragraphs, you insert a **<hr>**. Sometimes, it's good to use horizontal rules between different sections of your listing.

Codes for Graphics

Adding pictures and other graphics to your listings really brings some excitement to the normally plain-text world of eBay. If you want to insert a graphic in your listing, you need to know the address of that graphic (in the form of a Web page URL) and then use the following code:

```
<img src="URL">
```

There is no "off" code for inserted graphics. Note that the location is enclosed in quotation marks—and that you have to insert the **http://** part of the URL.

As an example, if your graphic is the file **graphic01.jpg** located at **www.web-server.com/mydirectory/**, you insert this code:

```
<img src="http://www.webserver.com/mydirectory/graphic01.jpg">
```

Including pictures in your listing will increase your item's sales potential. In addition, you can include other graphics in your listing—logos, starbursts, you name it. You use the same technique to link to any graphic image anywhere in your ad description.

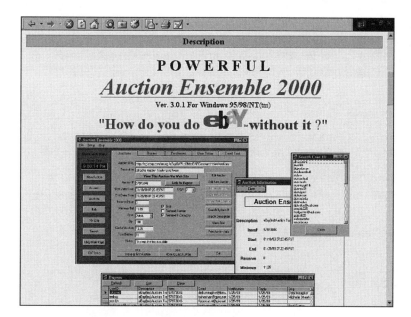

An eBay ad with a lot of graphics inserted in the description.

Codes for Links

Web pages are all about hyperlinks to other Web pages. Why should your eBay item listing be any different?

If you want to include a hyperlink to another Web page, use the following code:

```
<a href="URL">this is the link</a>
```

The text between the on and off codes will appear onscreen as a typical underlined hyperlink; when users click that text, they'll be linked to the URL you specified in the code. Note that the URL is enclosed in quotation marks and that you have to include the **http://** part of the address.

Here's what a representative hyperlink code looks like:

```
<a href="http://www.webserver.com/mydirectory/mypage.htm">This
is a link to my Web page</a>
```

You can also create a "mail-to" link in your listing; users would be able to send email to you by simply clicking the link. Here's the code for a mail-to link:

```
<a href="mailto:yourname@domain.com">click here to email me</a>
```

If you want to include a mail-to link to my email address (books@molehillgroup.com), the code looks like this:

```
<a href="mailto:books@molehillgroup.com">Click here to email the
author</a>
```

205

You can include links in your listing to your own personal Web pages (a great idea if you have other items for sale or additional images of this specific item) or to related sites. Many sellers also like to provide a direct email link in case potential bidders have questions they need answered.

Codes for Lists

If you have a lot of features to list for your item, you might want to format them in a bulleted list. Using HTML codes, it's easy to create a neatly bulleted list for your ad.

First, you enclose your bulleted list with the **<ul>** and **</ul>** codes. Then, you precede each bulleted item with the **<li>** code. (There's no "off" code for bulleted items, by the way.)

The code for a typical bulleted list looks like this:

```
<ul>
    <li>item one
    <li>item two
    <li>item three
</ul>
```

Bulleted lists are great ways to run through a list of attributes or specifications; it's a lot cleaner than just listing a bunch of stuff within a long text paragraph.

Code for Tables

In addition to making pretty text and inserting links and graphics, one of the other interesting things you can do with HTML is add a table to your item listing.

Okay, so tables sound boring. In reality, however, they let you break up your ad into two or more columns and add color backgrounds behind your text.

You start by enclosing your table with **<table>** and **</table>** codes. Then, you enclose each individual row in the table with **<tr>** and **</tr>** codes and each cell in each row with **<td>** and **</td>** codes.

A basic table with two rows and two columns (four cells total) is coded like this:

```
<table>
    <tr>
        <td>row 1 cell 1</td>
        <td>row 1 cell 2</td>
    </tr>
    <tr>
        <td>row 2 cell 1</td>
        <td>row 2 cell 2</td>
    </tr>
</table>
```

(Note that when you're dealing with complex coding such as this, it's sometimes easier to understand what's going on if you indent different levels of the code.)

Within any individual cell, you can insert any type of item—plain text, formatted text, bulleted lists, background shading, and even graphics. One neat effect is to use a simple two-column, one-row table to create the effect of two columns on your page. You can even shade the background of one of the cells or columns to set it off; it's a nice way to include more detailed information about your item.

You can format both the table as a whole and the cells within a table, to some degree:

➤ To dictate the width of the table border, use the **<table border="*xx*">** code, where *xx* is in pixels.

➤ To shade the background of a cell, use the **<td bgcolor="#*xxxxxx*">** code (which works like the color code for text).

➤ To dictate the width of a cell, use the **<td width="*xx%*">** code, where *xx* is a percentage of the total table width.

These codes gang together with the standard **<table>** and **<td>** codes in the table.

You Don't Need to Define the Document

If you already know a little HTML, you're probably wondering why I don't discuss the HTML codes you need to start and set up an entire HTML document (codes such as **<HTML>**, for example). The reason is that eBay already sets up the HTML page. When eBay generates an item listing page, that page includes all of eBay's "startup" HTML coding; your description is just inserted into the middle of the preset page. In fact, if you tried to insert the startup HTML codes in your listing code, you'd really mess up the coding for the entire listing page. So don't worry about setting up the page, and concentrate on formatting your description as effectively as possible.

Code You Can Use, for Real

Let's look at two examples of fancy ads created with simple HTML codes. You can use these codes exactly as printed in your own listings; just copy the code—word for word and character for character—into the Description box in the Sell Your Item page, and insert your own description in place of my generic sample text.

Second-Column Details

The first example is an all-text example, using a simple two-column, single-row table. The left column is designed to hold the ad's headline and the bulk of the descriptive copy; the thinner right column holds a bulleted list of item details and features.

Now, I said that you use a table to create this listing; the listing itself, however, doesn't really look like a table. Why is that? I set the **<border="*x*">** code to **0**—totally eliminating the border from the table. This way, you only see the two cells, which look like a two-column document. (Pretty sneaky, eh?)

Here's what the completed listing looks like.

A two-column ad, with bulleted copy in the subsidiary shaded column.

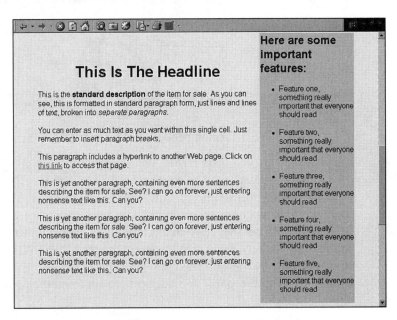

Here's the code you use to create that ad:

```
<table border="0">
    <tr>
        <td width="70%">
            <font face="Arial">
            <center><h1>This Is The Headline</h1></center>
            <p>
```

208

This is the **\<b\>**standard description**\</b\>** of the item for sale. As you can see, this is formatted in standard paragraph form, just lines and lines of text, broken into **\<i\>**separate paragraphs**\</i\>**.
\<p\>
You can enter as much text as you want within this single cell. Just remember to insert paragraph breaks.
\<p\>
This paragraph includes a hyperlink to another Web page. Click on
\<a href="http://www.molehillgroup.com"\>this link**\</a\>** to access that page.
\<p\>
This is yet another paragraph, containing even more sentences describing the item for sale. See? I can go on forever, just entering nonsense text like this. Can you?
\<p\>
This is yet another paragraph, containing even more sentences describing the item for sale. See? I can go on forever, just entering nonsense text like this. Can you?
\<p\>
This is yet another paragraph, containing even more sentences describing the item for sale. See? I can go on forever, just entering nonsense text like this. Can you?
\</font\>
\</td\>
\<td bgcolor="#DDDDDD" width="30%"\>
  \<font face="Arial"\>
  \<h2\>Here are some important features:**\</h2\>**
  \<p\>
  \<ul\>
    \<li\>Feature one, something really important that everyone should read
    \<p\>
    \<li\>Feature two, something really important that everyone should read
    \<p\>
    \<li\>Feature three, something really important that everyone should read
    \<p\>
    \<li\>Feature four, something really important that everyone should read

continues

```
            <p>
            <li>Feature five, something really important that everyone
              should read
          </ul>
          </font>
      </td>
    </tr>
  </table>
  </font>
```

Looks cool, doesn't it? I want you to notice just a few things.

First, you can put as much text as you like into either of the two cells, including paragraph breaks and bulleted lists and graphics and whatnot.

Second, in this kind of format, I find that it works best to use the thinner cell for a bulleted list of features and put your main text and graphics in the left-hand cell.

Third, I used a light gray background color for the right column, to set it off visually from the rest of the text. I also used a second-level headline (**<h2>**) in the right column, so as not to compete with the first-level headline (**<h1>**) in the left column.

Finally, notice that I changed the font face for all the text within each cell by using the **<font face="Arial">** code right after each **<td>** code. This affected all the text until the **</font>** code before each **</td>** code. (You can change the text for each cell individually, but you can't change the text for the entire table all at once.)

Big Picture, Colored Background

The next example is even easier than the first. You create another two-column, one-row table, but don't bother to set the column widths. This way, the columns size naturally, based on their contents.

The contents in this ad are pretty simple. The left column contains a picture of your item, and the right column contains a brief description (in large text). The table background is all blue, and you reverse the text out of the background by coloring the text white.

The whole thing is preceded by a large colored headline above the table. The completed ad looks like this:

Another table ad, with the picture on the left and the description on the right.

```
<h1><center><font color="#FF0000">This Is The Headline
<br>
On Two Lines, In Color!</font></center></h1>
<p>
<table bgcolor="#0000FF">
   <tr>
      <td>
         <img src="http://www.webserver.com/picture.jpg">
      </td>
      <td>
         <center><h2><font color="#FFFFFF">Look at this item!
         <p>
         It's really cool!
         <p>
         You should buy it!
         <p>
         Send me all your money <i>now!</i></font></center></h2>
      </td>
   </tr>
</table>
```

Can you get any simpler than that? Again, you can put as much text as you want in the right-hand cell. You can also add text to the left cell, either before or after the graphic. You can even add more regular text *after* the table—a good place, in fact, to put a link to your own personal Web page or a mail-to link to your email address.

Want another tip? Use these examples as templates, and then experiment, adding your own codes to see what results!

Easier HTML Editing

Most users enter HTML code directly into the Description box on the Sell Your Item page. This is okay if you only have a limited amount of coding (a few bold-faces and italics, a paragraph break or two). If you have a lot of HTML code, it might be easier to create the code in another application and then cut and paste it into the Description box. The only thing you have to remember is that the pasted code must be in plain-text format—you can't paste a Word document into the box.

I typically use Windows Notepad to create short amounts of HTML code. I'll actually save some boilerplate code in a Notepad file and then edit it for my individual ads. It's very easy to cut from Notepad and then paste into the Description box.

If you do some really heavy-duty coding, you might want to try Netscape Composer (which comes with the Netscape Navigator suite) or Microsoft FrontPage Express (which comes with Internet Explorer and Windows 98). The advantage of these programs is that they let you create an HTML document without coding; just create the document onscreen, as you would a document in Microsoft Word. You have to choose to view your Composer or Express file as raw HTML and then cut from that HTML view of your file to paste into eBay's Description box.

Let Somebody Else Do the Coding: Prepackaged HTML for eBay Ads

If all this talk of angle brackets and on and off codes leaves your head spinning, you have some options that won't leave your hands dirty with raw HTML.

AuctionDesigner.com (`www.auctiondesigner.com`) is a Web site that creates HTML listings for you, online, automatically. You have to pay a one-time $29.95 membership fee; then, creating an HTML ad is as easy as filling in the blanks in a template. AuctionDesigner.com will also serve as a image-hosting service for all those pictures you want to put in your ads.

Another similar service is Pongo WebWorks (pongohost.com). Pongo also offers eBay ad creation, as well as image hosting (for eBay pictures) and complete Web site design.

Several software programs do nothing but create HTML eBay listings:

➤ Auction Aid (firstdesign.com/auction/auctionaid.htm), priced at $8.50

➤ AuctionAssistant (www.blackthornesw.com/bthome/aafeat.htm), priced at $59.95

➤ Auction Secretary (www.the-store.com/auction2.html), priced at $39.95

➤ Ez-Ad-Pro (www.flash.net/~etx/turbo/ezadpro.htm), available for free

As you might imagine, AuctionAssistant and Auction Secretary offer a few more features than the other, more homegrown programs. I'm a particular fan of AuctionAssistant (discussed in more detail in Chapter 24, "Tracking Your Auctions with Auction Management Software). AuctionAssistant is a full-featured auction-management package that helps you create ads, upload ads, manage ads, automate your bidding process, and track the process of all your eBay auctions. In my opinion, if you're a high-volume eBay trader, it's worth the money.

You can often find other ad-listing and auction management programs on eBay by searching for **auction software**.

The Least You Need to Know

➤ eBay lets you use HTML code to customize the appearance of your item's description.

➤ HTML codes typically come in "on" and "off" pairs that either format surrounded text or insert special elements, such as graphics or hyperlinks.

➤ You can use HTML tables to create complex page designs with simple coding.

➤ If you don't want to do the HTML coding yourself, you can use special Web sites or software programs to automatically create HTML listing code.

Chapter 21

Undercover eBay: The Secrets That eBay Doesn't Want You to Know

---

In This Chapter

➤ Discover the questionable activities you can probably get away with

➤ Find out which activities are strictly forbidden by eBay—and will definitely get you kicked off the service

➤ Uncover the less-than-desirable things eBay doesn't want to know about its service

---

eBay is a terrific service and a fairly well-run business. In fact, eBay has built up a true community, with more than two million registered users buying and selling on a regular basis—the majority of whom have nothing but good experiences online.

However, all is not perfect in eBay land. There is a dark side to eBay that can occasionally surface, to the detriment of unwary users.

This chapter is where I tell you about eBay's dark side so that you'll know what to look out for if things start happening contrary to plan.

Activities eBay Frowns Upon

Welcome to the gray area.

There are several activities that you, the user, can engage in that eBay doesn't like but doesn't forbid. When users do these things, eBay just kind of looks the other way.

What activities are these? Basically, these tricks help you either win an auction, back out of an auction, or reduce the fees you pay to eBay. Go ahead and try them if you want to; eBay doesn't seem to care, and I refuse to pass judgment!

Sniping: Outmaneuvering Other Bidders at the Last Possible Minute

Sniping is a technique used to win auctions by swooping in at the last minute with a high bid. Although eBay discourages sniping (and doesn't really like to talk about it), sniping is rampant on its site. (By the way, you can get a step-by-step lesson in how to snipe in Chapter 22, "Winning an Auction: Strategies for Buyers.")

Sniping happens on eBay because the end time of each auction is rigidly enforced. If you know an auction ends at 12:01:30, you can time your snipe to hit at 12:01:29, leaving no time for any other bidders to trump your bid. Other auction sites, such as Auction Universe and Yahoo! Auctions, have flexible end times; if there is bidding within the last five minutes of an auction, the auction is automatically extended by another five minutes, giving extra time for other bidders to respond to a snipe.

Although eBay doesn't like sniping, it doesn't do anything about it; in fact, sniping appears to have tacit approval from eBay staff. Many experienced eBay users not only participate in sniping, but also regard it as a kind of game. Sellers like sniping, of course, as long as it helps to drive up the prices of their items. It's the community of less-experienced users—or those used to more traditional auctions—that is less likely to embrace sniping as a practice.

Deal Breaking: Getting Out of a Transaction

Auctions are supposed to be binding transactions; the seller agrees to sell a thing for a certain price, and the buyer agrees to buy it at that price.

All things binding, apparently, can be unbound.

There are numerous ways to back out of a transaction either during or after an auction. Whether you're a seller who decides not to sell, a bidder who decides not to bid, or a high bidder who decides not to buy, there are ways to wriggle out of the seller/bidder/buyer contract.

There are actually four possible situations where you might want or need to renege on your end of a transaction. None of these tactics are illegal or break eBay's rules, although some bend the rules quite a bid; all will undoubtedly earn you negative feedback from the other party.

Here are the scenarios:

➤ **You're a bidder and you want to cancel your bid.** If you're the high bidder on an item, you can back out by retracting your bid. eBay says it's acceptable to retract a bid if the seller has substantively changed the description of the item after you made your bid or if you made a clear error in the amount of your bid. (That last one is your excuse.) Just use the Bid Retraction form (pages.ebay.com/aw/retract-bid.html), think of the best excuse possible for backing out, and brace yourself for negative feedback. Bid retraction is frowned upon, but there's nothing anybody can do about it—and it's better than the next option, backing out on a winning bid after the sale.

➤ **You've placed the winning bid, and you don't want to actually buy the item.** This one is trickier but still doable. What you want to do is contact the seller directly, via email, and explain your situation. Tell the seller you're sorry, you can't really afford the price, your sister just died, your house burned down, or whatever works for you. (The truth is always good....) Sellers are, more often than not, decent and reasonable human beings—and if you're very nice, they might not even leave negative feedback about you. (Nah, forget it. You'll get negative feedback if you try this one; trust me!)

You Don't Pay, eBay Doesn't Charge

eBay will refund listing and selling fees to sellers if high bidders renege on their commitments. If this happens to you, just fill out a Final Value Fee Credit Request (pages.ebay.com/aw/credit-request.html).

➤ **You want to end an auction without selling the item.** It's easy to get out of an auction before the auction is over. All you have to do is cancel all the bids in your auction and then end your auction early. Here's what to do: First, go to the Canceling Bids page (pages.ebay.com/aw/seller-cancel-bid.html) and cancel the first bid on your item. Return to this page as many times as necessary to cancel all the bids on your item. Next, go to the Ending Your Auction page (pages.ebay.com/aw/end-auction.html) and follow the instructions. Voila! Your auction is over. (Again, get ready for the negative feedback—which is even worse if you had a lot of bidders on your item.)

➤ **The auction is over, and you don't want to really sell the item.** This issue is between you and the high bidder. Email the high bidder as soon as possible, telling him or her you've decided not to sell and giving the best excuse you can think of. If the high bidder insists on mailing you payment, do not accept the payment; return the check or money order directly to the bidder. As long as you don't accept payment, you don't have to ship. Expect some very negative feedback, however!

Activities eBay Forbids

As opposed to those activities eBay doesn't like but tolerates, there are a whole slew of activities eBay simply won't allow. Most of these offenses involve manipulating auction results, whether by the seller or an overly interested bidder. If eBay catches you doing any of these, you'll either be temporarily suspended (kind of a first warning) or permanently banned from the service.

Of course, you have to be caught before you can be punished. The main way eBay finds out about these activities are from other users—the real victims of these offensive behaviors.

If you suspect any of these bidding offenses in any specific auction, you can take several steps:

➤ Leave negative feedback on the suspected offender via eBay's Feedback Forum (pages.ebay.com/aw/feedback.html).

➤ Notify eBay's SafeHarbor Investigations (SafeHarbor@ebay.com); make sure you include all relevant information and copies of all email correspondence with the suspected offender.

➤ File a complaint with eBay's Fraud Reporting System (crs.ebay.com/frs/start.asp).

➤ File a formal complaint with your local US Post Office or Attorney General; if you do this, you should send a copy of your complaint to

eBay Inc.
ATTN: Fraud Prevention
2005 Hamilton Ave., Ste. 350
San Jose, CA 95125

Remember, all of these activities are unethical and can get you kicked off eBay permanently—and some are even blatantly illegal.

Shill Bidding

Shill bidding, quite simply, is bidding on your own item in a deliberate attempt to artificially drive up its price. A shill bid can involve the use of secondary eBay registrations, user aliases, family members, friends, or associates to pump up the price; other bidders then have to top a higher price to stay in the game.

One of the more common ways to bid on one's own items is to maintain a second email address, generally through one of the free Web-based email services, such as HotMail. Using this second email address you can then obtain a second eBay membership under a different name. Using this apparently unrelated user ID, it's easy to bid on your own items.

Multiple Accounts *Are* Allowed

Even though the presence of multiple user accounts is one possible factor in shill bidding, eBay does allow sellers to have more than one registration. This is subject to several provisions, chief of which is that there can never be any interaction between the registrations, especially in the areas of bidding and feedback. In addition, eBay requires that the registered user information must be identical for all accounts. (Of course, this begs the question: How can eBay tell you have multiple accounts if you enter different information for each registration?)

Bid Shielding

Bid shielding is the practice of using shill bidding (but not a shill associated with the seller) to artificially increase the price of an item temporarily, in an attempt to protect the low bid level of a third bidder. Essentially, the artificially high bid scares off other bidders, and then the shill retracts the super-high bid at the last moment, leaving the bidding wide open for the initial, lower bidder.

Let's say you want to bid on an item but only want to pay $10 for it. After you make your bid (at the beginning of the bidding before anyone else has a chance to bid), you immediately enlist a shill or use an alias to place a $100 bid on the item. If no other bidder tops the $100 high bid, the auction continues with no additional bidding. At the last possible moment, the shill retracts the high bid, automatically putting the bid level back down to the second-highest bid—which, if you're lucky, is the original $10 bid, and you win the auction at a very low price.

Bid Siphoning

Bid siphoning happens when a third party (unrelated to the seller or bidder) emails bidders in a currently open auction, offering a similar or identical item at a price below the current bid level. This siphons off potential sales away from the registered seller and makes an end-run around eBay's fee system.

Bid Discovery

If you're losing an auction and you want to know what maximum bid level has been specified by the current high bidder (which is not divulged by eBay), here's what unscrupulous bidders say you can do:

1. First, you place a very high bid on the item—well over the current high bidder's assumed maximum bid level. This works to increase the current (now former) high bidder's bid to its maximum bid level.

2. Second, you retract your bid. This returns the high bid to the former high bidder, but at that bidder's maximum bid level. (Their bidding is now maxed out.)

3. Then, to win the auction, all you have to do is bid a tad above the current high bid (which is also the high bidder's maximum bid, remember).

Artificially Raising the Number of Bids

Auctions with 30 or more bids are designated as HOT! auctions and get special attention in eBay's listings. Sellers like to have HOT! auctions, and some will manipulate the number of bids on their items to reach the 30-bid level.

By using shills, aliases, and associates, it's easy to increase the number of bids on an item. Once the number hits the HOT! level, the seller sits back and lets the bidding take its new natural course (which is typically an accelerated course because HOT! status draws more attention to your item).

Unwanted Bidding

Sellers don't have to sell to any specific bidder. In fact, it's somewhat common for a seller to specify that he or she will refuse to sell to users with negative feedback ratings—or to email specific bidders warning them away from bidding.

If you've been warned away from an auction yet persist on bidding on that seller's items, you're breaking eBay's rules. If the seller reports you to eBay, you can be indefinitely suspended from the service.

Backing Out of Transactions—Repeatedly

If you bid on an item and never send payment, you create an incomplete transaction (not to mention block legitimate bidders from buying an item and keep the seller from getting paid).

If you're selling an item but you back out of the sale (without accepting payment), you also create an incomplete transaction. Of course, if you back out of the sale after you accept the buyer's money, then you commit a criminal offense (as well as create an incomplete transaction!).

Although backing out of one or two transactions won't win you any friends, it also won't get you kicked off eBay. However, if you back out of a lot of transactions—as either a buyer or a seller—then eBay will toss you off. It's chronic incomplete transactions that eBay notices.

Auction Interference

Another no-no still happens on occasion: One bidder sends threatening emails to other bidders to warn them away from a seller or an item. You're not allowed to interfere with in-process auctions—and you're *definitely* not allowed to threaten other users! eBay will bump you if they find out.

Auction Interception

This trick is out-and-out fraud. You represent yourself as another eBay seller, intercepting the ended auctions of that seller (generally with forged email messages) and convincing buyers to send you payment for the items. Getting caught at this one will cause you more trouble than just a simple eBay expulsion.

Spamming

eBay doesn't like you to send bulk email (spam) to masses of other users. If eBay finds out, it'll kick you off, simple as that.

Things eBay Doesn't Want You to Know

So far this chapter has outlined things eBay doesn't like you to do. Now, it's time to talk about things eBay doesn't want you to know—things that might cause you to have a little less faith in its auction services.

Person-to-Person Auctions: Are They Really Person-to-Person?

eBay likes to present itself as "the world's largest personal online trading community," offering "one-to-one trading" among "individuals—not big businesses." That is mostly true, but not completely true.

A large number of merchants, both large and small, operate via eBay. Some are small collectibles or antiques dealers operating out of their homes; others are larger store-front merchants who have discovered the benefits of selling online.

That's not to say that eBay is a merchant selling its own merchandise, as is Onsale or First Auction, or even that it courts independent merchants to beef up its listings, as does Amazon.com Auctions. I mention this purely to point out that eBay's vaunted "person-to-person" auctions aren't always that personal.

Buying from a merchant on eBay isn't necessarily a bad thing, by the way. You're probably safer (in general) dealing with an established merchant than you are with an isolated individual. In many cases, you can also pay by credit card when you deal with a merchant, which you typically can't if you're buying from an individual. Typically, if you don't win today's auction from that merchant, the same item might be relisted again tomorrow, inventory permitting.

221

How can you tell whether you're bidding on a merchant-offered item? In many cases, you can identify merchant sellers by their use of Dutch auctions (to sell large quantities of a single item), links to their business Web sites, and better-looking listings. Heck, most merchants just come out and give their business name and address in their auction ads.

eBay Feedback: Is It Meaningful?

Frequent eBay users take their feedback seriously. To these eBay "pros," anything that isn't positive feedback is negative. Even so-called neutral feedback is viewed as damaging to reputations.

Because of this, you'll feel immense pressure to leave glowingly positive feedback about every eBay member you deal with. In fact, you might even be threatened into leaving positive feedback: "If you don't leave me positive feedback, I'll leave negative feedback about you." It's all about the numbers and the stars beside the names.

This sometimes escalates into "feedback extortion." This happens when another user demands some concrete action from you, at the threat of leaving negative feedback if you don't perform. For example, a bidder might demand that a seller sell an item to him at a lower price, or he'll leave negative feedback. It's extortion, pure and simple, and it should be reported to eBay authorities.

What happens when there is so much pressure to leave positive feedback that everyone on eBay has nothing but positive marks? It's kind of like grade inflation, where everyone gets an A; what does an A really mean when everyone gets one? It's the same way with feedback; if it's all positive, how do you know who the real good guys are?

Fraud: How Bad Is It?

A growing number of eBay critics charge that fraud is rampant on the site. They accuse eBay of turning a blind eye to users who make false bids, sell fake items, or fail to deliver paid-for merchandise. These critics go on to charge that complaints to eBay are often ignored and that known violators are able to easily create new memberships using new identities.

eBay replies that these types of problems affect only a small percentage of the two million or so auctions it hosts each day. The company claims that it is quick to investigate and act on alleged improprieties. Yet eBay also admits, less forcefully, that the company cannot monitor every single auction on its site for illegal activity. Instead, it relies on its members to bring problems to its attention.

There have been several documented instances of large-scale fraud among eBay users. For example, an Oklahoma City man recently bilked eBay users for at least $30,000 worth of baseball cards he didn't deliver.

Until recently, eBay refused to reimburse users who lost money in bad transactions, clinging to its role as an impartial facilitator of transactions and not a party to the transactions themselves. eBay's policy is to urge those who believe they've been taken to report problems to local law enforcement authorities—and cases such as this are clear instances of mail fraud because the users trying to buy the products sent their money through the mail.

In response to the concerns about fraud, eBay recently instituted the SafeHarbor program (discussed in Chapter 16, "Protecting Yourself on eBay"). In addition to other features, this program provides a $200 insurance policy for most eBay transactions.

SafeHarbor aside, users also complain that eBay is slow to act on reports of forbidden practices, such as shill bidding. Many observe that eBay is particularly negligent in identifying users with multiple memberships, bidding on the same auction under different pseudonyms. eBay continues to be the focus of an ongoing federal investigation for "possible illegal transactions." The New York City Department of Consumer Affairs is also investigating eBay for alleged trades involving counterfeit items.

In eBay's defense, CEO Margaret Whitman said "eBay has zero tolerance for fraud." The company recently added a 24-person team to look into complaints of fraud and to work with law enforcement agencies to prosecute scam artists. Are these charges nothing more than the result of simple growing pains? Or are they symptoms of much deeper problems? Only time will tell.

Fraud—On a Seven-Figure Scale

For a spectacular example of fraud by an eBay bidder, look no further than the story of the 13-year-old boy who placed $3.1 million worth of bids on eBay in April, 1999. Andrew Tyler of Haddonfield, New Jersey, bid $24,500 for a red 1971 Corvette convertible, $500,000 for a Van Gogh painting, $900,000 for an antique bed, and $1.2 million for that medical office in Florida mentioned back in Chapter 14. Fortunately for some of the sellers, Andrew's bids for the Van Gogh and the medical office weren't high enough to win—but he did have the high bids for the Corvette and the antique bed.

As you have no doubt guessed, all of Andrew's bids were fictitious. (The savings from his allowance didn't quite add up to a seven-figure number.) Andrew wasn't totally repentant, as he told the *Philadelphia Inquirer*: "It's sort of weird that it's so open to everyone. They don't ask you for your credit card or any proof that you're over 18."

In defense of eBay, Andrew did break several rules (he was under 18 and was a multiple deadbeat bidder) and has been kicked off the service for doing so. Still, it was fairly easy for this enterprising teenager to break those rules—how hard would it be for someone slightly more savvy to deliberately defraud the honest buyers and sellers of the eBay community?

Selling Illegal (and Possibly Immoral) Items: How Responsible Is eBay?

Because eBay is largely unpoliced, with anonymous sellers transacting with anonymous buyers, there have been numerous instances of illegal items changing hands on the site.

Until recently, eBay had a very active Firearms category, which included sales of assault weapons. In response to community concerns, eBay decided to close the category and ban the sale of firearms on its site. eBay has also been responsive in cracking down on the sales of other illegal items, such as Cuban cigars and pirated computer software, although reports of illegal merchandise on the site continue to surface.

Beyond auctions of possibly illegal items, eBay also treads on some thin moral ground with its large Adult Only category. Although eBay does require age identification to view items in this category, some pretty explicit stuff is described—and pictured—among the thousands of listings for X-rated books, magazines, and products.

Is eBay responsible for what its users buy and sell on its site? Some claim not; after all, eBay itself does not directly sell items to the public. (However, it does profit from its user-to-user transactions; remember all those listing and selling fees?) Others say that eBay has some responsibility to protect users from fraud and illegal transactions.

Unfortunately, there are no clear answers to these questions today. Critics and analysts simply can't agree to what extent eBay and other online auctions are responsible for the actions of their users. I suppose that means that pretty much anything goes, for the time being—and that buyers certainly should beware.

Security Leaks: How Vulnerable Is Your Private Information?

eBay allows users to insert HTML code into their item descriptions; this is what creates the colorful and visually attractive ads you see from some sellers. This capability, however, might create a security problem that would allow malicious eBay users to steal the user names and passwords of other users.

The problem, dubbed "eBayla," surfaces when an eBay member using a JavaScript-enabled browser bids on an item that incorporates specially doctored HTML code. This code modifies the item listing so that when an eBay user bids on the item, the bidder's eBay user name and password are secretly emailed to a third party—who can then use this information to post new auctions and place bids under the victim's name.

eBay characterizes the hole as an "occasional byproduct" of the service's user-focused design.

For what it's worth, these types of security holes seem to be common occurrences on e-commerce Web sites and with the latest generation of feature-rich Web browsers.

eBay is not unique in having such problems, although it's still a little unnerving just how easily eBay's security can be compromised.

System Outages: How Can You Bid When the Site Is Down?

What do you do when you there's five minutes left in an auction, you're ready to make that final bid, and all of a sudden, you can't access the eBay Web site?

System outages, which prevent both buyers and sellers from accessing in-process auctions, have been plaguing eBay as it tries to cope with its massive growth. It's natural, I suppose, for large masses of users to simply overwhelm the eBay's Web servers, but on a site where timing has a critical impact on winning and losing, sluggish performance can cost users big bucks.

What does eBay say about system outages? It offers an Automatic Auction Extension Policy for any "hard" system-wide outage lasting two or more hours. When the whole system goes down, eBay automatically extends for 24 hours any auctions scheduled to end during or in the hour after the outage.

What if it's only you who can't get into the system? Because the problem could be anywhere between you and them (across the entire Internet), eBay says it's not its problem. So if you have a flaky ISP, you could be in trouble.

Customer Service: How Responsive Is eBay to Customer Complaints?

You have a problem with fraud. Or you spot an illegal item. Or you have your user name stolen. Or you can't log on to the site during a crucial bidding period. So you decide to complain to eBay.

Good luck.

eBay's customer service department is extremely overwhelmed. It fields more than 65,000 email questions every week and often takes days—or longer—to manage a simple response. If you need immediate help, you're probably not going to get it.

The company-recommended alternative is to post your question on one of eBay's support message boards, such as the General Support Q&A board. The problem is that if eBay doesn't like your question (or the way you ask it), you could be kicked off the service!

There have been several reports of users getting suspended from eBay because of "inappropriate" (eBay's words) comments they posted publicly on the General Support Q&A board. What eBay deemed "inappropriate" ranged from criticisms of management to references to recent press coverage, all in response to a recent system outage.

On one hand, eBay says to use the Q&A board instead of emailing; on the other hand, it tells you not to air your complaints publicly on the Q&A board. Which is it, guys?

Putting It All in Perspective

Let's put all this in perspective. Because of its soaring popularity, eBay is experiencing almost unmanageable growth in terms of both users and listings. It's hard to keep your head above water when you're growing that fast. So it's possible—in fact, it's probable—that the majority of eBay's problems are byproducts of this rapid growth.

To be fair, even at its worst, buying something through eBay is no less safe than buying something at a local garage sale or through a newspaper classified ad—or through another online auction site.

Yes, it's unnerving to read of some of these issues, and it's downright disturbing to realize just what some users can get away with if they try hard enough. But the majority of eBay users have had nothing but positive experiences on the site. After all, almost four million active users can't be all wrong.

The Least You Need to Know

➤ Several activities are discouraged yet not forbidden by eBay—including sniping and backing out of in-process and completed auctions.

➤ Many more activities are forbidden on eBay, yet some users still actively engage in them—such as shill bidding, bid shielding, and bid siphoning.

➤ Perhaps because of eBay's rapid growth, it has been accused of all manner of undesirable activities, from committing fraud to selling illegal merchandise to discriminating against users who complain too much.

➤ On balance, eBay offers most users a positive experience, day in and day out.

Part 4

Buy Low, Sell High: Secrets of Successful Online Auctioneers

This is the part of the book you've been waiting for. Do you want to know how to virtually guarantee a winning bid on that special item? Do you want to know how to win an auction without bidding a single penny more than you have to? Do you want to know how to get the highest bids possible for the merchandise you're selling? If you answered yes to any of these questions, read the chapters in this section. You'll learn the secrets and strategies that will put you a step ahead of other online auction users—with a few extra bucks in your pocket, to boot!

Chapter 22

Winning an Auction: Strategies for Buyers

In This Chapter

➤ Discover the two major strategies for winning online auctions

➤ Uncover the secrets employed by successful online bidders

➤ Learn how to snipe, step by step

You want to be a player. You want to bid with the best of them. When you bid, you want to win. When you win, you don't want to overpay.

This is the chapter you've been waiting for. Discover the secrets and strategies that will help you be a successful online auction bidder!

Two Different Strategies for Success

You can adopt two major strategies when bidding in online auctions:

➤ The early bidder strategy
➤ The late bidder strategy

Both have their adherents, and both can win auctions. Which one you use depends as much on your personality as it does on the merits of the strategies themselves.

Supporters of the early bidder strategy claim that by establishing yourself early as a dominant player, you can scare off other bidders and leave yourself a clear playing field. Critics of this strategy maintain that all you really end up doing is bidding up the price earlier, and they point out that early bidders are still vulnerable to sniping.

Supporters of the late bidder strategy claim that by not tipping your hand until that last possible moment, you avoid bidding up the price and don't give competitors time to react to your bid. Critics of this strategy question what happens to the price when there are multiple snipers in the same auction, and they just generally complain about the unfairness of not being able to respond to last-minute bids.

Anti-Sniping Sites

Of course, you can't use the late bidder strategy with some auction sites, such as Auction Universe and Yahoo! Auctions. Unlike eBay, these sites actually extend the close of any auction that has last-minute bidding; if sniping continues at every five-minute extension, the auction might never end!

The Early Bidder Strategy—Bid First, Bid High, Bid Often

The thinking behind the early bidder strategy is to establish yourself as a player early and to scare off other potential bidders with your aggressiveness. With this strategy, you want to bid early and high, therefore intimidating other bidders—because no matter what they bid, your high bid keeps going higher, by proxy. If your bid happens to be topped mid-auction, you want to immediately answer that with a higher bid. Your actions tell other bidders that this item is yours and that they'd better back off.

Let's look at an example of this strategy in action:

1. You see a new item listed that you want to buy. Its minimum bid price is $10; you think others will value the item up to $20, although you're willing to pay up to $25 for it.

2. You immediately place a bid for $25. Then, you sit back and monitor the progress of the auction—hourly, if you can.

3. You see other bidders make a stab at the item, but their bids don't top your maximum bid. (You can tell this because the current bid keeps increasing; it started at $10 but goes up with each subsequent bid.) The current bid rises to $12, to $15, to $18, to $20, and then to $25—your maximum bid.

4. Now is when you go on red alert. The next bid will top your bid, which means action will be required. When you see the bid go above your maximum—let's say it goes to $26—you immediately enter a new bid for $30. If you time it right,

that temporary high bidder will get a notice of his high bid, followed within minutes by an outbid notice. Your rapid strike sends a message to your opponent: You won't be beaten in this auction!

5. You continue in this fashion until the auction is over, at which point you have probably scared off most other interested bidders. With this strategy, most of the action comes in the middle of the auction; by the time the auction ends, there's nobody left standing but you.

Using this strategy requires that you scan the new auctions in your favorite categories daily—if not several times a day. You want your bid to be the first bid on the item and the last.

In addition, this strategy requires constant vigilance. You need to constantly track the status of your auctions, and some sort of auction-tracking software might be useful. (For constant monitoring, check out AuctionTicker, discussed in Chapter 24, "Tracking Your Auctions with Auction Management Software.")

If you play this strategy properly, you will become a feared and respected bidding pro. Other bidders will automatically withdraw from the contest when they see your name. You will be not unlike the famous gunslingers in the old west, intimidating your opponents with the sheer force of your reputation.

Use this power wisely.

The Late Bidder Strategy—Be Sneaky and Snipe

The late bidder strategy is the exact opposite of the early bidder strategy. With this strategy, stealth and subterfuge are required to disguise your interest, as is the patience to hold your bid until the last possible moment. No one must know that you want this item, no one can suspect what you are willing to bid, and no one can be prepared for your last-minute strike against the people who've been bidding throughout the life of the auction.

You must be like the wind and strike like lightning.

The thinking behind this strategy is simple. By not disclosing your interest, you don't contribute to bidding up the price during the course of the auction. By bidding at the last minute, you don't leave enough time for other bidders to respond to your bid. The late bidder makes one bid only—and makes it count.

Let's look at an example of late bidding:

1. You find an item you want and make a note of the time the auction closes—to the second. Then, you arrange your schedule so that you're free when you need to bid.

2. Five minutes before the auction closes, you log on to the Internet and access the auction in question. You note the current bid price; let's say it's $25. You feel that a $30 bid will safely win the auction, so you prepare a maximum bid of $30.

3. With about 30 seconds left in the auction, you send your bid. You immediately pop up as the high bidder in the auction—and then the auction closes. By the time the former high bidder gets the auction's automatic outbid notice via email, the auction is already over—and you've won!

The experienced late bidder doesn't even look at new auctions listed today. Instead, you want to scan the auctions that are closing today. Then, you need to plan the timing of your bid; you'll need to be at your computer, logged on to the Internet and at the auction in question, ready to press the button at just the right moment.

For this strategy to be successful, you need split-second timing and fast reflexes. Some late bidders find that their success is enhanced by the use of automated sniping software, such as BidSniper Pro. (For details on this and other automated sniping software, check out Chapter 24.)

This whole process of swooping in at the last possible moment is called sniping. Some bidders (those who don't snipe!) despise sniping, saying it takes all the fun out of the auction process. Experienced snipers say that sniping itself is fun, that it can be kind of a game to see just how late you can bid and still make it count before the auction closes.

Whether you like it or not, sniping works. After all, if you place a high enough bid at the last second, there's no time for anyone to respond with a higher bid. The last high bidder always wins, and a sniper stands a very good chance of being the last high bidder.

Can a sniper lose an auction? Yes, under these scenarios:

➤ First, there might be another sniper in the queue who places a higher snipe than your maximum bid. A last-second bid of $35 will beat out a last-second bid of $30.

➤ Second, your snipe might be too early, allowing time for the previous high bidder to receive an outbid notice and respond with a higher bid.

➤ Third, your snipe might not be high enough to beat out an existing high bid. If the current bid is $25 but the high bid (not known to you) is $35, you'd be beat if you "only" bid $30.

➤ Fourth, you might be participating in an auction (such as those on Auction Universe or Yahoo! Auctions) that automatically extends the auction close because of last-minute bidding—making your last-minute bid not really a last-minute bid.

If you've ever been outbid on an item at the very last moment, you know that sniping can win auctions. Even if you hate sniping, the only way to beat a sniper is to snipe yourself.

Successful Sniping, Step by Step

Want to learn how to deliver killer snipes, auction after auction? Here's a step-by-step guide to always get your bid in just under the bell. In following these steps, know that the optimum timing for a snipe is 10 seconds before the auction's close; it's simply impossible for anyone else to respond in that short amount of time.

1. Don't bid! Resist the temptation to place a bid when you first notice an item. Make a note of the auction (and its closing time), but don't let anyone else know your intentions.

2. Five minutes before the close of the auction, log on to the Internet, and access the auction in question.

3. Open a second browser window to the auction in question. (Both Internet Explorer and Netscape Navigator let you open more than one browser at a time; with your main browser already open, just launch the browser again.)

4. Display the Windows clock on your desktop, and configure it to display both minutes and seconds. (Conversely, just grab a watch with a second hand or a stopwatch.)

5. In your first browser window, enter your maximum bid and click the submit button to display the confirmation screen. *Don't confirm the bid yet!* Wait on the confirmation screen....

6. In your second browser window, press the refresh or reload button to update the official auction time. Keep doing this until the time remaining until close is 60 seconds.

7. Now, using either the Windows clock or your watch or stopwatch, count down 50 seconds, until there are only 10 seconds left in the auction. (You might want to confirm the synchronization midway through your countdown by refreshing your second browser window again.)

8. When exactly 10 seconds are left in the auction, click the Confirm Bid button in your first browser window to send your bid.

9. Wait 10 seconds, and then press the refresh or reload button in your second browser window. The auction should now be closed, and (if your sniping was successful) you should be listed as the winning bidder.

continues

continued

Why bid 10 seconds before close? It takes about this long to transmit the bid from your computer to the online auction site and for the bid to be registered. If you bid any earlier than this, you leave time for the auction to send an outbid notice to the previous high bidder—and you don't want that person to know that until it's too late to do anything about it.

30 Sure-Fire Tips for Placing a Winning Bid—And Getting the Most for Your Money

Whichever strategy you employ, you can do other things to increase your chances of winning an auction without overpaying for the item in question. I describe 30 tips that can help anyone be a better bidder at any online auction.

Tip #1: Search eBay—Second

eBay has so much traffic that you quite often find yourself competing with a large number of bidders for the item you want. The more competing bidders, the higher the final price—that is, the more you end up paying if you're the winning bidder. The thing is, if you could find a similar item on a less popular auction site, you'd be competing with fewer bidders—and the final price would likely be lower.

Before you automatically start searching eBay for the item you want, check out some of the smaller auction sites first. Try Auction Universe, Yahoo! Auctions, Amazon.com Auctions, or Classifieds 2000 Auctions. If (and that's a big if, considering that less traffic also equals fewer items listed) you can find what you want there, you'll stand a better chance of winning the auction at a lower price.

Tip #2: Do Your Research

Don't bid blind; make sure you know the true value of an item before you offer a bid. Look around at other auctions of similar items; what prices are they going for? Research the price of similar items offline; sometimes, you can find what you're looking for at a discount store or in a catalog or at another online site—where you'll probably get a real warranty and a better return policy. Shop around, and don't assume that the price you see at an auction is always the best deal available.

Be informed, and you won't bid too high—or too low.

Tip #3: Don't Bid on the First Item You See

Probably several other items on the same auction site are similar to the first item you saw. Look at the entire list of items before you choose which one to bid on. Seldom is the first item you see the one you really want or the best deal.

Tip #4: Know When to Say No

Be disciplined! Set a maximum price you're willing to pay for an item, and *don't exceed it!* It's okay to lose an auction.

Don't automatically rebid just because you've been outbid. It's too easy to get caught up in the excitement of a fast-paced auction. Learn how to keep your cool; know when to say no.

Tip #5: Don't Let the Robots Bid Things Up

If two or more people are bidding on the same item, the proxy bidding software used by most online auctions can automatically (and quickly) rocket up the price until the bidder with the lower maximum bid maxes out. It's kind of an automated bidding frenzy conducted by two mindless robots.

Some bidders refuse to participate in proxy bidding. If the price is to increase, they want to do it manually. How do you defeat the automatic bidding software? Simple—make sure your maximum bid is the same price as the next incremental bid and no higher. It might take a bit more work, but it puts you in total control of the bidding process.

Tip #6: There Are Other Fish in the Sea

In 99.9 percent of the auctions, that "one-of-a-kind" item really isn't one-of-a-kind. In fact, some sellers (especially merchant sellers) will have multiple quantities of an item, which they release to auction in dribs and drabs over time. In addition, some collectibles are bought and sold and bought and sold by multiple buyers and sellers over time, continually changing hands via new auctions. If you don't get this particular item, there's a good chance you'll get to bid on something similar soon.

Tip #7: If It Sounds Too Good to Be True, It Probably Is

A rare copy of *Action Comics* #1 for only $25? A brand-new Pentium II computer for only $100? There has to be a catch. That *Action Comics* is probably a facsimile reprint, and the brand-new Pentium II is actually a remanufactured unit missing some key parts. Be suspicious of improbable or impossible deals; always ask questions that confirm or reject your suspicions.

Tip #8: Ask Questions

If you're unclear about any aspect of an item you're interested in, ask the seller a question via email. In addition to answering your specific question, some sellers have additional information or pictures they can send you one-on-one. There's no excuse for ignorance; if you're not sure, ask!

Tip #9: Check the Feedback

Check out the seller's feedback rating. Make sure the seller of the item you want has a good feedback rating—and avoid any who don't. On eBay, click the seller's numerical feedback rating to display actual comments from other users who have dealt with this user before. The best way to avoid bad sellers is to find out that they're bad sellers beforehand.

Tip #10: Search; Don't Browse

If you know what you're looking for, don't go through the time-consuming hassle of clicking and loading and clicking and loading to access a particular item category. Using an auction's search function will find what you want a lot quicker.

Tip #11: Search Smart

Searching for an item on eBay or Auction Universe is easy; finding what you really want is hard. You're more likely to find what you're looking for if you can use the auction site's advanced search capabilities to fine-tune your query. Some specific search tips can help you perform more effective—and efficient—searches:

➤ **Use advanced options.** Almost every auction site offers some sort of advanced search page. Find it and use it. These advanced searches typically offer a lot more options that you can use to fine-tune your search on that site.

➤ **Narrow your search.** Some of the more popular categories on big sites such as eBay will list thousands of items. If you do a search on **beanie baby**, you'll be overwhelmed by the results; narrow your search within these large categories to better describe the specific item you're looking for.

➤ **Make your queries precise—but not too precise**. When you're deciding which keywords to use, pick words that are precise, but not overly restrictive. If you must use a very general word, modify it with a more specific word—or you're apt to generate a huge number of results that have little relevance to the specific information you're searching for. As an example, **model** is a pretty general keyword; **Star Wars Death Star model** is a much more precise query. On the other hand, if you search for an **old Star Wars Death Star model partially assembled without instructions not painted**, you probably won't return any matching results. If you get fewer results than you want, take some of the parameters out of your query to broaden your search.

➤ **Get the right order.** When constructing your query, put the important stuff up front. Put keywords or phrases that describe your main subject at the start of your query; put less important words and phrases last. Search engines search for the first words first and rank results according to how they match these more important keywords.

➤ **Use wildcards.** If you're not sure of spelling, use a wildcard to replace the letters in question. Also, wildcards help you find variations on a keyword. For example, if you want Superman, Supergirl, and Superdog, enter **super*** to find all super words.

➤ **Truncate**. If you're not sure whether you're looking for plurals or singulars, then truncate your words and use wildcards. For example, search for **bab*** to return either a single baby or multiple babies.

➤ **Vary your vocabulary—and your spelling.** Don't assume that everyone spells a given word the same way—or knows how to spell it properly. Also, don't forget about synonyms. What you call pink, someone else might call mauve. What's big to you might be large to someone else. Think of all the ways the item you're looking for can be described, and include as many of them as possible in your query.

➤ **Fine-tune your results.** Did the search engine return an overwhelming number of matching items? If so, you need to fine-tune your search to be more specific. Look at the results generated from your initial search. Think about the good matches and the bad matches and why they ended up in the results list. Then, enter a new query that uses additional or different keywords and modifiers. Your goal is to make the next list of results a higher quality than the last.

➤ **Different day, different results.** Remember that new items are constantly added to any given auction site, and closed auctions are constantly removed from the listings. If you didn't find anything that matched your query today, try again tomorrow; you'll probably find a different list of items for sale.

More Search Secrets? Read the Book!

If you want to learn even more secrets of effective searchers, read my new Que book, *The Complete Idiot's Guide to Online Search Secrets*. It's jam-packed with more than 400 pages of secrets, strategies, and shortcuts to help you find just about anything on the Internet.

Tip #12: Search for Last-Minute Bargains

Check an auction site's "auctions ending today" page for the best buys. Scan the list for items with no bids or few bids, and pick off some bargains that have slipped others' attention.

Tip #13: Bid in Odd Numbers

When you bid, don't bid an even amount. Instead, bid a few pennies more than an even buck; for example, if you want to bid $10, bid $10.03 instead. That way, your bid will beat any bids at the same approximate amount—$10.03 beats $10 even, any day—without you having to place a new bid at the next whole bid increment.

Tip #14: Don't Be a Deadbeat

Don't bid unless you really intend to buy. Nobody likes a deadbeat—and if you do it often enough, you'll get kicked off the auction site, permanently.

Tip #15: Keep Track of Your Auctions

Don't let your auction activity get away from you. Use the auction's standard buyer listing pages to look at all your auctions on a daily basis, or use auction management software to track your auctions automatically.

Tip #16: Use My eBay

If you're an eBay user, the best way to track all your auction activity on a single page is via My eBay. My eBay can also track your favorite auction categories, as well as your account status—and let you access the pages you use most often, without having to click through useless parts of the site. Personalize My eBay the way you like and then bookmark it; it's a great home page for the heavy auction trader.

(Most major auction sites have their own equivalents of My eBay, personalizable pages you can use to track your activity on their sites.)

Tip #17: Read the Fine Print

What methods of payment can you use? What about shipping? Any other details that might impact your decision to bid? Read the entire item listing before you place your bid—so you don't get surprised by the fine print in any auction.

Tip #18: Don't Forget Shipping Costs...

When you're placing your bid, remember that you'll actually have to pay more than you bid; you have to pay shipping and handling to put the item in your hands. If S/H costs aren't detailed in the item listing, figure them out yourself, or email the seller to get a reasonable estimate. That ultra-cheap $2 item looks pretty expensive if you have to add $5 shipping and handling to the base price.

Tip #19: ...But Don't Overpay for Shipping

Not only should you not get taken by surprise by shipping costs, but you also shouldn't be taken advantage of by unrealistic shipping and handling charges. Get a ballpark feel for shipping on a specific item from the seller's location to where you live. Expect a little overage on the seller's part (she has to buy packing materials, labels, and such), but not too much of an overage. If you know shipping should be in the $2 range, accept a $3 charge—but question a $5 charge.

Tip #20: Money Orders Cost Money

The seller says that money orders or cashier checks speed shipment. Depending on your bank, it might cost a few dollars to cut a money order or cashier's check. Make sure you factor these costs into your total expenditure—and question whether you really want to pay to cut a money order for a $5 item.

Tip #21: Watch the Finish

Don't get outbid at the last minute. Most auction activity occurs at the very end of the auction. Track the last hour of your most important auctions, and be prepared to react quickly to last-second bidders and snipers.

Tip #22: Use a Middle Man for Expensive Items

If you buy a high-priced item through a person-to-person auction, consider using an escrow service. Although you'll pay for the service (in the neighborhood of 5 percent, typically paid by the buyer), it's a good safety net in case the seller doesn't ship or the item isn't what was described. In addition, you can use escrow services to accept credit card payments when the seller doesn't or can't accept credit cards directly.

Tip #23: Ship It Safe

If you bought a rare or high-priced item, ask the seller to insure the item for shipping. Pay the extra cost; it's worth it in peace of mind alone.

Tip #24: Pay Quickly

Don't delay—*pay!* Look, the seller needs the money, and the sooner you pay, the sooner you'll get what you paid for.

Tip #25: Document Everything

In case something goes south, it helps to have good records of all aspects of your transaction. Print copies of the confirmation email, plus all email between you and the seller. Make sure you write down the seller's user ID, email address, and physical address. If the transaction is ever disputed, you'll have all the backup you need to plead your case.

Tip #26: Communicate!

Don't assume anything; communicate what you think you know. If you have questions during an auction, ask them. When the auction is over, email the seller. When the seller emails you, email him or her back to confirm. Email the seller when you send payment and again to confirm receipt of the item. The more everyone knows, the fewer surprises there are.

Also, remember that not everyone reads his or her email daily, so don't expect immediate response. Still, if you don't receive a response, send another email. If you're at all concerned at any point, get the seller's phone number or physical address from the auction site and call or write him or her. A good phone conversation can clear up a wealth of misunderstandings.

Tip #27: Be Nice

You're dealing with another human being, someone who has feelings that can be hurt. A little bit of common courtesy goes a long way. Say please and thank you, be understanding and tolerant, and treat your trading partner in the same way you'd like to be treated. Follow the golden rule; do unto other auction traders as you would have them do unto you.

Tip #28: If You Win It, Inspect It

When you receive the item you paid for, open it up and inspect it—*immediately!* Don't wait a month before you look at it and then expect the seller to rectify a situation that was long considered closed. Okay the item, and then send the seller an email saying you got it and it's okay. If you sit on it too long, it's yours—no matter what.

Tip #29: If You Get Ripped Off, Tell the Auction Site About It

If you have a problem with a seller, first try working it out between the two of you. If things don't get resolved, then contact the auction site with your grievance. Most sites have formal procedures to work out these kinds of problems; if nothing else, you can leave negative feedback and let other users know about a bad seller. If worse comes to worst, don't hesitate to contact your local or state authorities about a really bad transaction—and make sure the auction site knows that you're doing so.

The Most Important Tip for Participating in Online Auctions

Have fun!

Tip #30: Use All the Tools at Your Disposal

You have many tools available to help you experience a pleasant and successful auction. Use all the tools the auction site provides, use email to contact the seller directly, use meta-auction sites to conduct cross-site searches, and use auction management software to help you track your in-process auctions. You don't have to go it alone; use any and all things that help you bid smarter and more successfully.

The Least You Need to Know

➤ Experienced online bidders follow two major strategies: early bidder and late bidder.

➤ With the early bidder strategy, you bid early, bid high, and respond immediately if you're outbid; the goal is to intimidate other bidders and force them to exit the auction early.

➤ With the late bidder strategy, you don't bid at all until the very last seconds of an auction; the goal is to leave other bidders no time to respond to your last-minute bid.

➤ Sniping—a literal last-second bid—is the tool of choice for late bidders.

Chapter 23

How to Get the Most for Your Merchandise: Strategies for Sellers

---

In This Chapter

➤ Discover the two major strategies for selling via online auctions

➤ Learn how to stand out from the two million other items up for auction

➤ Uncover the secrets employed by successful online sellers

You have things to sell. You want to make sure you actually sell them and that you get the highest price possible. But you're also competing with more than two million other items up for auction at the same time. How do you stand out from the crowd, attract a bunch of bidders, and goose up the high bids?

This chapter is for you. Discover the secrets and strategies that will help you be a successful online auction seller!

Two Different Strategies for Success

You can adopt two major strategies when putting an item up for auction:

➤ **The high road strategy** Supporters of the high road strategy go after bidders who don't mind paying a little more for something good. Your's won't be the cheapest item on auction, but it will be the best—in terms of value to the ultimate buyer. Whether it's the rarity of your item, its superior condition, or your superior service, you have to make it worth the bidders' while to pay a little bit more. Better stuff commands higher prices.

➤ **The low road strategy** Supporters of the low road strategy sell on price. They give buyers a lot for their money, in terms of quantity—but not necessarily quality. A low price grabs the bidders' attention, even if the merchandise is a little ordinary. Lower prices move more merchandise.

Both have their strengths and weaknesses, and which one you use depends on the type of item you have for sale, your competition, and your own way of doing things.

The High Road—High Price, High Quality, High Value

Use the high road strategy when you have something truly unique to sell. Maybe it's an ultra-rare Beanie Baby, a mint-condition stamp, or a complete run of a certain comic book or magazine. Whatever—position your item as one-of-a-kind and high quality, and set your initial price accordingly.

When you create your high road item listing, make it classy. Include a lot of details, and play up its rare and unique nature. Put "rare" in the title, and include at least one good-quality picture of your item. Consider making your item a featured auction. Try to attract the elite buyers with everything you do.

When you price your high road item, price it high enough to weed out the riff-raff. Price it high enough that serious buyers take you seriously. Price it high enough that you don't get a lot of initial bids.

When you list your high road item, make sure you back up the quality with superior support. Tell your bidders that you provide insurance with your shipping and that you offer a 30-day money-back guarantee. Solicit their email questions—and then answer them promptly. And follow through on your promises; make sure the end-of-auction communication is prompt, courteous, and complete. Ship the item in a new (that is, not re-used) box as quickly as possible.

When taking the high road, present the illusion of quality—and perception will become reality. The result will be higher bids from higher-class online auction citizens.

The Low Road—Low Price and a Lot of Excitement

Use the low road strategy when you want to generate a lot of attention fast—or when you have an item that is more common than it is rare. You want to grab bidders' attention with a low price and hope the resulting bidding frenzy will increase the price to a more acceptable level.

When you set your low road price, think cheap. Think really cheap. Think so ridiculously cheap that bidders would be crazy not to go for it. You want to get the bidding going fast, so your initial price should be significantly lower than what you expect the item to sell for. As a good rule of thumb, set your opening bid at 10 percent of the amount you expect the item to sell for. (For example, if you expect the item to sell for $100, your opening bid should be $10.)

When you create your low road item listing, be a salesman. Scream the deal at your potential bidders, and use every trick at your disposal to grab their attention. Use HTML to create an ad with bright colors, large fonts, and sizzling graphics. Put a lot of salesy buzzwords in your title, such as "new" and "free" and "deal." Consider throwing in other items to create an irresistible value pack—"three for the price of one" sort of stuff. Do everything in your power to attract the price shopper and the value hunter.

When taking the low road, you want to generate excitement, which will generate activity, which will generate bids.

Didn't Sell Your Item? You're Not Alone!

The "close rate" at most online auctions is around 50 percent—which means that half the items listed at any given time receive no bids and don't sell. This rate seems to be similar whether you're dealing with eBay, Auction Universe, Amazon, or one of the little guys. If you're closing more than half your items on their first listing, you're doing quite well; if you're closing less than half, you might want to rethink your listing and pricing strategies.

30 Sure-Fire Tips for Increasing Your Auction Revenues

Whichever strategy you employ, you can do other things to increase your chances of selling your item at the highest possible price. Here are 30 tips that can help anyone be a more profitable seller at any online auction.

Tip #1: Find the Right Site

Find the best auction site for your item. Don't automatically assume eBay will be the best site. For some items, Yahoo! Auctions or Auction Universe might be better—or you might even want a more specialized auction. Look around before you place your listing; look for where you find the most similar items selling for the highest prices.

Tip #2: Research Your Price

Don't sell without doing your homework first; make sure you know the true value of an item before you put it up for auction. Before you price your item, search for similar items at your chosen auction site. What are they priced? What are their final selling prices? Research the price of similar items offline; sometimes, you can get a feel for relative value if you compare your item to a newer version of the same. Be informed, and you won't set the price too high or too low; you'll set it just right.

Tip #3: Make Your Ad Stand Out

Do everything in your power to make your ad stand out from the two million other ads currently online. Work on both the title and the description, and consider employing HTML to create a more dynamic ad. (See Chapter 20, "Pretty Up Your eBay Ads with HTML," for more tips.)

Tip #4: Get All the Buzzwords in the Title

Make sure you have the right words and phrases in your title. If your audience looks for "laser discs," then say **laser disc**; if they look for "LDs," then say **LD**. If they look for both, then use both. Use all possible words (up to your auction's character limit) to hit all possible keywords your potential bidders might be searching for—even if some of the words are redundant.

Tip #5: A Picture Says a Thousand Words

Nothing increases your chances of selling an item like including a picture of it in your listing. Take a photo of your item, scan it in, upload it, and include it with your listing—even if it's just a plain text (non-HTML) listing.

Tip #6: Be Descriptive

Include as much descriptive text about your item as you can. The better you describe your item, the fewer mid-auction emails you'll get asking about it and the greater the chance that your ultimate buyer won't get any unpleasant surprises. In addition, you never know when that single "unimportant" detail is just the thing a specific bidder is looking for—so don't overlook any detail, no matter how small.

Also, don't forget to include all the details about shipping and handling (how much and who pays), payment methods, and the like. Don't leave anything open to interpretation.

Tip #7: Start and End in Prime Time

When you start your auction is important—because that effects when your auction *ends*. If you start a seven-day auction at 6:00 p.m. on a Saturday, it will end exactly seven days later, at 6:00 p.m. the following Saturday.

Why is when your auction ends important? Because some of the most intense bidding takes place in the final few minutes of your auction, from snipers trying to steal the high bid at the last possible moment. To take advantage of last-minute bidders, your auction needs to end when the most possible bidders are online.

If you end your auction at 3:00 in the morning, everyone will be asleep and you'll lose out on any last-minute bids. Instead, try to end your auction during early evening hours, when the most number of users are online.

Remember, though, that you're dealing with a three-hour time-zone gap between the east and the west coasts. So if you time your auction to end at 7:00 p.m. EST, you're ending at 4:00 p.m. PST—when most potential bidders are still at work. Conversely, if you choose to end at 9:00 p.m. PST, you just hit midnight in New York—and many potential bidders are already fast asleep.

The best times to end—and thus to *start*—your auction are between 9:00 p.m. and 11:00 p.m. EST, or between 6:00 p.m. and 8:00 p.m. PST. (Figure the in-between time zones yourself!) That way you'll catch the most potential bidders online for the final minutes of your auction—and possibly generate a bidding frenzy that will garner a higher price for your merchandise!

Tip #8: Be Honest

Be honest in your description of the item. If the item has a few flaws, mention them. Misleading a buyer will only cause you grief.

Tip #9: Link to More Information—And More Auctions

If you have more information available than you can put in the formal description, include a link to it in the listing. If you have a personal Web site that happens to list other items you have for sale, link to it. The more links, the merrier.

Tip #10: Make the Buyer Pay

Stipulate in your listing that the buyer pays all shipping and handling costs (and you might even want to detail these costs ahead of time in your listing). Also, make sure the buyer pays for any "extras" that might be added after the sale. If the buyer wants insurance, the buyer pays for it. If the buyer wants to use an escrow service, the buyer pays for it. If the buyer wants expedited shipping, the buyer pays for it. See the trend?

Tip #11: Go Long...

When it comes time to choose the length for your auction, go for the longest auction possible. The longer your item is up for auction, the more potential bidders who will see it—and the more potential bidders, the better your chances of selling it for a higher price. Don't cheat yourself out of potential sales by choosing a shorter auction.

Tip #12: ...Or Create a Short-Term Frenzy

On the other hand, if you have something really hot, create a bidding frenzy by choosing a very short auction length. If you do this, play it up in your item's title: **3 Days Only!** works pretty well.

Tip #13: There's No Reason to Reserve

I don't know of a single bidder who likes reserve price auctions. Why use something that scares some bidders away? Set a realistic minimum, and get on with it.

Tip #14: Single Items Are Best...

If you're looking for the highest total dollar, don't group items together. Lots seldom bring as much money as individual items sold individually.

Tip #15: ...Although You Can Unload Some Dogs in a Pack

On the other hand, if you have a lot of things to sell, selling in lots can reduce your personal overhead, as well as help you unload some less attractive items that you probably couldn't sell individually.

Tip #16: Don't Compete Against Yourself

If five people are looking to buy footstools today, don't give them five choices all from one person (you). If you have five footstools to sell, don't sell them all at once. Sell one this week, one next week, and one the week after that. Spread it out to create an illusion of scarcity, and you'll generate more total revenue.

Tip #17: Promote Your Auctions

Let people outside of your online auction site know about your auction. Mention your auction in relevant newsgroups and mailing lists; feature it on your personal Web site and send emails about it to all your friends. Include your item listing's URL in everything you do so anyone interested can click the link to view your auction. Do anything you can think of to draw traffic to your listing—and thus increase your chances of selling it.

Tip #18: Track Your Auctions

Don't let your auction activity get away from you. Use the auction's standard seller listing pages to look at all your auctions on a daily basis, or use auction management software to track your auctions automatically.

Tip #19: Use My eBay

If you're an eBay user, the best way to track all your auction activity on a single page is via My eBay. My eBay can also track your favorite auction categories, as well as your account status—and let you access the pages you use most often, without having to click through useless parts of the site. Personalize My eBay the way you like and then bookmark it; it's a great home page for the heavy auction trader.

(Most major auction sites have their own equivalents of My eBay, personalizable pages you can use to track your activity on their sites.)

Tip #20: Avoid Premature Cancellation

Know that many bidders wait until the very last minute to place a bid. (It's called sniping, and it's discussed in Chapter 22, "Winning an Auction: Strategies for Buyers.") If you cancel an auction early, you'll miss out on the bulk of the potential bids. So don't cancel!

Tip #21: Avoid Deadbeats

You don't have to sell to just anybody. You can stipulate that you won't sell to bidders with negative feedback or with feedback ratings below a certain level. If you receive bids from these potential deadbeats, cancel them. If the deadbeats continue to bid (after being warned off via email by you), then notify your auction site. You want to sell to someone who will actually consummate the transaction and send you payment; bidders with negative feedback are more likely to leave you high and dry.

Tip #22: Include All Your Shipping Costs

When figuring your shipping and handling costs, make sure you factor in all your costs—not just the shipping itself, but also the cost of the packaging, the labels, and the packing tape. Don't gouge your buyer (this isn't meant to be a profit center), but don't cheat yourself, either. If actual shipping costs are $3, think about charging the buyer $4 to cover your additional costs.

Tip #23: Use a Middle Man for Expensive Items

If you're selling a high-priced item, consider offering the buyer the option of using an escrow service. It's a good deal for you; the buyer pays for the service (in the neighborhood of 5 percent, typically), it provides a level of peace of mind for the buyer, and it lets you accept credit card payments that you otherwise couldn't accept.

Tip #24: Document Everything

In case something goes south, it helps to have good records of all aspects of your transaction. Print copies of the confirmation email, plus all email between you and the buyer. Make sure you write down the buyer's user ID, email address, and physical address. If the transaction is ever disputed, you'll have all the backup you need to plead your case.

Tip #25: Communicate!

Don't assume anything; communicate what you think you know. When the auction is over, email the winning bidder as soon as possible. Send a letter that reads something like this:

> Congratulations!
>
> You are the winning bidder on auction item number *123456, "Frizzbot Diddly Things."* Please send *$00.00 ($00.00 + $0.00* shipping/handling) to
>
> *Your Name*
> *Your Address*
> *Your City, State, and Zip*
>
> Please include your address and a copy of this email with your payment. Money order or cashier's check gets immediate shipment via *Preferred Shipping Method;* payment by check holds shipment for 10 working days.
>
> Please respond to this email (and include your address, please) to confirm your winning bid.
>
> Thanks again,
>
> *Your Name*

Email the buyer again when you receive payment and once more when you're ready to ship the item. The more everyone knows, the fewer surprises there are.

Also, remember that not everyone reads his or her email daily, so don't expect an immediate response. Still, if you don't receive a response, send another email. If you're at all concerned at any point, get the buyer's phone number or physical address from the auction site and call or write him. A good phone conversation can clear up a wealth of misunderstandings.

Tip #26: Be Nice

Remember that you're dealing with another human being, someone who has feelings that can be hurt. A little bit of common courtesy goes a long way. Say please and thank you, be understanding and tolerant, and treat your trading partner in the same way you'd like to be treated. Follow the golden rule; do unto other auction traders as you would have them do unto you.

Tip #27: Ship Promptly

Ship promptly after you've received payment (and after the check has cleared). Nobody likes to wait too long for something they've paid for.

Tip #28: If Nobody Buys, Relist—With a Different Listing

If you didn't sell your item the first time, try it again. Many auction sites let you relist unsold items at no additional charge; even if you have to pay again, you still want to sell the item, right? But remember that if it didn't sell the first time, there was probably a reason why. Was your asking price too high? Was your description too vague? Was the title too boring? Should you have included a picture or used HTML to spice up the listing? Whatever you change, change something to increase your chances of selling your item the second time around.

Tip #29: If You Get Stiffed, Ask for a Refund—And Don't Forget About Number Two

If you haven't been paid within three weeks, you can try to sell the item to the next highest bidder, if he's still interested. It never hurts to ask, in any case; just send the second-place bidder an email explaining that the high bidder was a deadbeat, and you still have the item if he's interested. If you're totally stiffed, contact your auction site for a refund of its selling fees—and to complain about the deadbeat who didn't pay. (And don' forget to leave detailed negative feedback about any deadbeat bidders!)

Tip #30: Use All the Tools at Your Disposal

You have many tools available to help you experience a pleasant and successful auction. Use all the tools the auction site provides, and use auction management software to help you track your auctions and automate your post-auction communications and activities. You don't have to go it alone; use any and all things that help you sell smarter and more successfully.

The Least You Need to Know

➤ Experienced online sellers follow two major strategies: the high road and the low road.

➤ With the high road strategy, you position your item as rare and unique, and you price it relatively high—but provide superior information and service.

➤ With the low road strategy, you price your item low enough to generate a flurry of initial bidding activity—and do everything you can to fuel the flames and attract even more potential bidders.

Chapter 24

Tracking Your Auctions with Auction Management Software

As online auctions have become popular, a cottage industry has developed around software that helps users better manage their bidding and selling. These auction management programs are typically published by small software developers—and, in some cases, by individual programmers—and are sold primarily online. In fact, you'll see many of these auction management programs sold via online auctions at eBay and other sites.

The Idiot's Overview of Auction Management Software

If you do a lot of trading at eBay or other online auction sites, you know how much of a hassle it is to create complex ad listings, manage all your auctions, place your snipes at just the right moment, and communicate with all the buyers and sellers you need to deal with. The solution is to automate some or all of these activities with special auction management software.

Table 24.1 outlines some of the more popular auction management programs currently available—including prices and features.

Table 24.1   Auction Management Programs

Software	Price	Ad Creation/ Submission?	Auction Tracking for Sellers?	Auction Tracking for Buyers?	Automated Email?	Automated Feedback?	Automated Searching?	Automated Sniping?
Auction Aid	$8.50	Yes						
Auction Assistant	$59.95	Yes	Yes		Yes	Yes		
Auction Ensemble 2000	$11.95		Yes	Yes	Yes	Yes		
Auction Express	$8.99		Semi	Semi		Semi	Semi	Yes
Auction Secretary	$39.95	Yes	Yes	Yes	Yes	Yes		
Auction Ticker	$19.95		Yes					
BidSniper Pro	$12.95							Yes
BidTrak	$24.95				Yes	Yes		
Easy Auction	$34.95		Yes		Yes			
eBay Auto Respond	$15.95				Yes			
eBay Auto Search	$10.00						Yes	
eBay Auto Submit	$25.00	Semi						
Robo-Feedback	$14.95					Yes		
TurboBid	$10.95							Yes

Run-Your-Own-Auction Software

Don't confuse this end-user auction management software with the heavy-duty professional software—such as Auction Master or EasyAuction—used to create and run online auctions.

If you want to start your own auction on your own Web site, you can check out a variety of auction packages at either BidFind (www.bidfind.com/af/ af-prog.html) or Yahoo! (dir.yahoo.com/Business_and_Economy/Companies/ Computers/Software/Business/Business_Management/Auctions/).

Auction Management Software—in More Detail

If the preceding table intrigued you, read some more information about the leading auction management programs. Note that most of these programs are sold by small companies or individuals and probably won't come in fancy packaging or with extensive user manuals—and you probably won't receive much in the way of technical or customer support if you have problems.

You also won't find these programs at traditional retail outlets. You can order them via Web sites or online auctions at eBay and other general auction sites. (Some companies link to their current auctions from their Web sites.)

Finally, be aware that the features and functionality of these programs are subject to change—and in fact do change often because these smaller software developers constantly update and upgrade their programs.

Which of these programs should you use? It depends on what you want to do:

➤ To create great-looking ads, I recommend AuctionAssistant.

➤ To automate your sniping, I recommend BidSniper Pro.

➤ To track the progress of all your auctions, I recommend Auction Ensemble 2000.

➤ To automate your post-auction emails and feedback, I recommend either Auction Ensemble 2000 or Auction Secretary.

Note that many of these programs work only with eBay auctions. If you regularly transact business on other online auctions, check out Auction Secretary, which generates simple HTML ads and provides auction management features across multiple auction sites.

Most of these programs (AuctionAssistant excluded) cost so little that you might want to check out several of them to see which you like best. Try a few and make up your own mind about their value.

Auction Aid

Auction Aid is a simplistic HTML ad creation program. You fill in the blanks, and Auction Aid does the rest. The selection of ad designs is rather limited (three formats plus different color combinations) compared to what Auction Assistant offers, but it's hard to beat the price. Auction Aid is available for $8.50 from `firstdesign.com/auction/auctionaid.htm`. It works with all auction sites that accept HTML code, including eBay, Auction Universe, and Yahoo! Auctions.

AuctionAssistant

Blackthorne Software claims that AuctionAssistant is "an automation program for sellers." I agree; this is the only program I know that can handle just about everything a seller needs handled.

To me, the best part of this program is the Ad Studio HTML ad creator, which lets you easily create great-looking, dynamic item listings using predesigned *Ad Themes*. An Ad Theme is a collection of colors, fonts, animations, sounds, and backgrounds that convey a common design.

Ad Studio's ads include frames, colors, pictures, animated graphics, and other design elements that make them really stand out from the pack. To create an ad, all you have to do is fill in a form and pick a theme; AuctionAssistant does everything else for you, up to and including uploading the HTML code to eBay's Sell Your Item page.

Creating a new ad listing with AuctionAssistant; fill in the blanks, and then click the Ad Studio button to choose an ad theme.

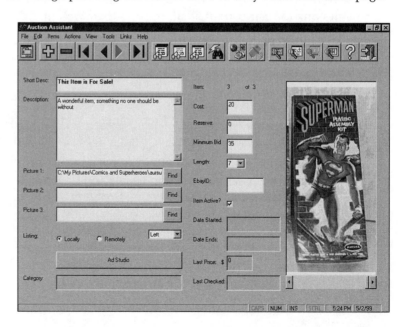

AuctionAssistant's auction management features are minimal but acceptable. Basically, it uses standard eBay seller listing pages to feed its own database of auction listings. It only tracks auctions in which you're a seller—and then, only those auctions where you used AuctionAssistant to create and place the ads. It doesn't offer any features for tracking auctions in which you're a bidder.

When your auction is over, AuctionAssistant does a very good job of automating all your end-of-auction communication. It will automatically send emails to winning bidders, track payments and shipments, and generate user feedback.

All in all, it's a slick package, and although it's priced a little on the high side, compared to other programs available, I recommend it for all large-volume eBay sellers.

AuctionAssistant (along with its companion program, AuctionTicker) is available from `www.blackthornesw.com/bthome/aafeat.htm` for $59.95. It is an eBay-specific program.

More Stuff for AuctionAssistant

Blackthorne Software also sells two collections of Ad Themes for AuctionAssistant's Ad Studio. Megaset #1 and Megaset #2 (`www.blackthornesw.com/bthome/msfeat.htm`) each contain more than 50 new Ad Themes, including New Item!, Hot Item!, Titanic, Fireworks, Pythonesque, PC Hardware, Military, International, Kids Stuff, and Baby Bear.

AuctionTicker

From the same company that produces the AuctionAssistant ad creator, AuctionTicker is a nifty program for tracking all your eBay auctions in real time. It fetches data from the eBay site at regularly scheduled intervals and then displays the results in a scrolling ticker on your desktop. You can even configure AuctionTicker to sound an alarm when an auction on your list is about to close.

Auction Ensemble 2000

Auction Ensemble 2000 delivers a lot of functionality in a fairly professional package—for a very low price. It will track all your auctions, whether you're a seller or a bidder, and automatically generate end-of-auction email and feedback. It will also track all payments and shipments automatically.

For more information about Auction Ensemble 2000, contact Chris Shackleford, the program's author, at apashack@yahoo.com. The program appears on auction at eBay for $11.95; it is an eBay-specific program.

Auction Express

Auction Express promises to be a full-featured auction management program—which is more than it delivers. Basically, all it does (in terms of auction management) is provide an HTML front end to common eBay functions. Instead of having to hunt for your eBay auction listings, for example, you can click a button in Auction Express, and it will load your auction listing page automatically.

That said, the program does have rudimentary sniping capability. Auto-Snipe lets you enter a single bid amount for an item, as well as determine how many seconds before the end time you want to bid. With this information loaded (and you have to enter all values manually), Auto-Snipe will automatically place your snipe for you at the designated time.

Auction Express is available from www.auctiontools.com for $8.99. It is an eBay-specific program.

Auction Secretary

Auction Secretary competes directly with AuctionAssistant. It generates simple HTML ad listings (with far fewer options than AuctionAssistant, however), tracks all your auctions (whether you're selling or bidding), and handles all end-of-auction communication and feedback—including payment and shipping. The interface is professional and intuitive; even though it's a weak ad generator, it has very strong auction management features.

Auction Secretary is available from www.the-store.com/auction2.html at $39.95. Unlike many of the eBay-specific programs, it works across multiple auction sites.

BidSniper Pro

If you like to snipe but hate being tied to your computer as you wait for auctions to close, you need an automated sniping tool—a software program that will automatically place your bid at the last possible second before the end of an auction.

BidSniper Pro is such a tool, letting you schedule an unlimited number of snipe bids for automatic placement—even if you're not anywhere near your computer. All you have to do is enter the item number you want to snipe, your maximum bid amount, and your "snipe time" (number of seconds before the end of the auction you want to place the bid). BidSniper then resides in your Windows system tray, automatically connects to your ISP (before the scheduled bid time, just to be safe), and places your bid.

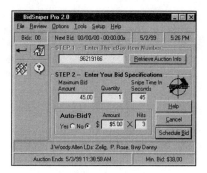

Getting ready to snipe an auction—automatically—with BidSniper Pro.

BidSniper Pro also includes BidWatch, which will look for higher bids placed after your snipe and (if so instructed) increase your bid accordingly to beat the other snipers. One can easily imagine multiple users, all employing BidSniper Pro's BidWatch feature, generating a flurry of automated one-upmanship in the closing seconds of a popular auction!

BidSniper Pro is available from www.datavector.net/prod02.htm for $12.95. It is an eBay-specific program—and one that I use personally!

BidTrak

BidTrak is an unusual auction management program for eBay sellers. It doesn't track your auctions per se; it intercepts eBay's end-of-auction emails to grab the names of your winning bidders and then prints shipping labels, tracks payment dates, and generates end-of-auction email and feedback.

BidTrak (along with its siblings Robo-Feedback and TurboBid) is available at www.flash.net/~etx/turbo/bidtrak.htm for $29.95. It is an eBay-specific program.

Easy Auction

Easy Auction is a custom database program that tracks all your eBay auctions, whether you're selling or bidding. It also generates end-of-auction emails and creates some sophisticated auction-tracking reports, including profit and frequency reports.

Easy Auction is available from users.netcon.net.au/microg/easya.htm (in Australia) for $34.95. It is an eBay-specific program.

eBay Auto Respond

eBay Auto Respond is a simple program that generates end-of-auction emails, creates shipping labels, and tracks addresses and shipping dates. Nothing more, nothing less.

For more information on eBay Auto Respond (along with its companion programs, eBay Auto Search and eBay Auto Submit), contact the program's author at roger@every-era.com. The program sells for $15 and is eBay-specific.

eBay Auto Search

eBay Auto Search lets you create a database of customized eBay searches and then have those searches executed automatically at a preset time. The program will even automatically connect to your ISP, conduct its search, and then disconnect when done.

For more information on eBay Auto Search (along with its companion programs, eBay Auto Respond and eBay Auto Submit), contact the program's author at roger@every-era.com. The program sells for $10 and is eBay-specific.

eBay Auto Submit

eBay Auto Submit doesn't create HTML ads; in fact, it doesn't create ads at all. What it does is automatically submit—according to your designated schedule—ads that you've created offline. I have trouble finding the value in this unless it's deathly important that all your ads adhere to some special start and end time.

For more information on eBay Auto Submit (along with its companion programs, eBay Auto Respond and eBay Auto Search), contact the program's author at roger@every-era.com. The program sells for $25 and is eBay-specific.

Robo-Feedback

Robo-Feedback does one thing and one thing only: It automatically generates feedback for your eBay transaction partners. The program (along with its siblings BidTrak and TurboBid) is available at www.flash.net/~etx/turbo/feedback.htm for $14.95; it is an eBay-specific program.

TurboBid

TurboBid, like BidSniper Pro, automates the sniping process. Select the auctions you're interested in, set your bid price, and tell TurboBid how many seconds before the end of the auction you want to snipe. It will automatically dial your ISP, place the snipe, and disconnect when done.

TurboBid (along with its siblings BidTrak and Robo-Feedback) is available from www.flash.net/~etx/turbo/robobid.htm for $10.95. It is an eBay-specific program.

Searching for Even More Auction Management Software

Perhaps the best place to search for auction software is on eBay and the other auction sites themselves. Use the auction site's search engine to search for **auction software** (or, on eBay, **eBay software**) and see what comes up. Many small publishers sell their programs via Dutch auctions online. In addition, you can find a large selection of auction-related software at Auctions Online Software (guestservices.hypermart.net/software.htm).

The Least You Need to Know

➤ To generate sophisticated HTML ad listings, use AuctionAssistant.

➤ To track and manage all your auctions across multiple auction sites, use Auction Secretary.

➤ To automate your sniping, use BidSniper Pro.

Chapter 25

Searching Multiple Auctions with Meta-Auction Sites

In This Chapter

➤ Learn how to use metasearch engines to search across multiple auction sites

➤ Discover the directory sites that list all the other auction sites

➤ Find out about online auction-related mailing lists and newsletters

---

Once you venture outside of eBay, Auction Universe, or any other large general-purpose auction site, how can you find that item you'd like to bid on—or the site where it might be listed?

The answer is simple: Use a meta-auction site. These sites serve as directories to hundreds of other auction sites and (in many cases) let you search across multiple auction sites for particular items. Some even let you manage all your bids and auctions directly from their sites.

Find What You Want Anywhere with Metasearch Sites

To me, the most useful meta-auction sites are those that offer metasearch capabilities—that is, the capability to perform a single search across multiple auction sites. If you're looking for a specific item, you only have to search for it once; the metasearch engine queries a number of different online auctions and then tells you which (if any) sites list the item you're looking for.

Use these meta-auction sites with a degree of caution, however. Quite frankly, not all of these search engines catch all the items that are really up for bid. That's partly because different auction sites use different search parameters (a common metasearch snag) and partly because some of these meta-auction sites haven't quite worked all the bugs. Because of their hit-and-miss performance, I still prefer to do my searching on the individual auction sites themselves.

What's a Metasearch?

A metasearch site is one that searches multiple search sites with a single query and then compiles and consolidates all the results into a single listing. Some of the more popular general metasearch sites on the Web include Metacrawler (www.go2net.com/search.html), Dogpile (www.dogpile.com), InferenceFind (www.infind.com), and SavvySearch (www.savvysearch.com).

Auction Watchers

Auction Watchers (www.auctionwatchers.com) is a site that specializes in searching for computer-related equipment. It searches 1st Class Auction, Auction World, DealDeal, Egghead's Surplus Auction, OnSale, uBid, and WebAuction.com. You can choose to search (using a standard search box) or browse through Auction Watchers' preselected and presearched categories.

iTrack

iTrack (www.itrack.com) is one of the newest auction search and tracking sites. It lets you enter three different searches (eight if you pay for the advanced service) across several big auction sites (eBay, Amazon.com Auctions, Auction Universe, and Yahoo! Auctions initially, with more sites promised). iTrack conducts a daily search with your parameters and emails you the results every morning; you can click the links in the email to go directly to any specific auction.

I like the iTrack service, and find that it works better than eBay's Personal Shopper service. I find myself using iTrack to keep a daily lookout for hard-to-find items across several sites.

Bidder's Edge

Bidder's Edge (`www.biddersedge.com`) is one of my favorite meta-auction sites; it has a clean design and several nifty features. Currently, Bidder's Edge tracks auctions from 20 different sites, including Auction Universe, Auction Warehouse, Bid.com, DealDeal, eBay, FirstAuction, OnSale, Surplus Auction, uBid, and WebAuction. Note, however, that although it tracks all categories from merchant auctions, it only tracks select categories (Beanie Babies and Furbys only, as of this writing) from person-to-person auction sites such as Auction Universe and eBay.

You can use Bidder's Edge to search for items, or you can browse through Bidder's Edge's preselected and presearched categories. If you find an item you want to track, click the + button to add it to your My Auctions list. If you find a type of item you'd like to look for in the future, click the $ button to add it to your Deal Watch list—and Bidder's Edge will notify you when a similar item comes up for auction.

Even though its search features are rather limited for person-to-person transactions, I still like the way Bidder's Edge works. In the future, as it expands the categories it tracks, this site will become a very useful tool.

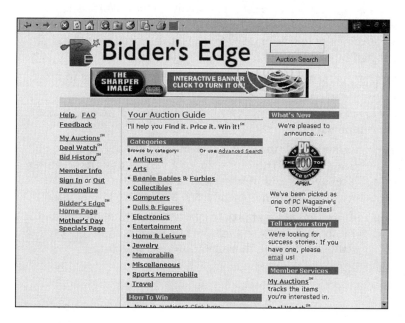

Use Bidder's Edge to search for items across multiple auction sites.

BidFind

BidFind (`www.bidfind.com`) searches more than 200 different auction sites, from A1 Auction to WowAuction (including eBay and OnSale). You can search for items or browse BidFind's preselected and presearched categories. Note, however, that BidFind does a much better job searching the smaller auction sites than it does in searching eBay. In fact, even though BidFind lists eBay as part of its search, I wouldn't be surprised to find out that this wasn't actually so.

To me, the most useful part of BidFind isn't its metasearch capabilities, but rather its list of more than 200 different auction sites—complete with descriptions and links to the sites themselves. You can access this list directly at www.bidfind.com/af/af-list.html; it's a pretty comprehensive list of a wide variety of different types of online auctions.

Lycos Auction Search

Lycos Auction Search (www.lycos.com/auctions/) is Bidder's Edge under the Lycos name. It looks and works just like Bidder's Edge—plus it links directly to Lycos' own developing auction service.

More, More, More: Auction News and Directories

What if you don't need to search across multiple auctions but want more information about online auctions; which ones are available, how to use them, and so on? Then, you should check out one of the following sites:

➤ **Auction Guide** (www.auctionguide.com)   The main Auction Guide site lists real-world (non-online) auctions around the world; Auction Guide's Online section (www.auctionguide.com/1guide/online/online.htm) specifically lists online auctions, sorted by category.

➤ **AuctionInsider** (www.auctioninsider.com)   This site lists and links to more than 150 different online auctions.

➤ **Auction Peak** (www.auctionpeak.com)   Get news and tips on how to make more money from online auctions.

➤ **Auction Tribune** (www.AuctionTribune.com)   Formerly known as the Auctions Online Supersite, Auction Tribune includes a variety of useful features, including auction news, eBay tips and information, a list of the top-10 rated auctions, and a directory of more than 100 different auction sites.

➤ **BidFind** (www.bidfind.com/af/af-list.html)   In addition to its metasearch engine, discussed previously, BidFind also includes the most comprehensive list of online auctions available, with more than 200 different sites listed.

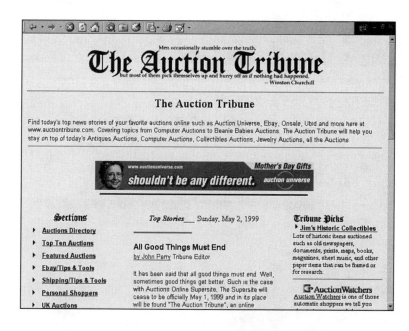

Auction news and tips—plus a directory of online auction sites—at The Auction Tribune.

Check Out These Auction Newsletters and Mailing Lists

Another good way to keep track of online auction happenings is to subscribe to one of the online newsletters and mailing lists dedicated to various aspects of the online auction phenomenon. Here are just a few resources to check out:

➤ **Bid Fortune** online newsletter from Auction Peak; see `auctionpeak.listbot.com` to subscribe.

➤ **eBaySellers** mailing list; see `www.onelist.com/subscribe.cgi/eBaySellers` to subscribe.

➤ **eBayUsers** mailing list; see `ebayusers.listbot.com` to subscribe.

The Least You Need to Know

➤ Meta-auction sites let you search for items across multiple auction sites; these sites include Bidder's Edge and Auction Watchers.

➤ Sites offering directories of online auctions include BidFind and The Auction Tribune.

➤ Several online newsletters and mailing lists target online auction users, including Bid Fortune, eBaySellers, and eBayUsers.

Chapter 26

Protecting Yourself from Unscrupulous Buyers and Sellers

In This Chapter

➤ Uncover which auction sites offer greater levels of buyer protection

➤ Discover which methods of payment are safer than others—and why

➤ Learn how escrow services can offer additional protection to both the buyer and seller

➤ Find out who to contact if you get cheated in an online transaction

If you're a seller—and you're smart—you really don't have a lot of risk with online auctions. Yeah, a deadbeat bidder could fail to make payment, but you still have the merchandise—and you hold on to that merchandise until you receive payment and the payment clears.

If you're a buyer, however, it's a different story. The online auction environment is pretty much "buyer beware" territory. You agree to buy an item, almost site unseen, from someone whom you know practically nothing about. You send that person a check and hope and pray that you get something shipped back in return—and that the thing that's shipped is the thing you thought you were buying, in good condition. If you don't like what you got—or if you received nothing at all—the seller has your money, and what recourse do you have?

I know that sounds pretty dire, and in reality, online auctioning is as safe as buying something from a local garage sale. Still, as a buyer, you can do things to protect yourself when dealing with online auction sellers.

Protecting Yourself Before You Buy

The first thing to do is choose carefully where you bid. You get different levels of protections at different online auction sites.

Protecting Yourself at Merchant Auctions

If you're bidding in a merchant auction (for computer equipment, for example), it's easy enough to choose a well-known and reliable auction site. You're much safer at Egghead's Surplus Auction, for example, than you would be at Bob's Big Discount Auction. There are enough reputable merchant auctions around that you don't have to take your chances on a fly-by-night site.

All merchant auction sites operate differently, so make sure you familiarize yourself with their warranties and policies before you bid. Some sites offer a 30-day guarantee or returns policy; on others, all sales are final. If you're uncomfortable with the policies of a given site, don't bid there; find another site that offers you more post-sale protection.

If you're not sure about a given site, check it out before you buy. It's not a bad idea to contact the state or local consumer protection agency and Better Business Bureau where you live, as well as the same agencies in the state where the company is located.

Protecting Yourself at Person-to-Person Auctions

Your options are not the same when dealing with a person-to-person auction site—because, ultimately, you're dealing with the individual seller, not with the commercial site itself. However, there are differences between the sites, in terms of protection and insurance offered to the buyer.

The three safest person-to-person auction sites today are eBay, Auction Universe, and Amazon.com Auctions for three reasons:

➤ eBay's SafeHarbor insures most of your transactions up to $200 (with a $25 deductible). This insurance is free to all members in good standing.

➤ Amazon.com Auctions insures most of your transactions up to $250 with no deductible. This insurance is free to all registered users.

➤ Auction Universe offers all buyers free protection on items sold by Bid$afe Gold members (who pay a $19.95 yearly fee) up to $3,000 per item.

If you get into trouble on these three auction sites, you have automatic recourse. File a claim, and get some or all of your money back.

However, there is more you can do to protect yourself before you bid. Almost all person-to-person auctions provide some sort of feedback mechanism about their users. Check the seller's feedback before you bid; if it's overwhelmingly positive, you can feel safer than if the seller has a lot of negative feedback. In fact, read the individual feedback comments, and studiously avoid those sellers who have a history of delivering less than was promised.

You can also take the extra step of verifying the seller's identity. Get all the information about the seller you can from the auction site, and then email him and ask for more. Get a phone number and a street address, and check him out. If the seller won't work with you—or if the information doesn't check out—then, don't deal with him!

Protecting Yourself During the Transaction

Did you know that how you pay for an item can increase or decrease your protection during a transaction? It's true; some methods of payment are safer for you than others.

Pick How You Pay

The least safe methods of payment for a buyer are cash, cashier's check, or money order; they provide no money trail to trace if you want to track down the seller. (In fact, any seller requesting payment in cash is probably up to no good from the get-go.) Paying by check gives you a minor trail to trace, but once the check is cashed, it's still pretty much a done deal.

A safer way to pay is by credit card because you can always go to the credit card company and dispute your charges if the item you bought was misrepresented or never arrived. Paying by credit card is generally an option in most merchant items and with some small merchants selling on person-to-person sites, such as eBay. Unfortunately, credit card payment is seldom available when purchasing from private individuals.

You might occasionally have the option of C.O.D (cash on delivery) payment. This is a good route to take if you can. You don't actually part with your payment until you receive the merchandise—and you can't stiff the seller, either, because if you don't pay the delivery guy, he doesn't give you your stuff.

Use an Escrow Service

A final option, increasingly popular in more expensive person-to-person auctions, is the use of an escrow service. This is a company that acts as a neutral third party between the buyer (you) and the seller, holding your money until you receive the seller's merchandise. If you don't get the goods (or the goods are unacceptable), you get your money back; the seller gets paid only when you're happy. As a side benefit, escrow services also allow you to pay by credit card—even if you're buying from a non-card-enabled individual.

Here's how a typical escrow transaction works:

1. At the end of an auction, you and the seller contact each other and agree to use an escrow service. The escrow service's fees can be split between the two parties or (more typically) be paid by you, the buyer. Fees differ widely from service to service.

2. You send payment (by check, money order, cashier's check, or credit card) to the escrow service.

3. After your payment is approved, the escrow service instructs the seller to ship the item.

4. You receive the item, verify its acceptability, and notify the escrow service that all is hunky-dory.

5. The escrow service pays the seller.

Some of the most-used online escrow services follow:

➤ **i-Escrow** (www.iescrow.com)   This service accepts American Express, Carte Blanche, Diner's Club, Discover, MasterCard, and Visa, as well as cashier's checks, money orders, personal checks, or bank/wire transfers. Fees run $5 for items under $100, 5 percent for items priced from $100 to $5,000, and 3 percent for items costing between $5,000 and $10,000.

➤ **Internet Clearing Corporation** (www.internetclearing.com)   This service accepts American Express, MasterCard, and Visa only. Fees run 3.5 percent each for both the seller and buyer (that's a total of 7 percent between the two of you) for items up to $5,000 (with a minimum fee of $5) and 2 percent for items costing between $5,000 and $10,000.

➤ **SecureTrades** (securetrades.com)   This service accepts cashier's checks, money orders, or personal checks only—no credit cards. Fees run 5 percent of the purchase price with a $5 minimum. SecureTrades also offers what it calls a Merchandise Holding Transaction, where the seller ships the merchandise to SecureTrades, who holds it until your payment is cleared; fees for this type of transaction run 10 percent plus a set fee of $10 (up to $499), $20 (from $500 to $999), or $30 (over $1,000).

➤ **TradeSafe** (www.tradesafe.com)   This service accepts American Express, Discover, MasterCard, and Visa, as well as cashier's checks, money orders, personal checks, or bank/wire transfers. Fees differ depending on whether you're paying by check or by credit card. The check fees run $15 for items priced up to $400; 4 percent for items from $401 to $2,375; and a flat $95 for items priced over that. The credit fees run $8 plus 4.25 percent of the purchase price for items priced up to $1,300 and $12 plus 4.25 percent of the purchase price for items priced above $1,300.

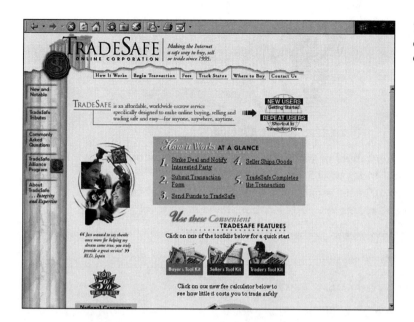

TradeSafe—perhaps the easiest-to-use online escrow service.

Protecting Yourself After the Sale

What do you do if you don't use an escrow service and you receive unacceptable merchandise—or no merchandise at all?

First, know that no person-to-person auction site accepts any responsibility for any transactions conducted on its site. It's not the buyer or the seller, only a relatively disinterested third party.

However, that doesn't mean you shouldn't contact the auction site if you're the recipient of a sour deal. All online auction sites have ways you can contact them in the event of a bad deal. At the very least, the sites will start tracking the seller's other activities and perhaps kick them off the site if a pattern of fraudulent activity can be shown.

In addition, you should leave formal negative feedback about any bad sellers you encounter; it's your duty to warn other buyers before they get suckered.

Beyond the auction site, you can contact other agencies if you've been disadvantaged in a deal. For example, if mail fraud is involved (which it is if any part of the transaction—either payment or shipping—was handled through the mail), you can file a complaint with your local U.S. Post Office or state attorney general's office. You might also want to contact your local police if you had a large amount of money ripped off or if your credit card numbers were stolen. You can file a complaint with the Federal Trade Commission (FTC) by contacting the FTC Consumer Response Center via phone (202-382-4357), mail (Consumer Response Center, Federal Trade Commission, Washington, DC 20580), or the Internet (www.ftc.gov/ftc/complaint.htm). Although the FTC doesn't resolve individual consumer problems, it can and will act against a company if it sees a pattern of possible law violations.

Find the Right Office

To find particular representatives of your local government, check out the About.com Alphabetical Index of U.S. Government Web Space (usgovinfo.about.com/blindex.htm). It has direct links to just about every conceivable government agency on both a national and local level.

The Least You Need to Know

➤ Online auctions are generally as safe as a local garage sale—with the caveat that the "buyer beware."

➤ Different online auctions offer different levels of buyer protection; merchant auctions are typically safer than person-to-person auctions.

➤ You're safer if you pay by credit card or use an escrow service.

➤ If you do get ripped off, contact the auction site, your local authorities, and the FTC.

Chapter 27

Shipping It Out— Without Spending a Fortune

In This Chapter

➤ Learn the right way to pack, seal, and label your packages

➤ Find out which shipping services are best for your individual needs

➤ Discover why you should insure your packages—and what to do if things go wrong

The auction's over, you've received payment from the high bidder, and now, it's time to pack your item and ship it off. If you don't have much experience in shipping items cross-country, this might be the most daunting part of the entire auction process. Don't worry, though; if you've ever wrapped a Christmas present or mailed a letter, you have all the skills you need to ship just about anything anywhere in the world.

Pick, Pack, Seal, and Label

Before you ship, you have to pack—which doesn't sound terribly difficult. However, if you pick the wrong container, don't cushion the contents properly, don't seal it securely, or mislabel the whole thing, you could risk damaging the contents during shipping—or, even worse, sending it to the wrong recipient. Even if you think you know how to pack and ship, you still probably want to read the following sections. You never know; you might pick up a few useful tips!

Pick a Box

The first thing you need to do is put your item in the appropriate shipping container. Easy, right? Not really—and the consequences of choosing the wrong container can be disastrous.

First, you have to decide whether to use a box or an envelope. If you have a very large item to ship, the choice is easy. But what if you have something smaller and flatter, such as a laser disc or a coin? Your choice should be determined by the fragility of your item; if it can bend or break, choose a box; if not, an envelope is probably a safe choice.

Whichever you choose, pick a container that's large enough to hold your item without the need to force it in or bend it in an inappropriate fashion. Also, make sure that the box has enough extra room to insert cushioning material.

On the other hand, the container shouldn't be so big as to leave room for the item to bounce around. Also, you pay for size; you don't want to pay to ship anything bigger than it needs to be.

If you're shipping in a box, make sure it's made of heavy, corrugated cardboard and it has its flaps intact. Thinner boxes—such as shoe boxes or gift boxes—simply aren't strong enough for shipping. When packing a box, never exceed the maximum gross weight for the box, which is usually printed on the bottom flap.

If you're shipping in an envelope, consider using a bubble-pack envelope or reinforcing the envelope with pieces of cardboard. This is especially vital if your item shouldn't be bent or folded.

Buying Boxes

Where do you find shipping containers and materials? If you're shipping via the U.S. Postal Service, then Express Mail and Priority Mail boxes, envelopes, and tubes are available for free from your local post office. Most post office locations also sell various types of boxes, padded mailers, mailing tubes, and other packing materials, as do office supply stores and specialty box and shipping stores.

You can also reuse boxes that were shipped to you, either from other eBay users or from online or direct mail retailers. (You'd be amazed how many times a box can be reused!) If you choose a previously used box, make sure you remove or cross out any old shipping labels, and make sure the box is in good shape, with no weak spots or cracks.

Pack the Box

Here's what you don't do: Drop your item in an empty box and then seal it up. A loose item in a big box will bounce around and get damaged, guaranteed. (Imagine your box being tossed around by a bunch of gorillas in a parking lot, and you get an accurate picture of what most packages endure in the shipping process.) No, you need to carefully pack your item to minimize any potential damage from dropping and rough handling.

How do you pack your box? Professional shippers use Styrofoam "peanuts"; we amateurs tend to use crumpled-up newspapers and other materials found around the house. However, packing needs vary for different types of items; you can use these packing tips when it's time to ship your next item:

➤ Cushion your package contents with shredded or rolled newspaper, bubble wrap, or Styrofoam peanuts. You can also use plain (non-buttered!) air-popped popcorn for cushioning; it's inexpensive and environmentally friendly and tastes good when you're watching a movie!

➤ Whatever cushioning material you use, don't skimp on it. Pack your items tightly to avoid shifting of contents during transit, and make sure the cushioning material covers all sides of the items.

➤ If you're shipping several items in the same box, wrap each one separately and provide enough cushioning to prevent movement and to keep the items from rubbing against each other.

➤ Not only should items be separated from each other in the box, but they should also be separated from the corners and sides of the box to prevent damage if the box is bumped or dropped.

➤ If your item has any protruding parts, cover them with extra padding or cardboard.

➤ Stuff glassware and other fragile hollow items, such as vases, with newspaper or other packing material. This provides an extra level of cushioning in case of rough handling.

➤ When shipping jars and other items with lids, either separate the lid from the base with several layers of bubble wrap or tissue paper or (better still) pack the lid in a separate small box.

➤ When shipping extremely fragile glass or ceramic items, consider double-boxing the item; pack the item tightly in a small box, and then place that box in a slightly larger box with even more cushioning material between the boxes.

➤ When shipping framed photographs or artwork, take the glass out of the frame and wrap it separately.

➤ When shipping electronic items (including many toys, such as Furbys), remove their batteries. Wrap and place the batteries next to the items in the shipping container.

➤ When shipping computer parts—circuit boards, video cards, memory chips, and so on—pad the item well and pack it in an Electro Static Discharge (ESD) bag to prevent damaging static buildup.

After you think you're done packing, gently shake the box. If nothing moves, it's ready to be sealed. If you can hear or feel things rattling around inside, however, it's time to add more cushioning material!

Seal the Box

After your box is packed, it's time to seal it. A strong seal is essential, so always use tape that is designed for shipping. Make sure you securely seal the center seams at both the top and the bottom of the box. Cover all other seams with tape, and be sure not to leave any open areas that could snag on machinery.

What kind of sealing materials should you use?

➤ **Do** use tape that is designed for shipping, such as pressure-sensitive tape, nylon-reinforced craft paper tape, glass-reinforced pressure-sensitive tape, or water-activated paper tape. Whichever tape you use, the wider and heavier, the better. Reinforced is always better than non-reinforced.

➤ **Don't** use wrapping paper, string, masking tape, or cellophane tape.

One last thing: If you plan to insure your package, leave an untaped area on the cardboard where your postal clerk can stamp "Insured."

Label the Box

The best-packed box won't go anywhere if you get the label wrong. For fast and efficient delivery, keep these points in mind when addressing your package:

➤ Write, type, or print the complete address neatly.

➤ Learn how to print labels using your computer and printer. To print one-off labels with Microsoft Word, pull down the **Tools** menu, select **Envelopes and Labels**, and when the dialog box appears, select the **Labels** tab and fill in the blanks.

➤ Always use complete address information, such as the suffixes Dr., Ave., St., and Blvd.

➤ Include the recipient's apartment or suite number, if applicable.

➤ Always use correct directions, such as N, S, E, W, SW, and so on.

➤ Use the correct zip code—and, when possible, use the four-digit add-on, ZIP+4. Hyphenate the ZIP+4.

➤ Always use the proper two-letter state abbreviations.

➤ When addressing to a P.O. Box or rural route destination, include the recipient's telephone number on the label.

➤ When shipping outside the U.S., include a contact name, telephone number, and postal code on the label—and don't forget to include the country name!

➤ If you're using any special services of the U.S. Postal Service (Priority Mail, First Class Mail, insurance, and so on), note this above the destination address and below and to the right of the return address.

➤ Always include your return address information.

➤ Place the delivery label on the top of the box. To avoid confusion, place only one address label on the box. If using a packing slip, place it on the same surface of the box as the address label.

➤ Do not place the label over a seam or closure or on top of sealing tape.

➤ To avoid ink smudges, place a strip of clear packing tape over the address label.

➤ If you're reusing a box for shipping, remove or cross out all old address labels or markings on a used box.

How to Ship It

You have a number of choices when it comes to actually shipping your package. You can use the various services offered by the U.S. Postal Service (regular mail, Priority Mail, Express Mail) or a third-party shipping service, such as UPS or Federal Express. You can deal directly with any shipping service or use a local shipping store to handle the shipping (and even the packing) at a cost.

Find That Zip Code

Don't know the zip code for the address you're shipping to? Then, look it up at the U.S. Postal Service's Zip Code Finder at www.usps.gov/ncsc/.

Which service should you use? Ultimately, you have to strike a compromise between cost and speed. As an example of how the major shipping firms compare on a similar job, Table 27.1 compares the costs of shipping a 1-lb. box from New York to Los Angeles.

Table 27.1 Comparison: Shipping a 1–lb. Box from New York to Los Angeles

Service	Cost
USPS Priority Mail (2 days)	$3.20
UPS Ground (2 5 days)	$5.55
FedEx 2Day (2 days)	$10.00
UPS 2nd Day Air (2 days)	$10.00
USPS Express Mail (1 day)	$15.75
FedEx Standard Overnight (1 day)	$20.25
UPS Next Day Air (1 day)	$22.75
FedEx Priority Overnight (next morning)	$24.00

Compare Online

If you want to compare shipping costs for a variety of services, check out SmartShip (www.smartship.com). This site not only lets you compare shipping costs, but also it provides tracking services for all major carriers.

Which shipping services do I use? For small items, I default to USPS Priority Mail; it's inexpensive and relatively fast, plus I get free packing materials from my local post office. For really large items, I go with UPS. If a buyer insists on immediate shipment (and is willing to pay for it), then I go with FedEx. But I find that, 9 times out of 10, Priority Mail does the job for me.

Using the U.S. Postal Service

The U.S. Postal Service (USPS) offers several different shipping options:

➤ **Priority Mail** This is the preferred shipping method for most experienced auction sellers. The cost is affordable (a flat $3.20 for most smaller packages), and items generally arrive in two or three days.

➤ **Express Mail** This is the USPS' fastest service, offering guaranteed next-day delivery 365 days a year, including weekends and holidays. Merchandise is automatically insured up to $500.

➤ **First Class Mail** This is an option if your item fits into a standard envelope. It also provides the benefit of shipping directly from your mailbox, without necessitating a trip to the post office.

You can find out more about USPS shipping at the USPS Web site, located at www.usps.gov. This site includes a postage calculator (postcalc.usps.gov), a zip code finder (www.usps.gov/ncsc/), and the capability to order shipping supplies online (supplies.usps.gov).

Using UPS

UPS is a good option for shipping larger packages but frankly is a little costly for smaller items. UPS offers a variety of shipping options, including standard UPS Ground, Next Day Air, and 2nd Day Air.

You can find out more about UPS shipping at its Web site, located at www.ups.com. You can access its cost calculator directly at www.ups.com/using/services/rave/rate.html.

Using Federal Express

Federal Express is probably the most costly shipping service, but it's also the fastest. Its most popular shipping options are Priority Overnight, Standard Overnight, and 2Day.

You can find out more about FedEx shipping at its Web site, located at www.fedex.com. You can access its rate finder directly at www.fedex.com/us/rates/.

Using Other Shipping Companies

USPS, UPS, and FedEx are the three most popular shipping services in the U.S.; they're not the only services available, however. Among the other services available are

➤ Airborne Express (www.airborne.com)

➤ DHL (www.dhl.com), great for international shipments

➤ Emery Worldwide (www.emeryworld.com)

➤ Purolator Courier (www.purolator.com)

For a more complete list of shipping services, see the ShippingLinks page on the TradeSafe site (www.tradesafe.com/ShippingLinks.htm).

Using a Shipping Store to Ship a Package

All this talk about services and rates get your head spinning? You can always let somebody else worry about the details. Many local shipping stores (such as Mail Boxes Etc.—located on the Web at www.mbe.com) provide packing and shipping services—and do everything from sell boxes to pack your items to serve as a "middleman" between you and UPS or FedEx. You'll pay for their services—some can be quite costly—but you don't have to get your hands dirty or concern yourself with any of those niggling details. If you can't find a shipping store in your area, check out AuctionSHIP (www.auctionship.com), a national network of retail stores that provide packing and shipping services. They even offer discounted rates for online auction customers.

If Things Go Wrong...

If you're shipping a moderately expensive item (over $20, let's say), it's probably worth the slight additional expense to insure it. You might want to give the buyer the option of buying insurance or just do it yourself and include the costs in your normal shipping/handling fee. (It costs only $.75 to add insurance to most Priority Mail shipments.)

Remember, if an item is broken or lost during shipment, you, the seller, are responsible for it—and must reimburse the buyer for the full purchase price.

If you think the package might be lost in transit (it's taking too long to arrive), you can always avail yourself of the tracking services provided by all the major shipping services. In most cases, you can track any package directly from their Web sites by entering your package's tracking number.

If the package never arrives—or arrives damaged—then you have some work to do. Assuming you insured the package, you have to file a claim with the carrier. Information for claim filing appears on most of carriers' Web sites, but you might have to visit your carrier's local office to obtain the proper claim forms. While you're waiting for the claim to be paid, you need to communicate with the buyer so that both of you are in the loop about what's going on. When you get reimbursed from the shipping service (or possibly before, depending on what you work out with the buyer), you need to refund the buyer's money. If you have to do this, be fair; if the buyer paid by cashier's check, your refund should be via cashier's check also.

The Least You Need to Know

➤ The better you pack your item, the better the chances it will arrive in one piece.

➤ Use a sturdy box, pack it with plenty of cushioning material, seal it tightly, and fully label it.

➤ The most popular shipping method in the U.S. is the U.S. Postal Service's Priority Mail.

➤ For larger items, consider using UPS; for faster shipments, consider using Federal Express.

➤ Always insure more expensive items so you're protected if the item is lost or damaged in transit.

Chapter 28

A Final Word: Making Auctions Fun!

In This Chapter

➤ Discover the changes already happening at the major online auction sites

➤ Learn how to have fun while you're trading online

As big as online auctions are today, they're going to get a lot bigger—fast. You're also going to see a lot of interesting and important changes in the online auction space—changes that will make online trading safer, more efficient, and more fun.

Read on if you want to know what I think about the future of online auctions—and how you can make your online trading more enjoyable.

The Future of Online Auctions

The Internet is all about change, and the online auction space is no exception. Here are my predictions of what you'll find in the online auctions of the near future—all of which are overwhelmingly positive, in my opinion.

Auctions Go Local

We're already seeing the start of this trend with City Auction, the Auction Universe Network, and eBay's tests of local auction sites. When auctions go local, you'll finally be able to buy and sell those things that you can't easily ship across the country. (For example, I have a used desk sitting in my garage that would be pointless to list with eBay today—but would be a great item to list on a local auction site.)

Auctions Go Upscale—and Big Ticket

Online auctions can be about more than cheap junk and collectibles normally sold at garage sales and flea markets. In the real world, auctions have always included the high end of the marketplace; just look at the types of items typically auctioned by Sotheby's or Butterfield & Butterfield. Well, Sotheby's is moving online, and Butterfield & Butterfield was recently purchased by eBay, which means you can expect to see more upscale, exclusive, and expensive goods auctioned online. In addition, look for more bigger-ticket items at online auctions—cars, boats, property, and so on. Before long, just about anything you can buy or sell in the real world will be a viable item for online auctioning.

Auctions and Classifieds Merge

Auction Universe already has its FirstBidWins feature, where the first bid at the minimum bid wins and closes the auction; eBay is talking about implementing a similar feature. How long until online classifieds all get rolled into online auctions of one type or another? Not long, in my estimation.

Auctions Get Integrated into Online Communities

Online auctions develop their own online communities; perhaps someone should think about integrating auctions with existing online communities. Don't be surprised to see GeoCities or Angelfire add person-to-person auctions to the mix of services they provide to their personal Web page users.

Every Site on the Web Adds an Auction

Everybody wants an auction on his site. Online businesses are scrambling to add auctions to their normal e-tail services, and individual collectors want to auction off their own merchandise. Can you imagine a world where every Web site is running its own auction?

The Not-So-Big Auction Sites Consolidate to Survive

Don't be surprised by the next contradiction. At the same time that small Web sites are adding online auction features, some of the smaller auction-only sites are dying on the vine. When eBay has 2 million auctions a day, how long can a site with only 25,000 auctions a day survive? Expect to see some of the second-tier players consolidate through mergers or acquisitions, in the hope of acquiring the critical mass to be a viable eBay competitor.

Auctions Get Safer

Look at the trends—eBay's SafeHarbor, Auction Universe's Bid$afe, Amazon.com Auction's user guarantee. The safer people feel, the more they trade, which is a great incentive for the auction sites to add even more levels of consumer protection.

Merchant and Person-to-Person Auctions Blur

I look at Amazon.com Auctions, and I don't know whether a listing is a merchant auction or a person-to-person auction. Expect to see the other major person-to-person auctions offering more merchant auctions, in all categories—from computers to cars.

Five Ways to Make Online Auctions More Fun

Okay, enough of the Nostradamus routine, let's get serious about making auctions fun. Sure, some sellers are in it for the money, and some buyers are in it to feed their collectible obsessions, but a whole lot of people buy and sell at online auctions as a form of entertainment. Just as gambling can be an amusing pursuit (until you're too deep in the hole!), online auctions can feel like a game.

(Don't dismiss the connection between gambling and auctions. My eight-year-old nephew doesn't "bid" for his Beanie Babies on eBay; he *bets* on them, in his words.)

That said, you can do five things to make your online trading as enjoyable as possible.

Set Your Limits

Anything's more fun if you don't go broke doing it. Just as recreational gamblers establish a set amount of money they're going to spend, recreational bidders should also have a set amount of funds to devote to their online pastime. Spend only as much as you set aside, no matter what.

Don't Take It Personally

Some online traders take the whole thing very seriously—to the point of being abusive towards other users. If you run into one of these clowns, ignore him. Online auctions aren't a life-and-death experience, and losing an online auction won't end Western civilization as we know it. Not having the high bid doesn't say anything less about you, personally; remember that you win some and you lose some, and then move on!

Take a Break

If you're spending 10 hours a day tracking all your online auctions, you're not having fun. Get a life! Turn off the computer, read a book, go out and play with your kids and your dog; do anything you have to do to put online trading in its proper place.

Make It a Hobby, Not a Profession

Yes, some small merchants do view online trading as a profession; I'm not talking to them here. For you regular folks, the minute you start seeing dollar signs every time you type eBay's URL, you've passed beyond the hobbyist stage. Unless you're a professional trader, you should play around on online auctions because you like to do it, not because it benefits you financially. After all, nobody has to pay you to play ball with your kids, do they? (*Do they?*)

Have a Sense of Humor

Finally, keep it light. If you lose an auction, laugh it off. If another user does some incredibly bone-headed or insulting thing, take it for what it is and nothing more. You're here to have fun, so have fun! Don't be so serious—and you'll find that your positive attitude will rub off on other users, making the whole thing more enjoyable for everybody.

The bottom line: Have fun, and enjoy yourself. Life's too short to do otherwise.

The Least You Need to Know

➤ Online auctions will go through some major changes in the next year or two.

➤ Expect to see many new features on your favorite online auction site, including local auctions, big-ticket auctions, and more buyer and seller protection.

➤ When you're trading online, make sure you're having fun; there's no reason you can't enjoy yourself and make money online.

The Complete Idiot's Directory of Online Auctions

Site	URL	Type of Auction
1st Class Auction	www.1stclassauction.com	Computers
3D Auction	www.3dauction.com	Computers
4Tunes.com	www.4tunes.com	Music
4u2Bid Auction	www.ultra-web.com/auction/	General
A J Fine Arts Silent Auction	www.ajarts.com/ajarts/auctnhp.html	Art
A1Auction	www.a1auction.com	General
AB!C	www.auctionsbyabc.com	Canada, bottles
ActionBid Online Auctions	www.actionbid.com	General
Advantage Auction	www.advantageauction.com	General
Affiliated ReMarketing Web	www.remarketing.com	Computers
AFundRaiser.Com	www.afundraiser.com	Charity
AllJazz Jazz Record Auctions	www.alljazz.com	Music
Amazon.com Auctions (Big Five)	auctions.amazon.com	**General**
Ampersand Antiques	www.qwikhomes.com/antiques/	Antiques
Andy Pak's Sports Card Auction	www.azww.com/apak/auction.shtml	Sports
Antique Canada/Antiques Ontario	www.antique-canada.com	Canada, antiques, collectibles
Antique Country	www.antiquecountry.com	Antiques
Antique Trails	www.nidlink.com/~trails/	Antiques, collectibles
AntiqueGuns.com	206.151.91.7/antiqueguns/html/categories.htm	Antiques

Site	URL	Type of Auction
Art and Fine Art Sales	`www.art4sale.com`	Art
Art Auction International	`www.art-auction-intl.com`	Art
Art Planet Auction Listings	`www.artplanet.com/` `search-category.html?category=` `Auction+Houses`	Art
Artists Online Silent Auction	`www.onlineart.com/auction.htm`	Art
ArtNet Auctions	`www.auction1.artnet.com`	Art
At-Auction	`www.at-auction.com`	Computers
Auction Bidding	`www.auction-bidding.com`	Computers
Auction Depot	`www.auctiondepot.com`	Canada, computers
Auction First	`www.auctionfirst.com/` `html/categories.htm`	General
Auction Floor	`www.auctionfloor.com`	Computers
Auction House	`www.unclebob.com/main.htm`	Computers, business
Auction Hunter (Auction Universe Network)	`www.auctionhunter.co.uk`	U.K., general
Auction InfoCom	`auction.infocom.net`	General
Auction IT	`www.auction-it.net`	Computers
Auction Nation	`www.auctionnation.com`	General
Auction Network	`www.auction-network.com`	Collectibles, sports
Auction OK (Auction Universe Network)	`www.auctionok.com`	Local (Oklahoma)
Auction Online De Veiling	`www.auction-online.com`	Netherlands, general
Auction Sales	`www.auction-sales.com`	Computers
Auction Town	`www.auctiontown.webjump.com`	Computers, collectibles
Auction Universe (Big Five)	`www.auctionuniverse.com`	**General**
Auction Universe Network	`www.aun.com`	Local
Auction Watchers	`www.auctionwatchers.com`	Computers
Auction Works	`www.auctionworks.com`	Collectibles, antiques
Auction World	`www.a-world.com`	Computers
auction-123.com	`www.auction-123.com`	Stamps
AuctionAddict	`www.auctionaddict.com`	General
AuctionAdventure	`www.auctionadventures.net`	Collectibles, antiques

Site	URL	Type of Auction
AuctionBox Computer Auction	www.auctionbox.com	Computers
AuctionBuy	www.auctionbuy.com	General
AuctionComic.com	www.auctioncomic.com	Comics
AuctioNet.com	www.auctionet.com	Computers
AuctionGate Interactive	www.auctiongate.com	Computers
AuctionIsland	www.auctionisland.com	Collectibles
AuctionLand	www.auction-land.com	General
AuctionMax	www.auctionmax.com	Computers
AuctionPage	www.auctionpage.com	General
AuctionPort	www.auctionport.com	Collectibles
Auctions on the Net	www.advocacy-net.com/auctnmks.htm	Directory
Auctions Online Supersite	guestservices.hypermart.net/index.htm	Directory
Auctions Orlando (Auction Universe Network)	www.auctionsorlando.com	Local (Orlando, FL)
Auctions Unlimited	www.auctions-unlimited.com	Collectibles
Auctions VA Universe Network)	www.auctionsva.com	Local (Auction (Richmond, VA)
Auctionscape	www.auctionscape.com	General
AuctionsSouthFlorida (Auction Universe Network)	www.auctionssouthflorida.com	Local (South Florida)
AuctionsUK	guestservices.hypermart.net/uk.htm	U.K., directory
Auctionuniverse.co.uk (Auction Universe Network)	www.auctionuniverse.co.uk	U.K., general
AuctionVine	www.auctionvine.com	Wine
AuctionWare	www.auctionware.com	General
Auction-Warehouse.com	www.auction-warehouse.com	Computers
AutographAuction	www.autographauction.com	Autographs
Automobile Auctions Online	www.dealerschoice.com/conauc.htm	Automotive
AZ Auctions (Auction Universe Network)	www.azauctions.com	Local (Arizona)
Bargain News Auctions Online (Auction Universe Network)	www.bnauctions.com	General
Bargoon	www.bargoon.com	Canada, general
Basketball Bonanza	www.basketballbonanza.com	Sports
bbauctions.com (Auction Universe Network)	www.bbauctions.com	Beanie Babies

Site	URL	Type of Auction
Beanie Baby Bidding	`www.beaniebid.com`	Beanie Babies
Beanie Forum and Chat	`www.advant.net/beanie.htm`	Beanie Babies
Beanie Nation	`www.beanienation.com`	Beanie Babies
Beanie Universe	`auctions.beanie-universe.com`	Beanie Babies
Bid 4 Vacations	`www.bid4vacations.com`	Travel
Bid on Collectibles	`www.bidoncollectibles.com`	Collectibles
Bid to Buy	`www.bidtobuy.com`	General
Bid.com	`www.bid.com`	Canada/U.S., general
Bid-4-It	`www.bid4it.com`	Business
BidAway	`www.bidaway.com`	General
BidBonanza	`www.bidbonanza.com`	General
Biddernet Online Auctions	`www.biddernet.com`	Computers
Biddington's Art & Antiques Online Auctions	`www.biddingtons.com`	Antiques, art
BidFind	`www.vsn.net/af/`	Directory
BidMore	`www.bidmore.com`	General
Bidnask.com	`www.bidnask.com`	Computers
BidnBuy	`www.bidnbuy.com`	Computers
Bidstream.com	`www.bidstream.com`	General
BidsWanted	`www.bidswanted.com`	Computers, business
Bill Henderson's Sports Card Auction	`www.azww.com/hendo/auction.shtml`	Sports
Black Voices BV Auctions (Auction Universe Network)	`www.bvauctions.com`	General
Boekhout's Collectibles Mall	`www.azww.com/mall`	Sports
Boxlot Online Auction	`www.boxlot.com`	Collectibles, art
Brentwood Wine Company	`www.brentwoodwine.com`	Wine
Buck a Bottle Auction	`www.buckabottle.com`	Bottles, steins
Bullnet Online Auctions	`www.bullnet.co.uk/auctions`	U.K., computers
CanAuction	`www.canauction.com`	Canada, general
CCE-Auction	`www.cce-auction.com`	Coins
Channel 3000 Auctions (Auction Universe Network)	`www.channel3000auctions.com`	Local (Madison, WI)
Channel 6000 Auctions (Auction Universe Network)	`www.channel6000auctions.com`	Local (Portland, OR)

Site	URL	Type of Auction
Cheap Snowboards	www.cheapsnowboards.com/base.htm	Sports
Christie's Inc.	www.christies.com	Art, antiques, collectibles
CityAuction	www.cityauction.com	Local
Classifieds 2000 Auctions (Big Five)	**www.classifieds2000.com**	**General**
Coin Universe Auctions	auctions.coin-universe.com	Coins
CollectEx	www.collectex.com	Collectibles
Collectibles.Net	www.collectibles.net/auction/	Collectibles
Collectit.net	www.collectit.net	Collectibles, sports
Collectors Universe.com	www.collectorsauction.com	Collectibles, sports
Columbian.com Auctions NW (Auction Universe Network)	www.auctionsnw.com	Local (Southwest Washington)
ComicExchange	www.ComicExchange.net	Comics
Computer Paradise Unlimited	www.cpu2000.com	Computers
Courant CTAuctions (Auction Universe Network)	www.ctauctions.com	Local (Hartford, CT)
Cross Stitches Auction	www.xstitches.com	Cross stitching, needlepoint
Crusader29's Auction Page	home.earthlink.net/~crusader29/	War games/ miniatures
Curran's Cards and Auctions	www.curranscards.com	Sports
Cyber Horse Auction	www.cyberhorseauction.com	Horses
CyberAuctions	www.cyber-auctions.com	General
CyberSWAP	www.cyberswap.com	Computers
Cycle Auction Online	www.ep.com/ep/csp.html?csp=3758	Automotive
Dargate Auction Galleries	www.dargate.com	Antiques, jewelry
DC Values	www.dcvalues.com	Local (Washington, D.C.)
DealDeal	www.dealdeal.com	Computers
Dennis R. Abel Stamp Auction	www.drabel.com/cgi-bin/auctions/auction.cgi	Stamps
Digibid	www.digibid.com	Musical instruments
Digital Auction	www.digital-auction.com	Computers
DiversCasino	www.diverscasino.com	Sports
Domains Auction	www.domainsauction.com	Internet domains
Dr. Laura Schlessenger Foundation Auctions (Auction Universe Network)	www.drlauraauctions.com	Charity

Site	URL	Type of Auction
Dream Pages Online Auction	www.dreampages.com/auction/	General
eBay (Big Five)	**www.ebay.com**	**General**
eBid: UK Online Auctions	www.ebid.co.uk	U.K., general
edeal	www.edeal.com	General
eGolf.com	www.egolf.com	Sports
Eleventh Avenue Marketplace	www.eleventhavenue.com	General
emarketlive	www.emarketlive.com	Computers
Encore Auction	www.encoreauction.com	Computers, office
EworldAuction	www.eworldauction.com	Books, manuscripts, maps
EZBid.com	www.ezbid.com	Computers
Fainco Auction	www.faincoauction.com	Collectibles, antiques
Fair Auction	www.fairauction.com	Computers
fan2fan	www.fan2fan.com/html/categories.htm	Sports
First Auction	www.firstauction.com	General
First Internet Travel Auction	www.4a.com/auction/	Travel
Florida Auctions Online	www.comspec-marketing.com/auction/	Local (Florida)
France Auction Web	www.auction-fr.com	France, art
Gemtraders.com	www.gemtraders.com/auction/	Gems, jewelry
Gibson Musical Instruments	www.auction.gibson.com	Musical instruments
Global Auction Club	www.gaci.net	Computers, sports
Global Auction Online	www.global-auction.com	Collectibles
Global Auctions	www.globalauctions.com	Art
Going Once	www.goingonce.net	Computers
GoingGoingGone Travel Auctions	www.goinggoinggone.com/going/homego.htm	Travel
Golden Age	www.goldnage.com	Antiques, collectibles
Golf Auction USA	www.golfauctionusa.com	Sports
Golf Club Exchange	www.golfclubexchange.com	Sports
golfbids.com	www.golfbids.com	Sports
Golfpeddler.com	www.golfpeddler.com	Sports
goMainline	www.gomainline.com	Collectibles
Graham Auctions	www.grahamauctions.com	Canada, general
Great Deals Auction	www.great-deals.net	General

Site	URL	Type of Auction
Guitarauction	www.guitarauction.com	Musical instruments
Haggle Online	www.haggle.com	General
Hardware Canada	www.hardwarecanada.com	Canada, general
Heidelberg Editions International	www.hei-art.com	Art
Hobby Markets Online	www.hobbymarkets.com	Collectibles
Hollywood Auction	www.travel.to/Hollywood/	Charity, movie
Hybrid Liquidation	www.liquidation.com	General
Infinite Auction	www.sweetdeal.com	Computers
Innovative Auctions	www.innauction.com	Computers
Interactive Auction Online	www.iaoauction.com	Computers
Interactive Collector	auction.icollector.com	Collectibles, art, antiques
Intermodal Equipment Exchange	www.intermodalex.com	Business
International Wine Exchange	www.wine-exchange.com	Wine
Internet Auction	www.internetauction.net	General
Internet Auction List	www.internetauctionlist.com	Directory
JC Shopping Club	www.jcshopping.com	Christian, general
Jewelnet Auctions	www.jewelnetauctions.com	Gems, jewelry
Jim's Historic Collectibles	www.ica-ark.com/ jimhistoricpage.htm	Books, manuscripts, maps
John Morelli Auctioneers	www.abcliveauction.com	Antiques, collectibles
Jordan & Jordan Online Wine Auction	www.saarwein.com/auktion.htm	Germany, wine
Just Glass Auctions	www.justglass.com	Glass
K&B Sports Cards Auction	www.kbsportscards.com	Sports
Keybuy Auction House	www.keybuy.com	Computers
King's Attic	www.kingsattic.com	Vintage radios
Klik Klok On-line Dutch Auctions	www.klik-klok.com	General
LancAuctions (Auction Universe Network)	www.lancauctions.com	Local (Lancaster, PA)
lastminute.com	www.lastminute.com	U.K., travel
Lionel Toy Train Auction	www.buznorma.com	Model trains
LiveBid	www.livebid.com	General
LiveToPlay	www.livetoplay.com	Sports
Local Auction Online	www.localauctiononline.com	General
Los Angeles Times Auctions (Auction Universe Network)	www.laauctions.com	Local (Los Angeles, CA)

Site	URL	Type of Auction
LUNDS Auctioneers & Appraisers Ltd.	www.lunds.com	Canada, antiques
Lycos Auctions	www.lycos.com/auctions/	General
Magic Auction	www.magicauction.com	Magic supplies
Maine Market Auctions (Auction Universe Network)	www.maineauctions.com	Local (Maine)
Mallpark Live Online Auctions	www.auctions.mallpark.com	General
Manheim Online	www.manheim.com	Automotive
Martin Lawrence Galleries	www.martinlawrence.com/auction.html	Art
MCW Online Poster Auction	www.mcwonline.com	Movie
MFCP Auctions Midwest (Auction Universe Network)	www.auctionsmidwest.com	Local (Midwest)
Mid-Atlantic Sports Cards Baseball Auction On-Line	www.azww.com/midatlantic/auction.shtml	Sports
Mid-Atlantic Wine Auction Company	www.midatlanticwine.com	Wine
Militaria Collectibles Auction Haus	www.militaria-collectibles.com	Militaria
Minneapolis Star Tribune Strib Auctions.com (Auction Universe Network)	www.stribauctions.com	Local (Minneapolis, MN)
Mobilia	www.mobilia	Automotive
Monitor Auctions (Auction Universe Network)	www.monitorauctions.com	Local (McAllen, TX)
Morning Call Penn Auctions (Auction Universe Network)	www.pennauctions.com	Local (Allentown, PA)
Mountain Zone	auctions.mountainzone.com	Sports
My Shop	www.myshop.com	Toys
My Shop: Beanie Babies Auction	www.myshop.com/html/categories.html	Beanie Babies
Nando: Scoopy's Auction Universe (Auction Universe Network)	www.scoopysauction.com	General
National Corvette Museum Auction	auction.corvettemuseum.com	Automotive
NeedFulThings	www.needfulthings.net/auction.shtm	Local (Oklahoma)
Net4Sale	www.net4sale.org	General
Netis AuctionWeb (Auction Universe Network)	www.netisauctions.com	General

Site	URL	Type of Auction
NetWORLD Online Auction Center	`auctions.networld.com`	General
New Age Auction	`www.newageauction.com`	Crystals
New Age Sportscards & Autographs Auction	`www.newagecards.com`	Sports, autographs
New Spirit	`www.wehug.com`	Crystals, jewelry
NewsNet 5 Auctions (Auction Universe Network)	`www.newsnet5auctions.com`	Local (Cleveland, OH)
NFL Alumni Charity Auctions (Auction Universe Network)	`www.nflalumniauctions.com`	Charity
Non-Profit Auction	`www.nonprofitauction.com`	Charity
NowUBid	`www.nowubid.com`	General
Numismatists Online	`www.numismatists.com/hkP92aTc/`	Coins
OHI EXchange	`www.ohiexchange.com/`	Collectibles
Ohio Auction, The	`www.ohioauction.com`	General
OneWebPlace	`www.onewebplace.com`	Collectibles
Online Auction Services	`www.online-auction.com`	Computers, business
Online Auctions UK	`www.onlineauctions.co.uk`	U.K., appliances
OnLine Equine Sales Company	`www.online-equine.com`	Horses
Online Market & Auction	`www.theonlinemarket.com`	General
OnlyGolfAuction	`www.robotica-inc.com/quickauction/golf/index.asp`	Sports
OnSale	`www.onsale.com`	Computers, electronics
OnTrack Auction	`www.ontrackauction.com`	General
Outpost Auctions	`www.outpostauctions.com`	Computers
Palm Beach Auctions	`www.palmbeachauctions.com`	Antiques, art, collectibles
Past's Presents	`www.auction-land.com/antiques/`	Antiques, collectibles
Paulus Swaen Old Maps and Prints Internet Auction	`www.swaen.com`	Manuscripts, maps
PCAuctioneer	`www.pcauctioneer.com`	Computers
PeddleIt	`www.PeddleIt.com`	Toys
Peggy's Baseball Cards	`www.erols.com/pegbbcds/`	Sports
Philadelphia Online Philly Auctions (Auction Universe Network)	`www.phillyauctions.com`	Local (Philadelphia, PA)
Philatelic.Com Online Auctions	`auction.philatelic.com`	Stamps

Site	URL	Type of Auction
Philately Stamps	`www.philea.se`	Stamps
Phoebus Auction Gallery On-Line Auction	`www.phoebusauction.com`	Collectibles, art, antiques
Pick Your Seat	`www.pickyourseat.com`	Tickets
Pinbacks.com	`www.pinbacks.com`	Buttons
PIRSS On-Line A/E/C Auctions	`www.insa.com/auction/`	Construction materials
PlanetBike	`www.auction-land.com/planetbike/`	Bicycles
Popula	`www.popula.com`	Collectibles, antiques
Postnet Auctions (Auction Universe Network)	`www.postnetauctions.com`	Local (St. Louis, MO)
Pottery Auction	`www.potteryauction.com`	Pottery
Priceline	`www.priceline.com`	Travel
Quixell	`www.qxl.com`	Europe, general
RacersAuction	`www.racersauction.com/auction`	Automotive
Record Universe	`auctions.record-universe.com`	Music
Rhythm & Books	`www.auction-land.com/cdbooks/`	Music, books
RightAuction.com	`www.rightauction.com`	General
RMG Auction Services	`www.binary.net/treasure/AuctionInfo.html`	Gems
Robotica Computer Products Auction	`www.robotica-inc.com/quickauction/robotica/`	Computers
Rock Auction	`www.rockauction.com`	Musical instruments
Rotman Collectibles	`www.wwcd.com/rotman/`	Collectibles, sports
Royal Auction	`www.royalauction.com`	Collectibles, antiques, jewelry
Russian Auction	`www.russianauction.com`	Russia, collectibles
Sandafayre	`www.sandafayre.com`	Stamps
SellAll	`www.sellall.com`	Business
SellAndTrade.com	`www.sellandtrade.com`	General
Sellathon Auction Services, Inc.	`www.sellathon.com`	Collectibles, sports
Shop4u.com	`www.shop4u.com`	Business
ShopZone	`www.shopzone.co.nz`	New Zealand, general
SkyBid	`www.skybid.com`	Collectibles
Sloan's Auctions	`www.sloansauction.com`	Antiques, art
Software Auction Online	`www.gosao.com/door11.asp`	Computers

Site	URL	Type of Auction
SoldUSA	www.sportauction.com	Sports, collectibles
Sotheby's	www.Sothebys.com	Art, antiques, collectibles
SPEEDBID	www.speedbid.com	U.K., collectibles
Sporting News Auction House (Auction Universe Network)	auctions.sportingnews.com	Sports
SportingAuction	www.sportingauction.com	Sports
Sports Collectors Univserse	auctions.sports-universe.com	Sports
SportsAuction	www.sportsauction.com	Sports
SportsTrade	www.sportstrade.com	Sports
St. Lucie Marketplace (Auction Universe Network)	www.stluciemarketplace.com	Local (St. Lucie County, FL)
Stardoodles for Kids	www.stardoodle.com	Charity
Steal-A-Record	www.wizvax.net/mpekar/index.html	Music
Stein Auction	www.steinauction.com	Steins
Strickler's Sports Den	sportsden.hypermart.net	Sports
Surplus Auction	www.surplusauction.com	Computers
Teletrade Auctions	www.teletrade.com/teletrade/	Collectibles, sports
ThinkBID	www.thinkbid.com	Collectibles
Tickets.com	auction.tickets.com	Tickets
Time Tunnel	www.nextlevel.com/espace/	Music
Tradehall Global Trading Network	www.tradehall.com	General
Trader's Cove Online Auction	www.niximage.com/auction/	Canada, general
TradersPage	www.traderspage.com	General
TravelBids Travel Discount Auction	www.TravelBids.com	Travel
Travelfacts Auction	www.bid4travel.com	Travel
Triangle Auction (Auction Universe Network)	www.triangleauction.com	Local (North Carolina)
U.S. Government FinanceNet Auctions	www.financenet.gov/sales.htm	General
u-Auction-it	www.uauction.com	General
uBid	www.ubid.com	General, computers
UBID4IT	www.ubid4it.com	Computers
Universal Studios Online Auction	www.unistudiosauction.com	Movies
Unofficial Beanie Baby Online Auction	www.defend.net/beanie/	Beanie Babies

Site	URL	Type of Auction
Up4Auction	`www.up4auction.com`	Antiques, collectibles
Up4Sale	`www.up4sale.com`	General
USAuctions	`www.usauctions.com`	Computers
VegasToday.com	`www.vegastoday.com`	General
VermontAuctions (Auction Universe Network)	`www.vermontauctions.com`	Local (Vermont)
Vintage Sports Auctions	`www.davidrudd.com`	Sports
VintageUSA Direct Auction	`www.vintageusa.com/auction.htm`	Vintage clothing
Virtual Warehouse	`www.4sale-or-auction.com`	General
VTCO Auctions (Auction Universe Network)	`www.vtcoauctions.com`	Computers
Waverly's Online Antique Auction	`www.waverlys.com`	Coins, antiques
Wcollect.com	`www.wcollect.com`	Art, collectibles
WebAuction	`www.webauction.com`	Computers
WebAuctionWorld	`www.webauctionworld.com`	General
WebCharity.com	`www.webcharity.com`	Charity
Webquest's Auctions	`www.webquests.com/auction/index.shtml`	Collectibles
White's Guide Auction House	`www.whitesauction.com`	General
Wine Online	`www.winecollector.com`	Wine
Wine.Com Auction	`www.wine.com/bidwine/auction.cgi`	Wine
Winebid.com	`www.winebid.com`	Wine
WLAJ Auction (Auction Universe Network)	`www.wlajauction.com`	Local (Lansing, MI)
World Wide Auctions	`www.wwauction.com`	Collectibles
WowAuction	`www.wowauction.com`	Collectibles
WWMT Auction (Auction Universe Network)	`www.wwmtauction.com`	Local (West Michigan)
www.CoinAuctions.Com	`www.coinauctions.com`	Coins
www.StampAuctions.Com	`www.stampauctions.com`	Stamps
Yahoo! Auctions (Big Five)	`auctions.yahoo.com`	**General**
Yong & Dell's Sports Cards Auction On-Line	`www.azww.com/yong/auction.shtml`	Sports

Speak Like a Geek: Online Auction Terms

A

Amazon.com Auctions   One of the top general auction sites, located at www.auctions.amazon.com.

antique   Typically, items at least 100 years old—although some selected post-1900 items are often called antiques, as well.

antiquity   An artifact from the ancient world, commonly extending to the fall of the Roman Empire or the Middle Ages.

auction   A public sale of goods or property in which prospective purchasers bid until the highest price is reached.

auction house   A firm that conducts real-world (non-online) auctions.

auction interception   A situation where a user steals the identity of another seller and intercepts the ended auctions of that seller (generally with forged email messages), with the intent of convincing buyers to send the payment for the items to him instead of to the real seller.

Auction Universe   One of the top general auction sites, located at www.auctionuniverse.com.

auctioneer   The person who conducts an auction sale.

B

bid   To offer a certain price for an item on auction.

bid discovery   The process of surreptitiously finding out the maximum bid price specified by an item's current high bidder.

bid increment   The predetermined amount by which a bid will be raised; the difference between the current bid price and the next acceptable bid.

bid retraction   See *retract*.

bid shielding   The practice of using shill bidding to artificially increase the price of an item *temporarily*, in an attempt to protect the low bid level of a third bidder. Bid shielding typically does not involve a shill for the seller.

bid siphoning   A practice that involves a third party (unrelated to the seller or bidder) emailing bidders in a currently open auction, offering a similar or identical item at a price below the current bid level.

bidder   One who bids to purchase an item in an auction.

Bid$afe   The buyer-protection program offered by Auction Universe.

browser   A software program that lets your computer access HTML pages on the World Wide Web. Netscape Navigator and Microsoft's Internet Explorer are the two most popular browsers today.

C

catalog auction   A real-world (non-online) auction held in a location different from where the actual goods for auction are kept.

Classifieds 2000 Auctions   One of the top general auction sites, located at www.classifieds2000.com.

collectible   Anything a collector feels is worth collecting, regardless of age.

commission   See *final value fee*.

contemporary collectible   Collectible items from the 1990s.

D

deadbeat bidder   A winning bidder who does not deliver payment for the item won.

Dutch auction   An auction where multiple quantities of an identical item are sold.

E

eBay   The world's largest online auction site, located at www.ebay.com.

email   Electronic mail, a means of corresponding to other computer users over the Internet through digital messages.

escrow   The act of putting an item in the care of a third party until certain conditions are fulfilled; online escrow services "hold" an item until payment is received, and "hold" the seller's payment until the buyer receives the item.

F–G

FAQ   See *Frequently Asked Questions*.

feedback   Comments left by one user for another, relating their experience in dealing with the other user.

final value fee   The fee paid by a seller to an online auction site at the completion of auction, calculated as a percentage of the final selling price.

Frequently Asked Questions   Also known as a FAQ, this is a document that answers the most commonly asked questions about a particular topic. FAQs are often found in newsgroups and on some Web sites as a preparatory answer to the common questions asked by new users.

H

high bid   The highest current bid for an item; at the end of an auction, the high bid becomes the *winning bid*.

high bidder   The bidder placing the high bid.

home page   The initial page screen of a Web site.

HTML   HyperText Markup Language, the quasi-programming language used to create Web pages.

hyperlink   Special text or graphics on a Web page that, when clicked, automatically transfer the user to the another Web page.

I–J

initial bid   See *minimum bid*.

Insertion Fee   The fee paid by a seller for the initial listing of an item for auction, calculated on the initial bid price.

insurance   A protection against loss.

Internet   The global "network of networks" that connects millions of computers around the world. The World Wide Web and Usenet are both parts of the Internet.

Internet Explorer   Microsoft's Web browser.

K–L

keyword   A word which forms all or part of a search engine query.

listing fee   See *insertion fee*.

live auction   An auction, either online or offline, that takes place in "real time."

local auction   An auction limited to a specific geographic region or city.

M

maximum bid   The highest specified amount that a bidder is willing to pay for an item; the maximum bid may be higher than the current high bid.

meta-auction   An auction of auctions; any site that aggregates information from or about other online auction sites.

metasearch   A search of searches; a process where queries are submitted to multiple search engines simultaneously.

minimum bid   The smallest amount that can be entered as a bid amount on a specific item, set by the seller at the time of listing the item.

modem   Computer hardware that enables transmission of digital data from one computer to another over common telephone lines.

N

Netscape Communicator   The software suite that contains the Netscape Navigator Web browser.

Netscape Navigator   Netscape's Web browser.

network   Two or more computers connected together. The Internet is the largest network in the world.

O

online auction   An auction that takes place on the Internet.

online catalog   Listings from a real-world (non-online) auction. Auction catalogues are often placed on the Web for viewing prior to the auction itself.

onsite auction   A real-world (non-online) auction that takes place at the location of the goods for auction, rather than at the auction house.

outbid   The process of making a bid for an item that is higher than the current high bid.

P

portal   A Web site that provides a gateway to the Internet, as well as a collection of other content and services. Many portals, such as Yahoo! and Excite (via their Classifieds 2000 subsidiary), are now offering online auctions.

private auction   An auction where the bidders' identities are not divulged publicly.

proxy bidding   A system where bidding is done automatically (by "proxy"), based on a bidder-specified maximum bid amount and set bid increments; in proxy bidding, bidders let the online auction software determine the appropriate bid for any given circumstance.

Q–R

query   A word, phrase, or group of words, possibly combined with other syntax or operators, used to initiate a search with a search engine or directory.

relist   The process of creating a new listing for an item which did not sell during a previous auction.

reserve auction   See *reserve price auction*.

reserve price   The minimum price that a seller will accept for an item, higher than the initial bid price. Reserve prices are not disclosed to bidders in an auction.

reserve price auction   An auction where the seller has reserved the option to set a second price (the *reserve price*) that is higher than their opening bid. At the end of an auction, if the high bid does not meet or exceed the seller's reserve price, the seller does *not* have to sell their item to the high bidder.

retract   The act of a bidder canceling a current bid.

S

SafeHarbor   The buyer protection program offered by eBay.

search   To look for information in an orderly fashion.

selling fee   See *final value fee*.

shill bidding   The process of a seller bidding on his or her own item, in a deliberate attempt to artificially drive up the price of the item.

shilling   See *shill bidding.*

site   A unified collection of Web pages on the Internet.

snail mail   Traditional U.S. Postal Service mail.

sniping   The act of placing a surprise bid during the closing seconds of an open auction.

Sotheby's   One of the world's largest real-world auction houses, now located on the Web at www.sothebys.com.

spam   Email or newsgroup messages that are unsolicited, unwanted, and generally irrelevant.

spamming   The act of sending large numbers of unsolicited email messages.

starting price   See *minimum bid.*

U–V

URL   Uniform Resource Locator; the address of a Web page.

vintage collectible   Any collectible from 1989 or earlier.

W–Z

Web   See *World Wide Web.*

Web browser   See *browser.*

wildcard   A character used to represent one or more characters in a search query; * is the most common wildcard used on most online auction sites.

winning bid   The high bid at the end of an auction, providing that the bid is equal to or higher than the minimum bid or the reserve price (in a reserve price auction).

World Wide Web   A subset of the Internet that contains HTML pages.

Yahoo! Auctions   One of the top general auction sites, located at auctions.yahoo.com.

Index

311

X – Z